A HISTORY of ENGLISH SYNTAX

A Transformational Approach to the History of English Sentence Structure

TRANSATLANTIC SERIES in LINGUISTICS
Under the general editorship of
Samuel R. Levin
Graduate Center
The City University
of New York

ANALYTIC SYNTAX
OTTO JESPERSEN

THE STUDY OF SYNTAX
The Generative-Transformational Approach to the Structure of American English
D. TERENCE LANGENDOEN

INTRODUCTION TO TAGMEMIC ANALYSIS
WALTER A. COOK, S. J.

IRREGULARITY IN SYNTAX
GEORGE LAKOFF

CROSS-OVER PHENOMENA
PAUL M. POSTAL

DEEP AND SURFACE STRUCTURE CONSTRAINTS IN SYNTAX
DAVID M. PERLMUTTER

A HISTORY of ENGLISH SYNTAX

A Transformational Approach to the History of English Sentence Structure

ELIZABETH CLOSS TRAUGOTT
Stanford University

HOLT, RINEHART AND WINSTON, INC.
New York Chicago San Francisco Atlanta
Dallas Montreal Toronto London Sydney

Library of Congress Catalog Card Number: 73–172650
ISBN: 0–03–079600–8
Printed in the United States of America
2 3 4 5 **038** 9 8 7 6 5 4 3 2 1

Acknowledgments

I wish to acknowledge my tremendous intellectual debt to Charles J. Fillmore whose ideas underlie much of the present study; my deepest thanks to him for his critical comments on an earlier draft of this book. I am also grateful to Fred Householder for his invaluable suggestions regarding many particulars. Thanks are also due to Naomi Baron, Julian Boyd, Joseph Greenberg, Lilith Haynes, Charles Jones, Samuel Levin, Joyce Melville, and Edith Moravcsik for many stimulating discussions and comments which one way or another have found their way into this book; to Joyce Melville and Jeanie Luckau for their meticulous editorial help; and to all those scholars, far too numerous to mention individually, without whose work this book would never have taken shape.

Contents

INTRODUCTION

The aim of this book is to present a broad outline of the history of selected sentence patterns in English. Although there has been a great deal of scholarly research on the history of English syntax, little has found its way into introductory books on the development of the English language. Most such books provide extensive materials on phonology, morphology, vocabulary, and writing systems, but pay little attention to sentence patterns. A separate study devoted to syntax alone therefore seems fully justified, for use either on its own or as a supplement to the many introductory histories of English already available.

No one work two hundred pages long could possibly hope to cover adequately even the major sentence patterns and the changes they underwent. Drastic restrictions necessarily had to be imposed on the scope of the material. Which patterns to discuss and which to omit was a considerable problem, and doubtless many readers will miss their favorite phrase or sentence type. Various possibilities presented themselves, the extremes of which were, on the one hand, an encyclopedia of interesting changes and, on the other, a selection of a few sentence types for detailed discussion. The present study leans toward the latter approach. The decision to look at a limited set of structures in some detail rather than to sketch superficially as many structures as possible derives from the fact that this volume is conceived not so much as a handbook of Old English (OE), Middle English (ME), Early Modern English (ENE), or Modern English (NE) syntax, but as an investigation into the creative processes of language both ahistorically at any one period and also historically over successive periods. Discussion of typical sentence patterns is aimed at providing the reader not only with a sense of what syntactic resources were available at earlier periods of the language, and how many of those resources are still available in one form or another in present-day English, but also with a sense of what steps could have bridged the gap between one recognizable stage of English and another. The book, then, is intended to introduce the reader to some of the theoretical issues in the study of language and language change as well as to the factual data necessary for the understanding of English texts written prior to this century and for the study of style, whether that of a particular author or of a period. Any serious student of the history of English syntax should turn for further factual details and copious examples to the invaluable encyclopedic compendium by F. Th. Visser, *An Historical Syntax of the English Language;* but above all he should read texts and investigate for himself their syntactic structures.

In the hope of giving a reasonably unified view of the language at different periods, I have chosen not only a few select sentence types but also a few select works, mostly in "informal educated style." This unified view is necessarily an oversimplification. There are considerable differences from author to author within the same period, and even within the works of the same author; these are, however, largely variations due to differences in style, age, dialect, degree of learning, and the like. They often obscure the basic similarities that can be found at any one time. In a book as brief as this, heterogeneous materials might cloud the major trends and have therefore been avoided. We will be looking at "Alfredian" prose ca. A.D. 880 as typical of OE, at the prose of Chaucer and of the *Paston Letters* as typical of later ME, and at the prose of Shakespeare, Nashe, and Deloney as typical of ENE.

The first chapter provides some of the theoretical background necessary for discussing linguistic change: causes of change, conditions for change, and types of change, as well as practical considerations of how to evaluate the data. Subsequent chapters outlining changes in the history of English syntax characterize the syntax of the major periods of English and provide particularizations of the general properties of language change discussed in the first chapter. The second chapter sketches Modern English syntax and introduces in some detail the approach to syntax that is taken in the later chapters. These discuss sentence patterns in OE (Chapter 3), ME and ENE (Chapter 4), and developments in NE since 1700, including the growth of differences between British and American English, and the similarities between certain aspects of Black English and earlier English (Chapter 5). Chapters 2–5 are arranged in such a way that it is possible to use the material section by section as well as chapter by chapter; so a reader wishing to trace the history of negation, for example, may do so by referring solely to the relevant sections in each of the four chapters.

The unorthodox grouping of ME with ENE in Chapter 4 may surprise many readers. As the name indicates, ENE is usually considered part of NE. This grouping is based on very important similarities between the ENE and NE sound systems, between their word-formation systems, and between attitudes to language in the two periods. From a purely syntactic point of view, however, ENE is closer to ME from ca. 1250 on than to NE. The traditional grouping therefore does not apply very satisfactorily in a study of changes in English sentence structure and is not used here.

The theoretical approach to linguistic analysis in this book is that of transformational generative grammar. Familiarity with this approach would be helpful, but is not essential. Useful introductory books on transformational grammar include D. Terence Langendoen, *Essentials of English Grammar;* Ronald Langacker, *Language and Its Structure;* and, at a rather more advanced level, Noam Chomsky, *Language and Mind,* and D. Terence Langendoen, *The Study of Syntax* (in the present series). Within the broad philosophical framework of transformational grammar there have developed alternative views on the nature of the distinction between syntax and semantics and of the ways in which the relationship between the two should be expressed in a grammar. Being more concerned with defining informally some of the areas that must be considered in the study of sentence patterns than with the technicalities of how these areas should be formally specified in a grammar, I have not confined myself exclusively to any one theoretical model of transformational grammar; nevertheless, a great deal of the thinking behind this study is based on the theory of "Case Grammar" developed by Charles J. Fillmore in "The Case for Case" (in E. Bach and R. Harms, eds., *Universals in Linguistic Theory*).

1 LANGUAGE AND LANGUAGE CHANGE

A. THE PATTERNS OF LANGUAGE

One of the most remarkable properties of language is that, although we constantly hear sentences we have never heard before, we have little trouble in communicating with each other and coming to some understanding about what is an utterance of a language, say English, and what is not. If we understand each other at least partially, we must share some common knowledge, some set of patterns; otherwise there would be chaos and our understanding, if it occurred at all, would be random. It is such questions as: What kinds of patterns occur in all languages? and What are the particular patterns available in any one language? that most linguists are interested in. Over a period of time one can usually detect marked changes in the patterns of a particular language; in the span of twenty-five years these changes may not seem very significant, but, over a hundred years and especially over several hundred, the cumulative effect of the changes is often such that the patterns seem markedly different. Linguists are therefore also interested in such questions as: Why do linguistic patterns change?, In what kinds of ways can linguistic patterns change?, and What kinds of changes have the patterns of any one language undergone? Since this is a book about English, we will be making an investigation into some of the particular sentence patterns available in English at various periods, into the changes these particular patterns underwent, and into the causes of these changes, wherever it is possible to speculate about them. We will also inevitably have to refer to the universal patterns of which English provides just a small sample, and it is with presenting a sketch of the universal properties of language and language change that the present chapter is mainly concerned.

Language is first and foremost a verbal system of communication. Whether we communicate or not is chiefly the domain of the psychologist —or more strictly speaking, the psycholinguist. What is essential to linguistic study is the development of hypotheses about what the patterns of language are that enable us to communicate. These patterns constitute, in the broadest terms, the conceptual structure, the patterns of sounds (phonology) which we use to express the conceptual structures, and the sentence structure (syntax) that forms a bridge between sound and conceptual structure. The intermediary role of syntax is particularly well illustrated by the way in which language allows for both ambiguity and paraphrase. Among the things we know as language users is that certain sentences may have more than one meaning; that is, they may be ambiguous. For example, in *It is too hot to eat* are we commenting on the weather, reporting that some dish is too hot (spicy hot or hot in temperature?) for us to eat, or possibly even commenting on some animal that is too hot to eat his dinner? Vice versa, the same meaning may often be expressed in different ways, as in the case of *You can swim if you like* and *You may swim if you like.* There is, then, no one-to-one relationship between meaning and the phonetic representation we give that meaning.

Within the syntactic patterns themselves we need to distinguish between the highly abstract underlying form of the sentence and its surface form as a string of words. It is this string of words that sound sequences are the realization of, not of the most abstract patterns. Consider, for example, *The red ball is rolling down the hill;* conceptually this involves at least a speaker, an addressee, a topic (*red ball*), a comment (*rolling down the hill*), an activity in process (*is rolling*), a direction (*down the hill*), and a time focus (simultaneity with the time of the utterance). These different concepts are formulated and given an order in an underlying sentence that has roughly the form *I say to you that the ball which is red is rolling down the hill.* Various operations, or "transformations," may be applied to this underlying sentence: for example, the *I say to you* part can be deleted, as may the *which is* part of the relative clause (*which is red*), and then the rest of the relative clause (*red*) is placed before the noun. The sequence of words resulting from these operations is the surface structure: *The red ball is rolling down the hill.* This sequence of words in turn is realized as a sequence of sounds, including not only phonetic consonants and vowels but also stress and pitch. We may therefore think of the structure of language as containing the following levels:[1]

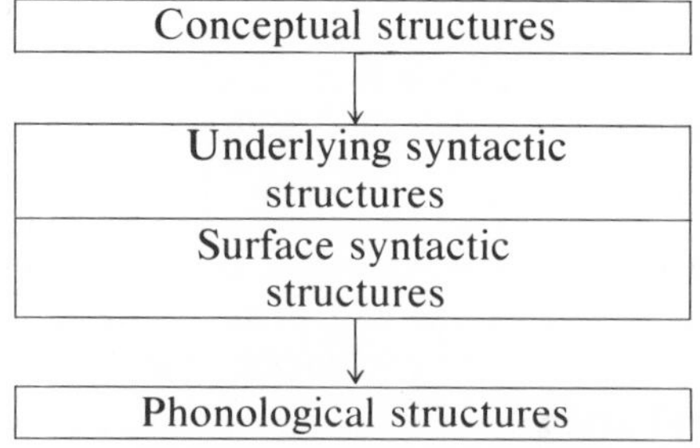

[1] This is only a very basic schematic representation. For further details see Langacker (1968:86–92) and Langendoen (1970:59–61). An alternative view of the relationship between conceptual and syntactic structures is provided in Chomsky (1964:16 and 1968:26).

Although the patterns that are available in language are finite, we can nevertheless construct a theoretically infinite number of sentences and a theoretically infinitely long sentence. This is so because, for every sentence we can construct, we can always construct one more that is different, even if in only one respect, and because for every addition to a sentence we can make a further addition, within limits to be discussed in Chapter 2, Section E. There are, of course, many psychological limits to the length of a sentence, such as attention and memory span. Any arbitrary limitation on maximal sentence length that one might propose would, however, be just as arbitrary as limitation on the length of a numeral. We are psychologically unlikely to be able to cope with large numbers unless we are mathematicians, but we would never for that reason wish to claim that the numeral system itself is finite; on the contrary, from a finite set of symbols and patterns (multiplication by tens, twos, and so on), we can construct an infinitely long numeral in the sense that for every large number we can think of a yet larger one.

The patterns of language that we intuitively know help us to recognize not only what is an utterance of the language, but also what is not. For example, we recognize that *She laughed me* is not a sentence of ordinary English; more subtly we recognize that *She is very gorgeous* is less acceptable than *She is absolutely gorgeous,* or that, even if we have not heard it before, *ungood* might well be an English word while *unbad* would probably not. Orwell uses *ungood* as a term in his hypothetical language of the future, Newspeak, in *1984;* he is responding to the pattern that allows us to negate a semantically positive adjective with *un–* (such as *happy–unhappy; true–untrue*) but usually not a semantically negative adjective (we do not find pairs like *sad–unsad; false–unfalse*).

The intuitive knowledge we have of our language, however unconscious, is called our "linguistic competence." The task a linguist has is to develop a theory or hypothesis about linguistic competence. This hypothesis is expressed in a "grammar" or model of what we know about a language; as a model, it makes no claim to represent competence directly or to account for what we do when we understand or make up a sentence. The linguistic patterns postulated in a grammar are formulated in what are called "rules." These rules are simply a description of the patterns; they state only what is (or rather what is postulated to be), never what should be. Although the linguistic patterns discussed in this book will be presented only informally, they could readily be presented abstractly as mathematically formulated rules; while such rules are significant conceptual aids to those trained to read them, they often provide the uninitiated reader with far more problems than aids; they are therefore avoided in the present study.

B. HOW DO WE ACQUIRE OUR KNOWLEDGE OF LANGUAGE?

One of the especially interesting things about language is that the linguistic patterns we can cope with are highly complex, and yet for most people they are almost completely unconscious. Even more remarkable is the fact that children aged five or six know nearly all the complexities of language in principle insofar as they can create new sentences that follow all the basic patterns of their language. They may, of course, not be able to deal with multiple subordinate structures, but they know the principles of subordination since they can understand and produce sentences like *I want you to go, I promise you to be back soon, I want the ball that is red,* and similar examples. They know, also, how to extrapolate the meaning from a new sequence of sounds, provided it is a sequence in their language. This suggests that we may have some innate linguistic ability that permits us to develop our linguistic competence (what we know about our language) at a very early age. We can hypothesize that we are born with at least a very abstract language acquisition device, a kind of blueprint in the mind which indicates which of all the noises we hear as infants are noises of the language and not some other noise; it also indicates what a possible linguistic pattern is and what the possible relationships between patterns are; it may even contain basic conceptual structures. When he is in contact with speakers of a particular language, a child hypothesizes about the structure of that language by matching in some way that is not yet known the sentences he hears with his innate knowledge of possible linguistic patterns and attempts to imitate the patterns he hears; eventually he learns the language or, strictly speaking, develops his own grammar or hypothesis about the language.

There has recently been a lot of discussion about the validity of the hypothesis that there are linguistic universals and that they are innate.[2] On one side of the argument are the behaviorists who, like Skinner in his book *Verbal Behavior* (1957), reject the notion of the availability of a highly structured language acquisition device and of innate language capacity and argue that children learn language only through stimulus and response networks of associations and similar behavioral systems. On the other side are those, among them the transformationalists, who question whether it will ever be possible, starting from a behaviorist theory of language acquisition, to determine how it is that a child learns such a highly complex system as a language simply from the meager data he hears.

The difficulty of constructing an adequate theory of language acquisition without a theory of innate language capacity is not the only justification for such a theory. Another is that many aspects of human reasoning and thought seem to be invariant. In fact, at the most abstract level, the categories of human reasoning and "natural logic" may overlap with or be one and the same thing as the categories of language.[3] Certainly grammatical categories such as affirmative versus negative sentences, and statement versus command versus promise seem to be essentially invariant across languages; so do such relations as Agent of, Patient of, and Instrument of action. Furthermore, certain constraints on the

[2] For fuller discussion of the issues see Chomsky (1968) Chapter 3.

[3] For a recent discussion of particulars see G. Lakoff (1970).

principles of expansion by subordination and coordination (see Chapter 2, Section E), and on such surface structure properties as ellipsis, word order, and so forth, seem to apply in all languages despite their apparent diversity. What differs from language to language are the particulars of surface realization, including whether inflection is used or not, and whether the prime word order is subject-verb-object or subject-object-verb. It is presumably highly general information concerning the categories and relationships of grammar and the constraints on possible sentence-formation that is available to the child in his language acquisition device. What he learns, in contact with other speakers of the language, is the surface manifestations of the abstract structures and the particulars that give the impression that languages are so diverse.

A further justification for postulating that children are born with a language acquisition device is that there seems to be a biologically determined point in a child's life after which creative hypothesis-making about gross linguistic structures diminishes; this maturation point is reached before puberty and is apparently only minimally affected by intelligence. Most noninnate, learned structures like mathematics, music, and painting are learned considerably later, or at least are considerably affected by intelligence.

The notion of an innate language acquisition device and of the interplay between it and empirical language experience is helpful in coming to an understanding of how language changes. Children learn from speakers around them, especially from their peers; the competence they develop in a particular language, say English, will probably differ in details, but not in very broad ways, from the language of their peers. The reason is that each child develops his own set of patterns to correspond to that of the people around him, within the limits of universal properties of languages. The ways in which his language will differ from that of those around him cannot be predicted in terms of specifics, but they do form a subset of the possible ways in which dialects of a language or successive stages of a language may differ.

C. WHY DOES LANGUAGE CHANGE?

The fact that each generation, or rather each child, learns the language anew and makes its own hypotheses about the patterns of the language is the main cause for language change. Chances are the child will not make exactly the same hypotheses as anyone else. Certain very broad generalizations can be made about the ways in which children's grammars tend to differ from those of previous generations; these will be discussed in Section E. Not only do the children's grammars differ from those of previous generations; children themselves develop successively more complex grammars before arriving, toward the end of the first decade of life, at what is essentially the grammar they will use all their life. Different structures in the language are learned at different times; for example, nouns and verbs are learned very early, but inflections like tense (for example, present in *He walks* versus past in *He walked*) are learned later and perhaps never become as fully internalized as those language elements learned earlier. The structures that a child learns late tend to change most readily in the history of the language; the form of the inflections is notoriously unstable in all languages.

Even if a child grew up in a very homogeneous linguistic community, he would be unlikely to speak exactly like anyone else since the data he hears is limited and skewed—skewed by the limits of what the speakers say and what he actually hears. He has to generalize and use his linguistic competence to construct utterances he has never heard before and he may generalize slightly differently from anyone else. But of course children never grow up in a strictly homogeneous linguistic community. Language structures differ considerably within one area and even within the speech habits of an individual.[4] If we took a random sample of a dozen speakers of English, we would find differences in their speech that could be accounted for by correlation with one or more such factors as: (i) difference in geographical origin—people in different parts of the country tend to speak differently; (ii) difference in socioeconomic group—linguistic habits vary from group to group; (iii) difference in education—the degree of a speaker's acquaintance with written styles and especially with literature can be influential (the Bible, Shakespeare, and other texts have had well-known effects on many generations of speakers; the teaching of grammar and logic also have obvious effects); (iv) difference in age; (v) culturally induced differences in sex—men and women in all cultures tend to speak slightly differently (in some cultures the distinctions are very great and affect the forms of address, the inflections used, and such things; in English they are readily recognizable in the use of pitch patterns, intensifiers like *very, quite, just,* and in vocabulary); (vi) contact with speakers of other languages—most speakers with reasonably proficient knowledge of another language will either consciously or unconsciously borrow forms from that language (as we shall see in subsequent chapters, vocabulary is very readily borrowed; sound patterns and syntactic patterns are far less readily borrowed, but their impact is far from minimal).

Heterogeneity in linguistic structure attributable to distinctions such as these can be observed by comparing the speech of two or more speakers of the same language. But variation is not confined to differences between speakers; it also occurs within the speech of one individual. No one person's speech is strictly homogeneous, although some people are far more consistent than others. Variability may result from the fact that different speeds of speaking are accompanied by different linguistic structures, both phonological and syntactic. Most importantly, being social creatures, speakers are more or less conscious of

[4] An excellent investigation of language and variability and its implications for the theory of language and language change is to be found in Weinreich, Labov, and Herzog (1968).

the functional value of different varieties of speech and vary their styles accordingly. Different linguistic patterns are rewarded, for example, in the school and on the ghetto street corner; linguistic patterns that one's peers approve may offend one's parents; different styles are appropriate in the law courts and in the local bar. To a greater or lesser extent all speakers adjust their speech to the social situation, some quite unconsciously, some consciously. Those who are conscious of the shifts often suppose they are using the norm that they have adopted in a particular situation, when in fact they are not, or have made only a partial adjustment to that norm. Others have considerable control over their behavior and can use their ability to switch styles for powerful rhetorical effect; consider, on the one hand, the many politicians who adopt at least some of the key speech habits of their audience on campaign trips and, on the other, radical students who switch to a nonprestigious style (including nonprestigious pronunciation and syntax as well as vocabulary) as a deliberate affront to the "Establishment."

In a very broad sense, then, all speakers are multilingual. Many millions of people in the world, especially in Africa and Asia, are multilingual in the obvious sense that they are proficient in more than one language; most of them gain this proficiency without formal education, being obliged by the necessities of making a living by trade to make use of a second, if not a third or fourth language. In linguistic communities where more than one language is spoken, one language is usually more prestigious than the others, at least in some areas and for some socio-economic groups, and multilinguals place different values on the different languages they use. Speakers using different dialects or different styles in different situations and placing different value judgments on them undergo essentially the same kinds of linguistic experiences as multilingual speakers, even though they are speaking the same language.

Given all the variations in the language they hear around them, children may develop hypotheses about the language that are quite different from those of older people. Children have the capacity, in other words, to "restructure" the language—that is, to reanalyze it and develop new sets of patterns. For example, in several languages, apparently independently, constructions like *He has bound him,* with the perfect auxiliary *have,* developed by the restructuring of patterns like *He has him (in a state of being) bound,* where *have* implies to have under one's control, to possess (see page 93). When enough speakers restructure in similar ways, radical changes in the language occur, and then we have what some linguists call "mutations" in the language.

The ability to analyze whole structures and generalize the analysis consistently to all kinds of contexts is not characteristic of language users after the language maturation point, that is, after the first decade of life. After that, speakers certainly go on analyzing the structures they hear and developing new hypotheses, but they do not internalize them sufficiently well either to generalize them to new contexts or to restructure their own grammar. That is why adult speakers who adopt characteristics from other dialects, whether geographical, socioeconomic, or whatever, rarely succeed in using these characteristics con-consistently; they innovate, but they do not usually mutate.[5] A well-known example is the way in which speakers who try to adopt in their teen-age years or later the rule that the form of the first person pronoun is *I* instead of *me* in *It's me* and *Me and you are gonna go tonight* tend to use it only sporadically; they often generalize the *me* → *I* rule sporadically too to other contexts and say *between you and I*. The latter kind of generalization to "incorrect" constructions (that is, to constructions where it is not used in the model dialect) is given the name of hyper-correction; it is an extremely common factor in language change.

Hyper-correction in particular, and language change in general, is most typical of urban communities where prestige pressures are most marked and where the greatest dialect mixture occurs. The most marked changes have always occurred in the biggest cities. London English from the Middle Ages on was particularly open to change as London was a cultural and economic center where people from all kinds of socioeconomic backgrounds gathered. In the United States, too, the large cities are the most noted for change. Within urban centers the greatest change among speakers from the early teens on is to be found in social groups that are upwardly mobile, since it is these speakers who attempt to imitate the speech of the upper middle-class peer group. In some very detailed studies of language change in New York City, William Labov has shown that innovation is most marked among lower middle-class teen-agers who in careful ("formal") styles attempt to imitate their upper-class peer group and in doing so hyper-correct in a marked way.[6] An example of the relative rapidity of change among lower middle-class teen-agers can be found in the use of *r* word-finally and before consonants, as in *car, card, dark,* and so forth. During the postwar years, upper middle-class teen-agers who had previously not used *r* in these positions came to do so sporadically; their lower middle-class peers imitated them in contexts where prestigious styles of speech were called for, as in formal situations and especially when reading aloud, and came to use *r* far more frequently than those they tried to imitate.

The desire to imitate others, which is basic to the dominance of prestige in language change, is also basic to the counterbalancing tendency for conservatism in language. The desire to imitate peers in a

---

[5] While adult speakers cannot usually restructure their own grammar, they can sometimes learn another, different, grammar very well, that is, add a whole new set of structures; hence the ability of some adults to learn to speak a second language with nearly as much proficiency as they have in their first language. Such speakers are often more proficient in the syntax than in the phonology of this new language; this suggests that an adult speaker's ability to develop new linguistic hypotheses is considerably greater in the syntactic than in the phonological area.

[6] See especially Labov (1966); Labov *et al.* (1968); Weinreich, Labov, and Herzog (1968); and Wolfram (1969).

prestige group leads to change; the desire to imitate peers in the same group leads to minimization of change. The conservatism of language users is most clearly seen in isolated communities with little outside influence, or in immigrant communities where a strong sense of attachment to the native culture persists.

The study of variation and its social correlates is only in its beginnings and is almost exclusively limited as yet to studies of present-day linguistic communities. While there is ample evidence that such variation has always existed and has been a major factor in linguistic change, it is almost impossible at the present stage of our knowledge to reconstruct exactly why and under what circumstances a particular change took place in the past. As it is clearly the less well educated who are the chief instruments of language change, and few records are available of their speech, we may in fact never be able to reconstruct the full picture of the conditions under which any one change or set of changes occurred. This book will therefore not be greatly concerned with particulars of why the language changed, although some speculation will be presented; instead it will be concerned primarily with what patterns have changed and what type of change was involved.

D. IS CHANGE INSTANTANEOUS OR GRADUAL?

The fact that there is so much heterogeneity between speakers and so much variability within one individual's speech and that one can, over a couple of decades, observe marked tendencies in a linguistic community gives the impression that change is gradual. Certainly, in the empirically observable performance of any one individual or group of individuals who come to favor one pattern already available to them over another also already available to them (as in the case of New York speakers who do and do not use *r* word-finally and before consonants), we can observe over time gradual quantitative change that is correlatable with such extra-linguistic factors as sex, age, class, and so on. In another way, however, change is instantaneous. There is nothing gradual about acquiring a pattern; the moment it becomes part of one's competence, even in the most limited way, one's competence is instantaneously changed, at least to the extent that the pattern is new. Changes at the level of the speaker's competence are therefore instantaneous; changes at the level of a speaker's performance—that is, at the level of the quantitative and situational use to which he puts the changes that have occurred—are gradual. In linguistic study we usually generalize beyond the individual to the speech community that has roughly the same set of speech habits. Obviously, the acquisition of a new pattern within this community will not be instantaneous for the community as a whole, though it will be for its individual speakers. Within historical studies covering time spans as great as those covered here, it is reasonable to speak loosely of certain speech communities acquiring a new pattern at approximately a certain date; it must be remembered though that not all individuals will have acquired it at the same time.

E. TYPES OF CHANGE

When we look at the kinds of differences that have occurred between grammar A at time X and grammar B at time Y, we will usually find that these changes involve either simplification or elaboration, very rarely just the rearranging of materials already available.

The balance of the two opposing tendencies is very important; if only simplification occurred, there would presumably be reduction in the available distinctions; but distinctions (as well as similarities) are basic to human communication. If only elaborations occurred, the language might become so complex that it would fall outside the domain of possible language as we know it.

The most obvious kind of simplification in language is loss of a pattern or "rule." For example, the rules that account for agreement of adjectives, demonstratives, numerals, and the like with the number, gender, and case of nouns have been lost. Loss has nearly always to be stated with very special reference to underlying functions, not to surface forms; for example, adjective agreement was lost at first only in constructions of the type *Noun is Adjective* (for example, *The boy is good*), not in *Adjective + Noun* constructions (for example, *the good boy*). Similarly, the *-m* ending of *whom* was lost at different periods according to whether *who* functioned as a question pronoun as in *Who(m) did you see?* or a relative pronoun as in *The man who(m) you saw;* again, the plural *-en* of verbs as in *They riden* was lost, but not the *-en* of the past participle as in *They have ridden.* Clearly, then, losses of this kind must be specified with very explicit reference to their underlying syntactic structure; they illustrate how very particular a change may be.

The more interesting cases of simplification have to do with the generalization of patterns which at one stage have limited use to more and more contexts. For example, a child will generalize the plural *-s* to all kinds of contexts in which it is not used in adult speech, such as *childs, gooses;* or he may generalize a pronominal form like *-body* from a statement like *Somebody is at the door* to a question as in *Whobody at the door?* It is generalizations of this kind that have led to the replacement of plural signaled by vowel alternation, as in OE *boc* "book," *bec* "books," by plural signaled by *-s.* That the pattern is not always totally generalized (we still have *man–men* and other pairs) is the result of various pressures like tradition, education, prestige, and also sheer quantitative frequency. It happens, for example, that nouns with vowel alternation for their plural and verbs with irregular past tense forms, like *bring–brought* and *sing–sang,* occur statistically very frequently in everyday speech; constant contact with the irregular forms reinforces that pattern and hinders generalization of the more usual *-s* plural and

-ed past tense, and may even result in the construction of new irregular forms like *He brang the book, He has tooken the book.* The term frequently used for generalizations of the sort described here is "analogy." Patterns that can be generalized to new elements are said to be "productive." The *-s* plural form is productive as this is the form most naturally used for any new noun introduced into the language; the plurals *-en* and *-ren* as in *oxen, children,* however, are unproductive as they are not used for new nouns.

If one pattern is generalized to more and more contexts, it follows that some other pattern is being replaced; eventually it may be lost altogether. Patterns that are being replaced, like vowel alternation for noun plurals, are said to be "recessive"; when they are lost in all but fixed phrases, they are "fossilized." The OE instrumental case was recessive when it was being replaced by the dative; it was fossilized when relics of it came to be used only in fixed phrases like *the more the better* or fixed words like *why* (see p. 122).

One of the principle conditions for simplification is the presence of variable rules in a grammar. Consider again New York speakers who both do and do not use *r* before consonants and word-finally (as we saw, this is particularly common among upwardly mobile lower middle-class teen-agers). As they have to make the choice, however unconsciously, between using *r* and not using it, these speakers have a dialect that is more complex than that of speakers who never use *r* in these positions, or who always use it. When choices of this kind are available in the grammars of large numbers of speakers, later generations often develop simpler grammars which eliminate the choice. Since, in the particular instance under consideration, the prestige dialect has *r,* we can postulate that the simplification will involve the generalization of *r* so that eventually *r*-lessness will drop out. On the other hand, we cannot be sure that such a change will take place; changes in attitude may bring it about that another dialect, this time an *r*-less one, acquires prestige, or some other factor may intervene.[7]

If the presence of choices in a grammar is a condition, though not necessarily a cause, for simplification, then so is the presence of redundant elements that carry no extra information. Language is highly redundant. In English there is about 70 percent redundancy in the sounds of an average utterance—change certain elements, and you will still get most, if not all, of the meaning. Reduction of redundancy is a change that will be discussed frequently in the following pages; one example is the reduction of multiple negation such as is to be found

[7] For example, ME long *ū* (the sound in *boot*) gave rise to *au* as in *house, out;* similarly Middle High German *ū* gave rise to *au* as in German *Haus* "house," *aus* "out." In German *ū* became *au* no matter what consonant followed; but in English, for some reason we do not know, *ū* failed to become *au* before such labial consonants as *p, b, f, v, m* or such velar consonants as *k, g, ng*. In German there are words like *auf* "up," *Daumen* "thumb," and *Haube* "cap, hood," but such vowel + consonant combinations do not occur in NE. One simply cannot predict all the limitations that will be put on a change, though one can predict the limitations that *may* be put on it.

in earlier English sentences like *I don't want no toys no more* to a structure with only one *n-*: *I don't want any toys any more*. Or consider the Black English form *Ten boy came* where *boy* is not marked for plural since *ten* functions as the plural marker and *-s* on *boy* is therefore redundant.[8] *Ten boy came* contrasts in the same dialect with *The boys came*. The *-s* here is functional, that is, it conveys meaning, and is not redundant; hence, presumably, its retention. Those languages like German, French, Russian, and Old English which have agreement of adjectives, articles, and so on with nouns for number, gender, and case are highly redundant; for example, in OE *þis mann* and in Old High German *dieser mann* "this man," the demonstratives *þis* and *dieser* agree with the noun in that they are marked as singular, masculine, nominative. Such redundancies are open to change, but again change may not necessarily occur; in English agreement has been lost except for number (for example, *this* man, *these* men), but in German it has not. Redundancies can even be increased in number; for example, it may be that the number, gender, case agreement rules of the early Indo-European languages themselves developed from a system without such redundancies, or at least with far fewer redundancies.

Elaboration, by contrast to simplification, involves increased complexity, such as the increase in redundancies mentioned at the end of the last paragraph. The simplest kind of elaboration is the addition of a pattern, as for example when the auxiliaries *have* and *be* came to be used in OE for the perfect as in *I have seen her, He is come* (see p. 91), or when a new auxiliary *do* came into the language in ME (see p. 137), or when in the last decade a pattern for deriving nouns from monosyllabic verbs came into use, giving us *be-in, love-in, teach-in*. Elaboration is also found when restrictions are imposed on a pattern, making the conditions for the use of that pattern more complex; an instance is the restriction on relative clause reduction that has come to operate in the last century or so and no longer permits us, in the written language at least, to say such things as *He is the man hijacked the plane* (see p. 185).

From our discussion of causes for change, it should be clear that simplification is brought about almost exclusively by children. After the language maturation point has passed, one can usually not restructure and simplify one's grammar, but can only add elements, most of which are never fully integrated. In other words, the adult speaker normally only elaborates. It is, of course, not impossible for children to elaborate, for example, by introducing new restrictions or new structures that do not involve simplification of the grammatical variability they hear around them, but such changes are unusual. Since it is the restructuring by children that brings about major changes or mutations, and since that restructuring nearly always involves simplification, simplification can be regarded as the main type of change.

---

[8] See Wolfram (1969:143f.).

Over large periods of time, processes of simplification can readily be seen. It is important to realize, though, that what is simplification in one part of the grammar may result in elaboration elsewhere. Many examples of this will be given in the course of this book. For example, we will consider how loss of case inflections on nouns was a simplification as far as the formation of nouns was concerned; it was, however, accompanied by various elaborations in the use of prepositions like *to* and *of*, instead of cases, and by increased restrictions in word order.

The kind of change illustrated by the development of *Preposition* + *Noun* phrases (for example, *of the cat*) as replacements of or alternates to *Noun* + *Case* (for example, *the cat's*)—that is, the change by which an inflection is replaced by a word—is called "segmentalization." This kind of change has occurred again and again in various parts of the grammar in the history of English. Another of the many examples of segmentalization is to be found in the development of the comparative form of the adjective. The older form is the inflection *-er*, as in *warm–warmer;* another form, *more*, is also available where there is no inflection but the word *more* carries the same function as the inflection *-er* (*beautiful–more beautiful*). The phrase with *more* developed in Old English (the form was *ma; -re* was later added, patterned on the *-er* of the inflected comparative); it was rarely used with anything but long words—nearly all words three syllables or more long are compared with *more* rather than *-er*. In this century the phrasal (segmentalized) form is gaining some ground even for monosyllabic words (such as *more sure, more strong*); an interesting stage is illustrated by the blend of the nonsegmentalized with the segmentalized form, for example, *more worser, more greater*, both forms typical of the sixteenth century. Blends of this type illustrate well a stage of the language when a system has not been fully internalized.

For nearly every type of change that one can mention, its opposite can also be found; but for any pair of changes one is more usual in the history of most languages. Simplification, for example, is commoner than its opposite, elaboration. Similarly, segmentalization has an opposite, "desegmentalization," and it is less common on the whole than segmentalization; in fact it is hardly found at all in the history of English. Desegmentalization is the process by which a phrase is replaced by a one-word unit. For example, the French future inflection *-erai* has its origin in a phrase consisting of *Verb* + *habēre* (*Verb* + "to have"); and some of the Proto-Indo-European case inflections like locative and instrumental seem to have derived from *Noun* + *Adverb* phrases.

The interaction of opposing types of change is governed in some as yet not clearly defined way so that certain distinctions are maintained in a language, whatever changes may be occurring. For example, in many languages case inflections have been drastically reduced; however, in few languages have plural inflections been lost. Perhaps this is because such properties as number (singular versus plural) have semantic function, while case does not in itself (for a discussion of the surface functions of case see p. 75). In general, if an element is functional and is therefore the chief carrier of meaning, that element will be retained at least until another one with the same function replaces it. On the other hand, if an element is not functional and does little or nothing to signal meaning, it will often be lost.

F. PROBLEMS

The historical linguist is faced with many problems, even when looking at bygone stages of a language as well documented as those of earlier English. Among these problems are two of particular importance for this book: (i) How does one determine whether one is dealing with successive stages of the same language or with successive languages? and (ii) How is one to interpret the available data?

Same or Different Language?

The more one considers the underlying properties of languages, the more similarities one sees. Hence the postulation of certain very abstract kinds of universals; hence also increasing difficulty in determining at what point there is sufficient disparity between two grammars to justify the claim that they are grammars of two different languages rather than two different dialects. As a generalization, we can claim that dialects are differentiated almost exclusively in very superficial ways whereas languages are differentiated in more underlying ways. Similarly, if grammars of later generations differ from those of earlier generations in many superficial ways, the same language is involved; but if the differences are more fundamental, different languages are involved. Such statements are, however, very impressionistic, and no one has established a truly satisfactory metric for resolving marginal cases; so extralinguistic evidence is often used to determine what may be categorized as a member of language A rather than of language B. For example, we call earliest OE around 700 English rather than one of the dialects of early German not so much on linguistic grounds but rather because its speakers had emigrated from the Northern European continent to the geographical location called England. When we delimit the periods of English and say that OE dates from approximately 450 to 1150, ME from approximately 1150 to 1500, ENE from 1500 to 1700, and NE from 1700 on, we are giving a rough guide to those periods of English that have the most linguistic coherence; nevertheless, these periods are also delimited by partially nonlinguistic criteria. The date 450 is established primarily on historical grounds: the Saxons invaded England at approximately this time and presumably spoke a dialect that evolved into OE; there are actually no OE documents until the late seventh century and these are charters mainly in Latin. The date 1150 has more linguistic viability; the annals for 1132–1154 of the *Peterborough Chronicle* (all written in one hand, apparently after the accession of Henry II in 1154) show a sharp break with the language of the documents before 1132. In the annals from 1132 on, but not before, we find, for example, the use of the definite article *þe* "the"; presumably *þe* was used in the spoken language considerably earlier, however. The end of ME, 1500, is chosen again as a rough guide, and mainly on nonlinguistic grounds: chiefly the development of printing (Caxton set up his press in 1486) and the beginning of the Renaissance in England. The end of the Early Modern English period, 1700, reflects in part such linguistic features as the modernity of the use of auxiliary verbs and the final stages of the Great Vowel Shift (originally phonologically distinct words like *sea* and *see* came to rhyme in most dialects at this time) and in part the development of such attitudes to grammar as led to Johnson's *Dictionary* and Lowth's *Grammar.* The following chapters will attempt to capture some of the clusters of similarities that make it justifiable for us to speak of "English" during all periods, and also the differences that make it justifiable for us to speak of three main periods: OE, ME, and NE. As stated in the introduction, syntactically ENE clusters quite markedly with ME and is included with it; if we were studying the sound patterns of the language, however, ENE would clearly cluster with NE. This illustrates well how important it is for a historical linguist to establish clearly the criteria by which he judges linguistic unity versus diversity. We cannot expect changes to occur at a uniform rate at all levels of the grammar.

The Data for Historical Linguistics

As the previous discussion has shown, much of the broad theoretical background for historical linguistics can be found in contemporary language. Specific changes that occurred in earlier periods, however, have to be deduced in other ways. Empirical evidence for historical linguistics is unfortunately very sparse; many languages (for example, most Amerindian and African languages) were not recorded at all until the last couple of hundred years; even if records were made, many have been lost or damaged; some (for example, Linear A and many Etruscan documents) are still virtually impenetrable. Much of historical linguistics concerns reconstruction of the language (i) from sparse texts, or (ii) by methods of comparative reconstruction where different but supposedly related dialects or languages are compared and abstract hypotheses are developed that provide the simplest formula for earlier, non-attested stages from which later, attested stages can be shown to have developed, or (iii) by internal reconstruction where certain variants in an attested stage (for example, the alternation between [s] and [z] in *house–houses*) may be used to hypothesize about patterns at an earlier stage, or (iv) a combination of two or more such methods.

In the case of English, and most Indo-European languages, we are fortunate in having extensive data not only of individual words, but also of whole sentences and even whole texts; without such data it is hard to reconstruct the history of sentence patterns, though it is by no means impossible. Dialectal differences between variants of the same modern language may give us considerable clues as to how sentence patterns develop; comparison of the syntax of different but related languages, even if as distantly related as Sanskrit and English, may lead us to hypothesize what the syntax of Proto-Indo-European was like. Some attempts have actually been made to reconstruct folk tales in Proto-Indo-European;[9] there has been much discussion about the validity of these reconstructions, but so long as they are considered to be on the same footing as any other reconstruction, they are useful, especially as challenges to our intellect and to our notions of what possible and plausible sentences of a language are and also what possible and plausible syntactic changes are.

In this book we will not be reconstructing sentence patterns on a purely speculative basis. There is plenty of material from mid-Old English times on that will exemplify most structures a linguist might wish to investigate in English. All the same, there are severe limitations on the extent of our study. One is that many of the texts available, particularly in the early periods, are translations, usually from Latin, and it is not always possible to evaluate how much of the language used is a direct word-for-word translation rather than idiomatic English. Texts have been chosen for the most part which seem to show little or no evidence of translation, but this does not ensure that what we read is what any author actually wrote since scribal practices were considerably freer than we would tolerate in these days of copyright. Take any two manuscripts of the same work and you will find words changed, words spelled differently, and even whole sentences rewritten; to change a text within reason was considered the prerogative of the scribe in all but a few cases (for example, Alfred in the preface to the *Cura Pastoralis* commands that no one shall change his words; so too does Orrm in the Introduction to the *Orrmulum* some three hundred years later). This would not trouble us greatly if it were not that scribes were often foreigners; this was particularly true in early OE times (many of the earliest scribes were Irishmen who spoke Gaelic) and in early ME times (when many of the scribes were French). We cannot be sure that the scribe has not changed a sentence to what he thinks is a reasonable English expression, when in fact it is a translation from his own language or some hybrid construction. On the other hand, the materials are so extensive and so varied, and so much overall uniformity is discoverable among texts of approximately the same period (insofar as we can date them) that our generalizations about English structure cannot be too heavily distorted by these problems. Certainly,

[9] An early attempt to reconstruct Proto-Indo-European was made by Schleicher in the latter part of the nineteenth century and was revised by Hirt in the thirties; a recent attempt can be found in R. A. Hall, Jr., "On realism in reconstruction," *Language* 36:203–206 (1960).

in a study as broad in outline as this they should not give us undue concern.

Another problem is that the written language is always conservative. Furthermore, until this century there has always been a considerable gulf between the so-called "conversational," everyday language and that of written texts. In ages when literacy is the privilege of a very small minority, elegance and rhetorical effect are of far greater importance than when practically everyone can read and write. Also, in ages when parchment is expensive and only a few copies of any text can be made since handwriting is the only medium of copying, only those works considered of special value will be treasured and duplicated. Hence most of the materials that come down to us from before the age of printing are biblical and liturgical works, moral tracts, sermons, histories, and some secular literary works. Very little remains of what might be considered "the language of the common man." So when we compare OE sentence structure to that of the present day, we are not always comparing comparable styles. The materials selected for this study have been chosen specifically for their relatively limited concern for literary elegance and rhetorical effect; poetry has for this reason been almost completely ignored. In general, it seems fair to say that the structures found in prose were also available in poetry, but that poetry had available to it additional devices not available for prose, such as restrictions imposed by meter, stanza, poetic form, and other considerations.

Most of the materials are as close to informal, "conversational," educated English as possible within the limits of the texts available that are both reasonably accessible and worth reading. Conversational language is of course basically spoken language and can only be approximated in the written medium; it is characteristically ephemeral and intended only for the immediate moment whereas written language is usually meant to last. Conversational language involves dialogue, interchange, and "orientation toward the addressee,"—hence question and answer, to a degree quite unusual in written styles other than those of sermons and fictional dialogue. It also characteristically involves ritual expressions and formulas such as those used for greetings, farewells, polite requests, commands, compliments, endearments, oaths, imprecations, exclamatory expressions, and the like, all of which change considerably over the centuries. Above all, it reflects lack of premeditation. Hence there are few markers of logical progression and there are many false starts, repetitions, and so forth.[10] We find various degrees of approximation to these characteristics of conversational language in letters, journals, picaresque tales, and dramas. It is therefore on documents of this type that the present study is based, where they are available.

---

[10] For good discussions of the characteristics of colloquial speech, see Wyld (1937) Chapter 10 and Salmon (1967).

2 A SKETCH OF SELECTED MODERN ENGLISH SENTENCE PATTERNS

A. UNDERLYING AND SURFACE STRUCTURE AGAIN

In Chapter 1 it was suggested that, in order to account for the language user's ability both to understand new utterances and to produce them, it is necessary to postulate that every language user has a built-in system of abstract patterns, called his linguistic competence. The particular part of this competence that is our concern here is the syntactic system that forms the bridge between the language user's conceptual structure and its manifestation in sound sequences. In this chapter we will look in a preliminary way at some of the more important syntactic patterns common to most speakers of present-day English. First of all, however, it may be useful to expand a little on the notion of the contrast between underlying and surface structure since this is fundamental to the thinking behind this book.

As we saw, the main reason for postulating that there is a contrast between underlying and surface structure is that some sentences with identical sound sequences have several meanings—that is, they are ambiguous—while some sentences which have very different sound sequences are paraphrases of each other.

Ambiguity is a purely descriptive term in linguistics. Most of us have been told at one time or another that ambiguity is a bad thing as it confuses the reader or listener; this is a prescriptive point of view, concerned with passing judgment on the effect of ambiguity in certain contexts, as in expository prose. Creative writers, on the other hand, may value ambiguity highly and regard it as essential to their art. The linguist, in describing language, places no value judgment on ambiguity at all; he is very interested in it, however, since it brings him face to face with the problem of how to demonstrate the relationship between conceptual structures and the forms in which they are expressed.

Ambiguity is particularly common in the written language where the pitch and stress patterns of the voice are largely not represented, but it is also frequently characteristic of spoken language. Take, for example:

2.1 We won't go. = (a) We predict our not going.
(b) We refuse to go.
2.2 They must be married. =
(a) They ought to get married.
(b) All the evidence suggests that they are married.
2.3 The doors were closed at three. =
(a) Someone closed the doors at three.
(b) The doors were in a state of shutness at three.

where each of the utterances 2.1–2.3 has at least the two meanings suggested, and where there is normally no surface linguistic difference in either the spoken or the written form to disambiguate the meanings.

Sometimes we find near-ambiguity when two or more very similar-looking surface forms have really quite different underlying structures. Consider, for example:

2.4 Bill made the boy a good father.
2.5 Bill made the boy a good liar.

Sentence 2.4 may itself be ambiguous between *He made a good father for the boy* and, though less likely, *He made the boy into a good father;* certainly 2.5 does not mean he was a good liar for the boy, but that he made the boy into a good liar. The same nominal expression, therefore, may have different roles or functions within the sentence. In 2.4 *the boy* (in the more obvious interpretation) is the beneficiary of Bill's adequacy as a father, but in 2.5 *the boy* is the person acted upon by Bill. Or consider the difference between the roles that *Dick* plays in:

2.6 Dick works in his garden every week.

and

2.7 Dick likes his garden.

In 2.6 *Dick* is the agent responsible for an action called working; in 2.7 he is the experiencer of a state of pleasure.

Sentences 2.4–2.7 illustrate how the same nominal expression may have different functions although it occurs in the same surface position. Vice versa, the same nominal expression (hereafter abbreviated NP for "noun phrase") may have the same function although it occurs in different surface positions. Consider, for example, such a well-known set of sentences as:

2.8 The window broke.
2.9 I broke the window.
2.10 I broke the window with a crowbar.
2.11 A crowbar broke the window.

In all these sentences the window undergoes the action of breaking—is the "patient" of the breaking; but some of the sentences are also concerned with who was the agent responsible for the breaking (2.9, 2.10) and by what means it was done (2.10, 2.11). The functions of the agent, patient, and means remain the same, whatever their position.

Each of the functions that an NP may have has a special name. The function of the doer responsible for the action is called the Agent function (*I* in 2.9, 2.10); the means of doing it is the Instrument (*crowbar* in 2.10, 2.11); the thing which is acted upon is called the Patient (*window* in 2.8–2.11). In all, there are about a dozen basic functional relationships for NPs. Agent, Instrument, Patient, and some other functions will be discussed in more detail in Section C.

When we look behind the surface form of a sentence to its more abstract properties, including the relationship of parts of the sentence to each other and the role or function they fulfill, we can then see that a particular sentence is simply one instance of a certain combination of more abstract elements, a particular surface manifestation or "realization" of a more general underlying pattern.

Sometimes the same underlying form may have several possible surface manifestations. For example, if I want to express in other surface forms the ideas underlying:

2.12 I allow you to go.
2.13 Maybe he will go.

for 2.12 I may select:

2.14 You may go.
2.15 You can go.

and for 2.13:

2.16 He may go.

Not only the sound sequences are different, but also the grammatical categories. *Allow* has the grammatical function of a main verb, as does *go; may* and *can,* however, are members of a very special set of verbs called "auxiliaries." In 2.13 *maybe* has the grammatical function of an adverb, but *may* in 2.16 is an auxiliary verb.[1]

[1] For discussion of the distinction between main verbs and auxiliaries see page 32.

If a given element has the surface form A in one context and the surface form B in another, we have a case of "suppletion." A simple instance is the relationship between *go* and *wen-;* the latter occurs only before the past tense *-t*, as in *He went; go* occurs elsewhere, as in *He is going, He has gone, He goes*. Other instances of suppletion are provided by the adjective *good* alternating with *bett-* before the comparative *-er* and by the adverb *well* alternating with *bett-* before the comparative *-er*. Perhaps less obvious but equally predictable are the quantifier variants *some/any,* as in:

2.17 I saw *some* lions near Kilimanjaro.
2.18 I didn't see *any* lions near Kilimanjaro.

and the auxiliary variants *must* and *can,* as in:

2.19 They *must* be students (in the meaning "All the evidence suggests they are students").
2.20 They *can't* be students (in the meaning "All the evidence suggests they are not students").

So far we have discussed some of the ways in which different underlying structures may have the same surface form and in which the same underlying structure may have different surface forms. It is also possible for underlying structures not to have any overt form at all. The classic example is provided by the "imperative" construction, as, for example:

2.21 Go!

Imperatives must be considered to contain at least an underlying addressee, *you,* as in *You, go!* If they did not, we could not account for why we say *Look at yourself in the mirror,* rather than **Look at you in the mirror,* since *-self* forms occur only when there are two nouns or pronouns referring to the same things, as in *I looked at myself.* As we shall see, there is actually a lot more to the underlying structure of sentences like 2.21, all of it usually without any surface manifestation at all.

We will be finding many more examples of different types of manifestations for the same underlying structure in the course of this book. The multiplicity of different forms available at any one time for the same or similar underlying structures is undoubtedly a condition for change.

B. THE SENTENCE AND ITS PARTS

However simple it may appear to be in its surface structure, a sentence can be thought of as having two parts. Consider, for example, a set of sentences like:

---

* An asterisk signals the form is "ungrammatical"—that is, not part of the structure of the language.

2.22 Frankie shot Johnnie.
2.23 Did Frankie shoot Johnnie?
2.24 Frankie, shoot Johnnie!

The action (shooting) and the participants (Frankie as Agent, Johnnie as Patient) are the same in 2.22–2.24. Where the sentences differ is in their force as speech acts; the first has the force of a statement, the second the force of a question, and the third that of a command. Thus a sentence contains one part that refers to events or states and the participants in them, and another that specifies, at least in the underlying structure, the type of speech act involved.

In the late fifties, the Oxford philosopher J. L. Austin developed a theory of speech acts that has influenced both philosophers and linguists to a considerable extent. The theory has recently been developed and modified by J. R. Searle in his book *Speech Acts*. According to the theory of speech acts, every sentence can be considered from three different points of view. Most obviously, when we speak we perform an utterance act—that is, we utter a sequence of sounds. But we do not just mouth words without meaning. For an utterance to be properly meaningful as an utterance of the language, we must not only perform an utterance act, but we must also refer and predicate—that is, perform a propositional act in which events or states and participants in them are referred to. Equally important, we must also perform what Austin calls an "illocutionary act"—that is, we cannot utter a meaningful sentence without stating, questioning, commanding, promising, or the like.

Austin is concerned primarily with what we do as speakers—with our performance, not with our internalized, intuitive knowledge or competence. Nevertheless, the theory of speech acts is important to a linguist writing a grammar of competence since our intuitive knowledge includes knowledge of what may or may not potentially constitute a speech act. The potential utterance act is specifiable in that part of the grammar of a speaker's competence which deals with sound sequences. The potential propositional and illocutionary acts are specifiable both in the part of the grammar dealing with abstract conceptual structures and in the part dealing with the grammatical categories and relationships of sentential structure, since both the potential illocutionary acts and the potential propositional acts impose significant limitations on possible semantic combinations and also on the choice of possible grammatical categories and the order in which they are given a surface form.[2]

---

[2] Most transformationalists agree that illocutionary acts must be accounted for in grammars. There is, however, considerable disagreement about where and how this is to be done. Proponents like Chomsky of the view that semantics is an interpretive component of the grammar argue that the potential illocutionary force of the sentence is to be accounted for in semantic interpretation, not in syntax at all. In his discussion of the illocutionary force of declarative sentences, Ross (1970) specifies the potential illocutionary force on the semantic-syntactic level; he does, however, suggest that an interpretive view might be equally or more viable, if one knew how to specify it.

The propositional part of the sentence will be called the "proposition"; the part specifying the kind of speech act will be called the "performative." The latter term is used instead of "illocutionary force" partly in the interest of brevity and partly because it is the preferred term in most transformational grammars.

Selected properties of the proposition and of the performative will be outlined below. Only those properties which are to be discussed in later chapters will be looked at in any detail. In this chapter the proposition is discussed first, as analysis of this part of the sentence is more likely to be familiar to readers than that of the performative. In later chapters, where sentences from real texts are used, it is preferable to describe the performative first as it has so many consequences for the surface structure of sentences.

C. THE PROPOSITION

Of the proposition one can ask whether it is true or false. For example, consider the assertion:

2.25 John arrived late.

I can ask either of you or of someone else:

2.26 Is it true that John arrived late?

Insofar as the proposition can be judged true or false, it has affinities with the propositions of logic; like them it may be negated, as in:

2.27 John didn't arrive late (equal to the logical proposition: 'It is not the case that John arrived late').

Furthermore, the verb and the functions which make up the proposition correspond roughly to the "predicate" and the "arguments" of logic, respectively.

Logic, however, is not language, although it is derived from language. A logical proposition in itself is neutral to such elements as time, place, and manner; but in language the proposition cannot be expressed without at least some reference to the time of its occurrence relative to the time of its utterance. In other words, the propositions expressed as sentences in natural languages cannot occur without a tense marker. Consider these examples:

2.28 *Bill ride his bicycle.
2.29 *Bill's riding of his bicycle.
2.30 Bill is riding his bicycle.

Only 2.30 is a complete English sentence; it alone not only expresses the fact that Bill is the actor-agent associated with the event called riding a bicycle (as do 2.28–2.29), but it also locates that event in a temporal span that is assumed to be prior to the time of utterance.[3] The function of tense modification is to indicate whether the speaker assumes that the proposition refers to an event that took place before the time of the utterance, whether he assumes it refers to an event taking place simultaneously with the time of the utterance, or at whatever time (for details see p. 42). The tense affects the whole core of the proposition (the verb and the arguments associated with it); in fact, the tense may be "predicated" of the core, as in *It is in the past that he went,* which is an extended surface form of *He went.*

Tense modification is not the only way to divide up the time span. Another way to think of events occurring in time is to concentrate on whether the event is truly over and completed:

2.31 He has arrived.

or whether the event has duration and continues as a relatively unified process over some extended period of time:

2.32 He was running for three hours.

or whether the event is recurring again and again in a series of unique happenings:

2.33 The mouse ran out of the hole for three hours.

(that is, kept repeatedly running out), and so on. Such delimitations of the time span are usually given the name "aspect." Like tense, aspect affects the whole core of the proposition; unlike tense, however, aspect is not required for a proposition to be expressed as a sentence in English.

The following diagram shows the relationship between the basic parts of the sentence as postulated here.[4] Parentheses indicate elements which may be present on the syntactic level but are not required:

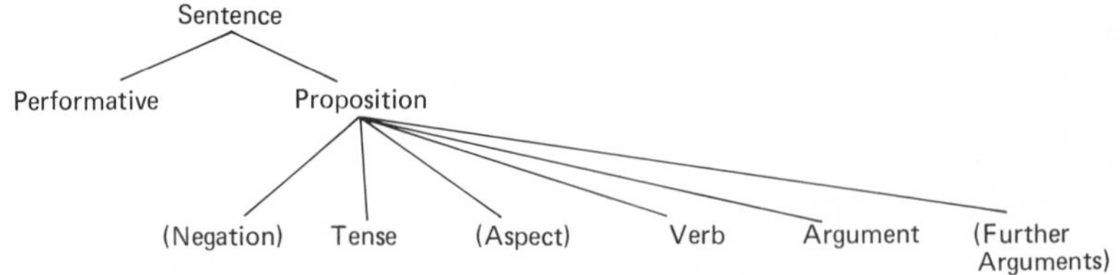

In the following paragraphs the main core—verb and "arguments"—will be discussed first; then tense, aspect, and negation, in that order.

[3] Dialects like Black English of the "street-speech variety" have sentences with the *form* of 2.28, but such sentences have the *function* of 2.30 and are interchangeable with them (Wolfram, 1969:134–137).

[4] Since tense (and also negation and aspect) can be predicated of a proposition, as in *It is in the past that he read the book, It is not the case that he read the book,* and so forth, some linguists give inde-

The Verb and Associated Arguments

The Verb

Verbs are the heart of the proposition. This can be seen quite readily if we substitute indefinite pronouns or even meaningless variables like *x, y,* and *z* for NPs. Consider, for example, the substitution of variables for NPs in 2.8–2.9:

2.34 *x* broke.
2.35 *y* broke *x*.

These sentences still make some sense. If, however, we keep the NPs and substitute variables for the verb, the sentences convey much less information:

2.36 The window *x*.
2.37 I *x* the window.

The centrality of the verb manifests itself in other ways as well; for example, many nouns are derived from verbs (for example, *to feel* → *feelings, to walk* → *a walk*). It is true that verbs can also be derived from nouns, for example, *to lord it over someone,* but such derivations are relatively rare.

Verbs can be grouped according to the number of arguments (NPs in particular functions like Agent, Patient, or the like) with which they may be associated, and also according to the types of function they either must be associated with or else may be associated with. A few verbs in English are not associated, at least overtly, with any functions at all, for example, *It rained, It is hot,* where *it* has no reference and

---

pendent propositional status to these constituents, as in:

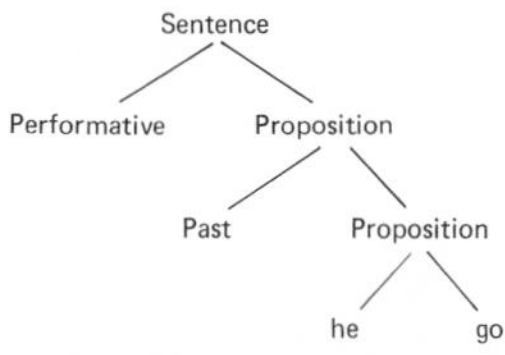

See especially Lakoff (1970), McCawley (1968), and Postal (1970).

While theoretically attractive, this model involves many devices for proposition-collapsing that have not undergone much change in the history of English and are therefore not important for this book. (There is, however, a rather interesting correlation at certain points between segmentalization and failure to collapse propositions together; the details of this correlation need considerable study.) In models in which the major constituents of the proposition are each given independent propositional status, no more than two nominal expressions may be attached to any one verb and, therefore, the treatment of nominal expressions and their functions is rather different from the one given here. Nevertheless, there is a considerable amount of overlap and of translatability from one model to the other. Both models eventually have to account for the same data, of course.

is used simply as a meaningless element to fill the subject slot.[5] Most verbs, however, always have one or more functions associated with them. When a verb is associated with only one function, it is called a "one-place verb" (traditionally an "intransitive verb"). When it is associated with more than one function, it is called a "multi-place verb." The number of functions associated with any one verb is of considerable historical interest as it may vary from period to period.

More important for the underlying conceptual structure of individual verbs than the number of functions associated with them are the types of function with which they must be associated. For example, *break, smash, open, close,* and similar verbs must be associated in surface structure with a Patient; they may also be associated with functions like Agent, Instrument, as illustrated by 2.8–2.11 above. Verbs like *look at, listen to,* however, must be associated with both an Agent and a Patient in surface structure:

2.38 *The house looked at.
2.39 I looked at the house.

Verbs that may be associated with Agents are action verbs: verbs which can be used in reply to *What did you do?* Most verbs are of this kind, but there are some which cannot be used in reply to *What did you do?* These nonaction verbs may be illustrated by:

2.40 I knew the answer.
2.41 I liked that story.

Not only may these sentences not be used in reply to *What did it/you do?;* they may also not be used in permissions. I cannot permit the soup to taste good, nor can I permit you to like the story (except in jocular locutions). Furthermore, these nonaction verbs do not occur with the auxiliary *be + ing,* for example: **I am knowing the answer,* **He is liking the story.*

Like verbs, constructions of the form *be + Adjective* can be of the action or nonaction type. Adjectives describing types of behavior tend to be "action adjectives": *What are you doing?, I am being true to my word,* or *I am being nice/good/considerate/noisy.* But most adjectives are of the nonaction type, for example, *I am blond. I am being blond,* if it occurs at all, means *I am behaving as if I were blond. Be sad, be happy,* and the like are basically of the nonaction type; *He is being sad* can only mean that he is behaving as if he were sad, and not that he is a sad person, and illustrates a derived use of *be sad.* Consider also the difference in meaning between *That little boy is very good* (goodness

[5] One can, however, claim that all propositions have at least one underlying argument if one takes the view that sentences like *It rained* have an underlying locative (*It = in some place*). See D. T. Langendoen (1966).

is inherent in him, characteristic of him) and *That little boy is being very good* (he is acting in a manner of which I approve; the sentence possibly even implies I did not expect him to act that way because he is really a naughty boy). The subtyping of both verbs and adjectives into action and nonaction types is one of the justifications some linguists give for considering *be + Adjective* a subgroup of verbs. Another justification is that there are many pairs of verbs and adjectives that mean the same thing, many of them suppletive, such as *I like you, I am fond of you; I desire it, I am desirous of it.* The analysis of adjectives as a subset of verbs can be shown to be particularly convincing when we consider the history of verbs and adjectives in English. Where in OE there were expressions like *Me hungered, Me thirsted,* we now have *I am hungry, I am thirsty.* In other words, a verb appears to have been "replaced" by an adjective. This type of replacement could be accounted for very easily if we considered adjectives to be a subset of verbs. According to such an analysis, *run, like, be noisy,* and *be blond* would all be verbs; the first two would be nonadjectival verbs, the third and fourth would be adjectival; the first and third would be action verbs, the second and fourth nonaction verbs.

It is also possible to consider the so-called "predicate nominal" (the second NP in an *NP + be + NP* construction) as part of the verb. For example:

2.42 He is a fool.

(where *a fool* is the predicate nominal) pairs with adjectival expressions like *He is foolish.* Like the pair *He is blond* and *He is being blond today,* there are pairs like 2.42 and *He is being a fool* (acting like one). As with adjectives, there are also historical justifications for treating *be a fool* as a nominal subclass of verbs; for example, predicate nominals, like predicate adjectives (Adjective in *NP + be + Adjective* constructions), agree in number, case, and gender with the first NP in languages like OE and Latin. Whether the analysis of predicate nominal constructions as verbs of the nominal type is correct or not, it is clear that these constructions have an underlying structure considerably different from that which the surface structure suggests. The question form of 2.42 is:

2.43 What is he?

not:

2.44 * Who is he? (This is, of course, a possible question, but a different one.)

Another way in which verbs are subcategorized is according to whether they are "main verbs" or "auxiliary verbs." This distinction is based primarily on the surface characteristics of the verbs, not on their underlying function. Since the interrelationship between main verbs and auxiliaries in the history of English will take up a substantial part of the following pages, it may be appropriate to take this opportunity to elaborate at some length on the distinction.

Main verbs are members of a very large class. New ones are constantly being added; in any dictionary of modern English they number thousands. If they occur in simple negative sentences or in questions requiring *yes* or *no* for an answer, they require *do,* as in:

2.45 He didn't walk to school.
2.46 *He walkn't to school.
2.47 Did he walk to school?
2.48 *Walked he to school?

Auxiliary verbs, on the other hand, form a small set: *will/would, can/could, shall/should, may/might, must, ought to,* traditionally called "modal auxiliaries"; and *have* and *be* when they require participial endings on the following verbs. *Have,* as an auxiliary, requires the past participle marker on the following verb, as in *He has gone. Be* requires either the present or the past participle marker on the following verb, depending on whether *be* expresses ongoing activity as in *He is going* or the passive relationship as in *He was seen yesterday. Have* and *be* may also occur without requiring participles, as in *I have a broken nose* and *He is a Yippie;* in such cases they are traditionally called main verbs since they can occur independently of other verbs. In other respects, however, they behave much like auxiliaries, so disturbing an otherwise clear-cut surface distinction between the two classes.[6]

The set of auxiliaries is definable by the following characteristics:

(a) As the term implies, they are "helping verbs," and cannot occur independently of other verbs. Sentences like *You may* are not exceptions since they assume another sentence in which a main verb is present, such as *May I leave?*

(b) Auxiliaries may all occur with *not/n't* immediately following them, for example, *He shouldn't go, He mustn't go, He isn't going.* The only main verbs that allow *not/n't* to follow them immediately are *be,* as in *He isn't young* and, in some dialects, notably British ones, *have,* as in *I haven't a book,* and *used to,* as in *He usedn't to go.* For all other verbs, *do* is required to support the negative, as in 2.45 versus 2.46.

[6]Recently, however, the main verb status of the *have* and *be* that do not require participles has been called into question since their occurrence is very largely predictable. Furthermore, they are interrelated in interesting ways as can be seen from *I have the book, The book is mine* where the NPs and their functions are the same and *have* or *be* is selected according to which of the functions is subjectivalized. For some discussion see Fillmore (1968:61–65), Lyons (1968:388–399), and Bach (1967). If *have* and *be* are not main verbs, they are, like *do* to be discussed below, predictable and therefore "dummy" auxiliaries.

(c) In so-called "yes–no questions," which require *yes* or *no* for an answer, auxiliaries occur before the subject, for example, *May he go? Has he left?* Other verbs require *do* as in 2.47 versus 2.48; again the exception is *be,* and for some dialects *have: Is he young? Has he a book?*

(d) Auxiliary verbs occur in tags: *He's going, isn't he? He'll leave, won't he?* but main verbs other than *be* and *have* require *do: He let go, didn't he?* not **He let go, letn't he?*

The verb *do* has been mentioned several times in the preceding discussion. There is a main verb *do* as in *do the shopping* which does not concern us here. There is also a *do* verb that has all the characteristics of the other auxiliaries except that it carries no meaning or information in itself as they do. This *do* is completely predictable in that when no auxiliary is available in the surface forms of such structures as negations, questions, and tag-questions, it is introduced to support tense: For example, consider:

2.49 I didn't do the shopping.
2.50 Did you do the shopping?
2.51 You shopped, didn't you?

In these sentences it is the *n't* that signals negation and the word order that signals the question forms; *do* is simply a place-filler or "dummy" auxiliary, and as such is quite different from the other auxiliaries, all of which carry at least some meaning. Further details of the use of *do* are given in Chapter 5, page 176.

Nominal Expressions

The functions of nominal expressions

AGENT. The Agent function is the function of the doer responsible for an action or event taking place. In a sentence like:

2.52 I ran down the hill.

I is the Agent of the running. Since Agents must be able to do something of their own volition, the kind of NP that can function as Agent is limited: the noun must be animate (or a personified nonanimate). Consider, in contrast to 2.52, a sentence like:

2.53 The can ran down the hill.

where the can is hardly its own Agent, unless we think of it in a fairy story with both intention and legs; the Agent, though not mentioned, is either somebody or some force like gravity. In either case, *the can* realizes the Patient function, the element to which something happened. In such a sentence as *The can broke the window, the can* is again not the Agent, but rather the Instrument which somebody (as Agent) used to break the window (the Patient).

PATIENT. The Patient is the broadest function. Usually it is the function of the recipient of the action. For example, in:

2.54 I opened the door.

the door is the Patient. In:

2.55 The door opened.

the door is also Patient—it does not open of its own agency, but is opened by somebody or something, for example, the wind. Sometimes a whole sentence may function as the Patient, so that one sentence is embedded within another sentence, as in:

2.56 I saw that he was going.

where *that he was going* is what I saw. Such sentences are called "complement sentences"; they are discussed more fully in Section E below.

INSTRUMENT. Instrument is the function expressing the means by which something is done, most explicitly the thing used to do something. Most often the Instrumental is realized by a prepositional phrase, typically *with x,* as in:

2.57 The cop sprayed Bill's eyes with mace.

Nonprepositional versions, however, also occur with the verb *use,* as in:

2.58 I used a pencil to mark it.

EXPERIENCER. Experiencer is the function of the animate being inwardly affected by an event or characterized by a state. For example, if I say:

2.59 I am sad.

I am not claiming that I am the Agent of sadness, nor even that I am the Patient, but that I am experiencing it. Similarly, *he* in *He is happy/distracted/hungry,* or similar phrases is the Experiencer of happiness, distraction, hunger, or other emotions.

If Experiencer is the only function with which a verb is associated, that verb will be a nonaction verb (see p. 30) and will not permit the *be + ing* auxiliary.

GOAL. The direction toward which something is directed functions as the Goal. Goal may be a location as in:

2.60 He walked to school.

or it may be a physical being such as a person to which something is directed, like *(to) her* in:

2.61 He gave the book to her.

and in *I gave her the book, I sold the car to her, I handed it to her.* When an Agent and a Goal manifested by a physical being are both present, as in the last examples, the Goal is traditionally called the "indirect object." In this book, however, the term "indirect object" will be used only for the prepositionless form of the Goal when it immediately follows the verb as in *I gave her the book* (see p. 38 below).

SOURCE. If the direction to which something is directed has the function of Goal, the direction from which something comes is the Source. Again, the Source may be a location, as in:

2.62 The apple fell from the tree.

It may also be a physical being, like *from me* in:

2.63 He bought a car from me.

POSSESSOR. The function of Possessor is expressed in many different ways in English; underlying all is the function of the animate being that has something in his possession at least temporarily.[7] The *he* underlying the various forms *he, his, him* is Possessor in each of the following sentences:

2.64 He has a car.
2.65 The car is his.
2.66 The car belongs to him.
2.67 That is his car.

A Possessor may possess something in the relationship called "alienable possession" (possession by contingency; possession may end). In English, sentences of the form illustrated in 2.64–2.67 involve alienable possession. A Possessor may also possess something "in-

[7] This covers both uses of Possessor in a sentence like *He has my book* (= he has in his temporary possession [with him] the book that I have in my continued possession [that I own]). Strictly speaking, underlying distinctions between owning and having in one's temporary possession should be made, but they involve more detail than we can go into here.

alienably" (inherently, so to speak). In English, inalienable possession usually involves body parts; in other languages it may involve other elements. Sentences of the form illustrated in 2.65 do not occur with this type of possession:

2.68 *The navel is his.
2.69 *That eye is mine.

Even sentences of the form 2.64 are odd for inalienable possession, unless the noun is modified by an adjective, as in:

2.70 He has a dirty navel.

DOUBLE FUNCTIONS. Sometimes an NP may have not just one but two functions in a sentence. To go back to 2.52, in *I ran down the hill, I* is certainly Agent, but in addition it also functions as Patient. To run as an Agent is to get oneself from A to B by running; similarly, to get up is to get oneself from A to B by raising oneself. In many languages, including French, a surface form of the Patient is to be found in the so-called reflexive, as in *Je m'en vais,* French for 'I am leaving', 'I'm getting myself out of here' (literally, 'I myself hence am taking'). In earlier stages of English we find similar constructions, as in OE, *He for him ham* 'He journeyed himself home', and in such archaic locutions as *He betook himself home.* The difference, then, between 2.52 and 2.53 is not solely that in the former the subject is the Agent and in the latter the subject is the Patient, but that in the former the subject is both Agent and Patient, that is, I am acting both for myself and on myself; the can is only being acted on.

Some other instances of NPs with dual function can be illustrated by *I sold her the car* (*I* = Agent and Source – I was responsible [as Agent] for a transaction that involved passing the car from me [as Source] to her) and *She bought the car from me* (*she* = Agent and Goal).

SUBJECT AND OBJECT. It is a characteristic of English that one of the NPs of the proposition is "subjectivalized." Possibly all languages allow some kind of subjectivalization, but the process must be defined for each language individually. As far as NE is concerned, subjectivalization means that one of the NPs is positioned at the beginning of the sentence and that it determines the number of the verb: in 2.9–2.10 and in sentences like *I smoked the joint,* the NP as Agent is subjectivalized; in 2.8 and in *The door opened,* the NP as Patient is subjectivalized; in 2.11 and in *Paint covered the walls,* the NP as Instrumental; in 2.59 and *He is thirsty,* the NP as Experiencer. If more than one NP is present, there are priorities determining which NP is most likely to be subjectivalized, depending on the function of the NP. If Agent is present, it is the most likely function to be subjectivalized. It does not have to be, however; for example, there is a special structure called the "passive" which is characterized precisely by the subjectivalization of an NP in some function other than Agent, usually Patient or Goal, in that order of priority. Besides:

2.71 The leader (Agent) handed a Molotov cocktail to a little boy.

we have the passives:

2.72 A Molotov cocktail (Patient) was handed to a little boy by the leader.
2.73 The little boy (Goal) was handed a Molotov cocktail by the leader.

Passives are preferred when the NP functioning as Agent is indefinite (*someone, something*) and in certain kinds of technical, especially scientific, writing. Otherwise the subjectivalization of Agent is greatly preferred, and to some extent accounts for the frequent association of subjects with Agents. For the association of subject with "topic," see the section on Determiners, page 41.

Sometimes there is no function to be subjectivalized (but see p. 30, footnote 5). If so, we find the subject position filled by a meaningless *it,* as in:

2.74 It is late.

This *it* has no reference; it does not imply that anything has already been mentioned. The *it* can be thought of as a pseudo-subject, simply filling a positional slot in the sentence. Consider also:

2.75 It appears that John is coming.

Here too *it* is a pseudo-subject, a dummy element with no meaning. *It* in:

2.76 It is obvious that he is a fink.

is a real subject, however, since it is a meaningful element substituting for *the fact.* For further discussion of this issue see Section E on complementation below.

In a sentence with two or more NPs, not only subjectivalization but also objectivalization operates. Objectivalization is a rule that selects an NP that has not already been assigned to subject position and places it after the verb, as in the case of *the window* in 2.9 and *roses* in *I like roses.* If Agent and Patient are both present in a sentence, Patient is most commonly objectivalized (the objectivalized Patient is traditionally called the "direct object"). If Agent, Patient and Goal are all present, Agent will normally be subject, Patient will normally be object, and Goal will normally be expressed in a *to* + *NP* phrase, as in 2.71.

Goal may itself, however, be placed without a preposition as the "indirect object" between the verb and the objectivalized Patient:

2.77 The leader handed a little boy a Molotov cocktail.

The prepositional expression of Goal is usually preferred if the NP is expressed as a noun as in 2.71; the indirect object form of Goal is preferred if the NP is expressed as a pronoun. Like subjectivalization, therefore, objectivalization, both "direct" and "indirect," has priorities to which we respond in registering such properties of sentence use as emphasis and appropriateness in discourse.

NPs that are not subjects or objects are normally expressed by a preposition plus nominal. The usual prepositions associated with particular functions in English are as follows, *by* with Agent as in:

2.78 It was done by me.

with with Instrument as in:

2.79 I did it with a hammer.

from with Source as in:

2.80 I took it from him.

to with Goal as in:

2.81 I gave it to her.

Patient and Experiencer usually have no preposition in English because they are normally subject or object, but occasionally *of* and *to* respectively appear as in:

2.82 I (Agent) robbed the manager (Source) of his money (Patient).
2.83 The argument (Patient) is not clear to me (Experiencer).

The Possessor is usually associated with *of.* It also has another form, however, that of the *-s* genitive inflection – the relic of a complex case system which we shall be looking at in the next chapter. So besides:

2.84 The wealth of the Rockefellers.

we speak (perhaps more commonly) of

2.85 The Rockefellers' wealth.

The genitive has various other functions. Thus besides the interpretation of *My aunt's picture* as 'My aunt has a picture', there is the interpretation, 'The picture that someone painted of my aunt'. In the former, she is Possessor of the picture; in the latter she is the Patient of the painting and the picture is the result of someone's action (in this latter function the construction is sometimes called the "objective genitive"). These and other functions of the genitive will be discussed in Chapter 3, and especially in Chapter 4.

We say that each function has a preposition associated with it and that the preposition is deleted (or simply not given a surface manifestation) when the NP in that function is subjectivalized or objectivalized. This may also be true for other available functions, including those not detailed here, such as Location, Benefactive, or others. Consider, for example, *The Cop* (Agent) *sprayed mace* (Instrument) *in his eyes* (Goal and Location) versus *The cop sprayed his eyes with mace.* Under certain conditions certain prepositions may be replaced by the genitive *-s* inflection; this does not apply to prepositions for all functions, however, but mainly to *of* associated with Patient, Experiencer, and Possessor.[8]

The structure of nominal expressions

The nominal expression, or NP, that functions as Agent, Patient, Instrument, and so on, consists of at least a noun or a pronoun. Various determiners like *the, a, this,* and *that,* and various quantifiers like *some, many, much,* and *few* may modify or expand the noun. Of these, only the determiners *the* and *a* will be discussed here. Nouns may also be modified by whole sentences, as in *The man I love has left me.* Here *(whom) I love* defines the noun and is called a relative clause. Relativization is one of the major devices for forming complex sentences and will be discussed in Section E.

NOUN SUBCLASSES. Nouns are constrained in various ways by their surroundings and they in turn impose constraints. These constraints can conveniently be accounted for by noun subclassification. One very important feature of nouns is whether or not they have intrinsically unique reference. Names such as *George, Jane, The Alleghenies,* and *Washington* all have unique reference and are intrinsically unique; the term usually given to this subclass is "proper nouns." Nonproper (or "common") nouns, which do not have intrinsically unique reference, are themselves divided according to whether or not they are "concrete." Concrete nouns like *boy, table, book* can occur in all but a very few sentence types, for example, **To go there is a book.* Those nouns that can occur in positions like *To go there is (a) . . .* are the nonconcrete (or "abstract") nouns like *nuisance, problem, bore, difficulty,* as in:

---

[8] The view that prepositions are replaced by *-s* inflection applies to NE; historically, *of* developed considerably later than the genitive inflection.

To ride the bus is a nuisance, Swimming is no problem, That he came was the difficulty, and so on.

Concrete and proper nouns can be cross-classified according to whether they are animate or not. Animate nouns can be pronominalized by *he,* or *she* (that is, can be subclassified according to gender), and can be subjects of *laugh, run, sleep, be sad,* and so forth. Only animate nouns may be used in the function of Agent, Experiencer, or Possessor. Nonanimate nouns are pronominalized by *it;* they cannot occur as subjects of verbs like *be sad* (when they do, we say they have been "personified"). Only nonanimate nouns may function as Instrumental.

Another subtyping of nouns concerns whether or not they can be modified by numerals. Proper nouns cannot ordinarily be counted. *Five Johns came in* is certainly a sentence, but it means 'Five people named John came in', not 'Five people who are John came in'. Nonproper nouns may be count or noncount (sometimes called "mass") nouns, such as *one cat, two people, three questions,* in contrast with the noncountable nouns like *milk, hope, love; *one milk, *two funs* are ungrammatical.

A further feature of nouns is whether or not they can be either singular or plural. Most count nouns can be either, but mass nouns have to be either one or the other; thus singular *book,* nonsingular *books,* but only singular *chastity* and only nonsingular *oats.*

DETERMINERS: DEFINITE AND INDEFINITE. *The* and *a* are usually called the "definite" and the "indefinite" article, respectively. Their prime function is to signal what assumptions the speaker is making about what knowledge is common to him and the speaker. For example, if I say to you:

2.86 Do you want the ticket?

and you don't know anything about any tickets, you nevertheless know that I assume you know about some tickets; so you can reply:

2.87 What ticket?

But if I say to you:

2.88 Do you want a ticket to "Dracula, Prince of Denmark"?

no such assumptions apply, and 2.87 would be inappropriate.

The assumes the noun has been referred to before, or is what is loosely called "given, known material." Known material includes "culturally known," for example, *the President, the sun, the moon.* On the other hand, *a* indicates that the speaker assumes the noun has not been previously referred to. This is why such a discourse as *There was once a king of Narnia* is natural at the beginning of a story, but not in the middle of a story in which this same king had been referred to earlier. It is also why the following sentences can only refer to two separate girls:

2.89 A girl is reading. A girl is crying.

If the same girl is being referred to, we have to say something like:

2.90 A girl is reading. The girl is crying.

(or 2.93 below).

If there are several NPs in one underlying sentence and only one of them is definite, then that NP is normally subjectivalized. Suppose I say:

2.91 A man walked into a room. A window was opened by the man.

The discourse is somewhat bizarre compared to:

2.92 The man walked into a room. The man (he) opened a window.

because the priorities for designating a nominal expression as already-mentioned are the same as those for subjectivalization: we expect Agent, Patient, and Goal to be designated as already-mentioned in that order, if all three are present in one proposition. Hence the frequent assertion that the subject is the "topic" (given information) of the sentence. Already-mentioned and subject do not always coincide, however. Consider, for example:

2.93 A cat ate the cheese.

where *A cat* is marked by *a* as first-mentioned but is the subject in the function Agent, while *the cheese* is already-mentioned, but is the object in the function Patient.

For reasons not yet entirely clear, certain adjectival verbs like *be tall, be loyal* must have definite subjects. I cannot say **A man is tall*, **A man is loyal* in the same sense as I can say *A man came in.* There is, of course, a sentence *A man is loyal,* but this means *All men are loyal.* The *a* used in this sense is the so-called "generic" and is substitutable by *the, all, any, every* or the absence of any article; as such it has a totally different function from the definite and indefinite articles. All the following are generic sentences and all are paraphrases of each other: *A dog is four-legged* (unambiguous generic), *The dog is four-legged* (ambiguous with *the aforementioned dog*), *All dogs are four-legged, Any/every dog is four-legged, Dogs are four-legged.*

PRONOUNS. The pronominal system, as well as the article system, in part also signals what is first-mention or nonfirst-mention in a discourse. Matching the *Indefinite Article + Noun* expressions, are the "indefinite pronoun" expressions such as *someone, something*. Matching the *Definite Article + Noun* expressions are the "personal pronouns" *he, she, it, they,* which all indicate "mentioned before." In a discourse like 2.90, the pronoun form is preferred to *the + Noun* since it avoids repetition of the noun. Compare:

2.94 A girl is reading. She is crying.

While the personal pronouns share much in common with expressions of the type *the + Noun,* they also have special properties of their own. In a discourse the pronoun form of the NP is optional if the NP is in identity with some NP in a previous sentence, as illustrated by 2.90. If two identical NPs occur in the same sentence, however, one must be pronominalized.[9] For example:

2.95 After John went to the theater, John had a hamburger.

implies that there were two different people called John. If the John who went to the theater also ate the hamburger, one of the two instances of *John* must be pronominalized:

2.96 After he went to the theater, John ate a hamburger.
2.97 After John went to the theater, he ate a hamburger.

If two identical NPs occur in the same underlying sentence, not just in combined sentences as in 2.96–2.97, then an additional rule applies: the second of the identical NPs is "reflexivized"—that is, *-self* is added to the pronoun. Therefore:

2.98 Marmaduke saw Marmaduke.
2.99 Marmaduke saw him.

both mean Marmaduke saw someone else. Not so for:

2.100 Marmaduke saw himself.

Tense

Conceptually, we think of time relations as a three-way system of past, present, and future. As far as the syntactic structure of English is concerned, however, there is a two-way distinction. As expressed by

[9] Unless the sentence is generic: *Whatever Isabel wants, Isabel gets.*

the so-called "tense-inflections," which are attached to the verb (or to the auxiliary verb, depending on the structure of the sentence), the distinction is between past (for example, *He ran*) and nonpast (for example, *He runs*). As expressed by general adverbs of time, the distinction is between present *now* and nonpresent *then* (*then* covers past and future, for example *He came then, He will go then*). Here we will be concerned only with the tense system.

The terms past and nonpast are often used to designate the inflectional tense system, although past tense does not always coincide with conceptual past (time prior to the moment of utterance), as in *If he came tomorrow, we could still leave on time.*[10] Tenses are purely grammatical markers; they reflect different points on a semantic scale as seen at the time of utterance, depending partly on the performative (question, prediction, and so on), partly on the time adverb, if any, in the sentence, and partly on the general context provided by the discourse. This is particularly obvious with nonpast when no overt auxiliary is present in the surface structure. In such circumstances, nonpast typically expresses states regarded as pertaining at least to the time of utterance (see p. 44 below), as in:

2.101 He likes those pictures.

or habitual and customary actions which could apply at the time of the utterance (see p. 44 below), as in:

2.102 They recycle their cans.

It can, however, also be used with a future time adverb, to designate that an event will occur after the time of utterance. This is particularly common when the event is (i) fairly definitely going to take place, (ii) going to take place soon, as in:

2.103 We go to Bodega Bay on Friday.

but hardly:

2.104 (?) We go to Bodega Bay in A.D. 2001, when we retire.

In combination with auxiliaries like *be + ing,* nonpast signals that the action is regarded as occurring at the moment of utterance, as in:

2.105 He is leaving (right now).

---

[10] Some grammarians might consider *came* in this sentence subjunctive because in earlier English verbs with subjunctive inflections were used in hypothetical conditions. In NE, however, *came* is simply the past tense, the function of which is to help signal hypothetical condition, not time prior to the utterance.

or, if a future time adverb is present, at some moment in the future, as in:

2.106 He is leaving Tuesday.

(see p. 45, footnote 13 below).

Aspect

Tense is a grammatical category typically locating a proposition in a time relative to the time of utterance. Another way to set the proposition in a temporal framework is to focus on the manner in which the spectrum is distributed or "contoured."[11] There is a wide variety of possible distributions or contours. Here we will look only at three kinds of aspect: distributive habitual,[12] perfective (involving completion), and progressive (involving duration, continuation, and so on). We will be concerned only with the kinds of manifestations these aspects have in terms of verbal inflection and auxiliaries. Aspectual relations can, however, also be found in adverbial expressions (the force of *already* is completive in *He is already here*); in word order (*load the truck with hay* implies that at the end of the action the truck will be completely loaded, whereas *load hay onto the truck* does not); and in the semantic structure of verbs (if I say *He will persuade you to go,* I am focusing on the completion of the act of persuasion and on your projected state of having agreed to go, while no such focus exists in *He will tempt you to go*).

Distributive Habitual

The habitual aspect focuses on the generality of the occurrence of an event or events; it may focus on the oneness of the habit, or on the fact that it recurs repeatedly, distributed over time, as in:

2.107 He goes to work every morning.
2.108 Whenever he comes, he is late.

The latter kind of habitual, called "distributive," is typically associated with adverbs like *again and again.* If the event has happened in the past and will continue to happen, the surface expression of distributive habitual is nonpast tense; past is used only if the events mentioned habitually occurred before some time prior to the time of utterance as in:

2.109 He went to work every morning.

In such cases, *used to* is preferred:

---

[11] On aspect and its relation to tense see Lyons (1968:313–317).

[12] Ideally, habitual and distributive should be treated separately, as not all distributive contours are habitual; for example, *The mouse ran out of the hole for three hours* where the running (in and out) is distributed iteratively over a particular period of time and is not habitual.

2.110 He used to go to work every morning.

Progressive

Progressive aspect, expressed by *be* requiring a present participle on the following verb (hereafter abbreviated *be* + *PrP*), emphasizes the simultaneity of a process with some moment in time. It is associable only with action verbs, since it concerns processes rather than states (for examples see the discussion of main verbs, p. 30). If the tense is past, then the process is simultaneous with a moment prior to the time of utterance; an overt time adverb is usually required. If none is present in the surface structure, the sentence is normally interpreted as having an underlying time adverb. For example, if someone says:

2.111 He was running down the road.

he assumes that the moment in time with which the running is simultaneous is known; otherwise the sentence needs to be completed by some such clause as *when x* . . . . If the tense is nonpast, then the process is assumed to be simultaneous with the time of utterance. Adverbs of time like *right now* occasionally occur; usually, however, they are given no overt form unless present time is to be emphasized.[13] Thus the usual surface form for progressives with nonpast is illustrated by:

2.112 He is running down the road.

not:

2.113 He is running down the road right now.

When associated with predictive auxiliaries like *will,* the process is assumed to be simultaneous with some moment in the future; the same kind of situation obtains for adverbs as with past tense progressives:

2.114 He will be running down the road.

This sentence either assumes the moment in time is known or else requires a *when x* . . . clause to follow.

Perfect

Perfect aspect is expressed by the auxiliary verb *have* requiring a past participle on the following verb (hereafter abbreviated *have* + *PP*). Perfect emphasizes that an event or state is completed. Consider, besides:

2.115 He went away.

the perfective:

---

[13] *He is running tomorrow* is predictive, not progressive.

2.116 He has gone away.

Sentence 2.115 states only that his going occurred before the time of the utterance; 2.116 emphasizes that the going is complete at the time of utterance. Perfect locates events or states within a period before the time of utterance and emphasizes the end-point; it does not, however, single out a specific moment in the past as past tense can. Hence it is not possible to say:

2.117 *He has gone at eleven o'clock.

although the following is fully acceptable:

2.118 He went at eleven o'clock.

Certain conditions have to apply for the use of perfect to be appropriate. For one, there must be what can be called "present relevance"; the subject of the sentence must be alive (or still in existence if an inanimate). Hence:

2.119 Columbus has discovered America.

is bizarre, while:

2.120 I have discovered a good place to fish.

is not. For another, it is usually appropriate to use the perfect only when the event is expected or at least has been discussed before. This is particularly clear in questions, as in:

2.121 Has John left?

which implies that the speaker expected John to leave, whereas:

2.122 Did John leave?

is neutral to such expectation.

Negation

The last constituent of the proposition to be discussed here is the optional negator. Negation has been of particular interest to grammarians and language philosophers for centuries because of its relationship to the concept of negation in logic. Only the barest outlines of the syntactic properties of negation can be given here. One kind of negation operates on the whole proposition, such as that in *He is not happy;* this is often called "sentence negation." Another type operates only on parts of the proposition. For example, the proposition in *He is unhappy* is affirmative, but the adjective constituent is negative; the whole proposition can itself be negated, giving *He is not unhappy.* Only sentence negation will concern us here.

It is fairly well established that in the different languages of the world, "affirmative," that is, non-negative propositions, typically have no surface marker to indicate that they are affirmative, though forms are available, such as *It is the case that x;* negative propositions typically have surface negative markers. In English, the surface manifestation is, in its most usual form, *not* (also reduced to *n't*). In its form *not,* negative is usually incorporated into the surface verbal phrase and placed directly after the auxiliary if there is one; if none is present, then *do* (which carries the tense) is introduced to support *not:*

2.123 He will not like what he sees.
2.124 He didn't like what he saw.
2.125 *He liked not what he saw (archaic only).

As was pointed out on page 32, the only exception to the standard positioning of *not* in all dialects of English is with the *be* verb, and in some dialects, especially British English, with verbs like *have* and *used to.*

Certain elements in the sentence other than the verb are affected by negation, notably indefinite quantifiers, certain indefinite time adverbs, and certain coordinators. Many of these elements are suppletive. Consider, for example:

2.126 I did*n't* buy *any* coffee. versus I bought *some* coffee.
2.127 She does*n't* like dancing and Bill doesn't *either.* versus She likes dancing and Bill does *too.*
2.128 He has*n't* left *yet.* versus He has *already* left.

Some of the elements that are affected by negation may attract the negative and absorb it, giving rise to what is known as "negative-absorption" or "negative-incorporation." Besides the negative sentence in 2.126, we therefore also find:

2.129 I bought *no* coffee.

The negative-incorporated form of *some–any* is *no,* of *somebody–anybody* is *nobody,* of *too–either* is *neither;* of *many* it is *few,* of *much* it is *little.* The negative-incorporated form must be used if a nonspecific indefinite is the subject:[14]

[14] *Someone is not at the window* is of course a possible sentence, but it involves a specific indefinite and means something like 'One of the group who should be at the window is not at the window'.

2.130 *Someone* is at the window.
2.131 **Anyone* is not at the window.
2.132 *No one* is at the window.

Elsewhere negative-incorporation is optional, as 2.126 and 2.127 demonstrate.

The effect of negation spreads from the proposition of which it is a constituent to certain subordinate sentence types; hence we find *anyone,* the suppletive form of *someone,* in:

2.133 It isn't conceivable that he would have time to see *anyone.*

but *someone* in the affirmative version of this sentence:

2.134 It is conceivable that he would have time to see *someone* (but not **anyone*).

In standard English negative-incorporation cannot, however, spread to subordinate sentences. For modern dialects and earlier stages of the language in which negative-incorporation in certain subordinate clauses is possible, see pages 96, 151, 194.

D. THE PERFORMATIVE

We turn now to discussion of the performative, that part of the sentence which specifies the type of potential performance act a sentence can constitute—that is, whether it can be used to make a statement, prediction, command, or the like.

While the question of truth can be raised with respect to the proposition, one can only raise the question of appropriateness with respect to the performative. There is a large set of verbs which are performative when used in the first person nonpast tense.[15] Such verbs include *pronounce, permit, command, christen, promise,* and *affirm,* as in:

2.135 I *pronounce* you man and wife.
2.136 I *permit* you to go.
2.137 I *command* you to tell me where the gun is.
2.138 I *christen* this boat *The Chimera.*
2.139 I *promise* to do it.
2.140 I *affirm* my belief in the equality of all men.

All of these verbs share the special property that when a speaker utters sentences like 2.135–2.140 he is not simply *saying* something about an event but is actually *doing* something; in saying 2.135 in the appropriate

[15] In semijocular mood Austin claims that the list of verbs is "of the order of the third power of ten" (1962:149).

circumstances, for example, he actually causes a couple to be married. Austin (1962:121) provides a useful formula for the illocutionary force of performatives: "In saying *x* I was doing *y*" or "I did *y*". To put it another way, saying 2.135 constitutes a marriage, saying 2.138 constitutes a naming, and so on. By contrast, consider:

2.141 The bottom dropped out of the stock market yesterday.

Saying 2.141 does not constitute a bottom dropping out.[16]

Of course there are certain circumstances when 2.135 might not constitute a marriage, as when the speaker has no authority to perform the ceremony, or the couple are already married to each other. In either case, the uttering of 2.135 would simply be vacuous. Under no circumstances, however, can one raise the question of whether it is *true* that the speaker pronounced the couple man and wife if he has said 2.135. Philosophers have given the name "felicity conditions" or "happiness conditions" to situations like this where an utterance (or part of it) can be judged only for its appropriateness, not for its truth.

Built into each performative are not only certain assumptions about the speaker's right to perform the speech act, but sometimes also certain assumptions about consequences that will follow from the speech act. One can say that a speech act is happily formed only if both types of assumptions are fulfilled—that is, only if the performative is being used by an appropriate person in an appropriate situation *and* if the appropriate consequences follow. Austin mentions, for example, the assumptions behind naming a ship; if I name it the *Queen Elizabeth* I assume I have the right to do so, and I also assume that "certain subsequent acts such as referring to it as the *Generalissimo Stalin* will be out of order" (1962:116).

A clear distinction must be drawn between the intentions and assumptions that are built into performatives, and those that are not. If I request or command you to do something as in 2.137, I intend you to do it. This intention is part of the meaning of *I command.* But if I command you to tell me where something is, not only with the intention that you will in fact tell me but also with the intention of distracting you from doing something else, the latter intention is obviously not built into the meaning of *I command* and is outside the grammatical system we are discussing here.

So far we have considered only performatives expressed by main verbs. Not all performatives have to be so expressed, however. For example, some can be manifested as auxiliaries. Besides 2.139 there is:

2.142 I shall do it.

Besides 2.136 there are:

[16] Though, as we shall see, it does constitute a statement or saying.

2.143 You may go.
2.144 You can go.

Once we see that performatives may have various types of surface manifestation, we can go on to generalize the notion of the performative or illocutionary force of the sentence not only to sentences with overt performative verbs like *acquit* and *promise* or ones with overt auxiliaries like *may* in performative function, but also to sentences without any overt performative marker at all. Consider 2.141 again, for example. This is clearly not a sentence with an overt performative. Nevertheless, it has certain properties that justify postulating that there is an underlying performative. Its force is that of a statement; in saying 2.141 I am stating something; or, to express it differently, 2.141 constitutes a statement. One cannot deny the fact that a statement was made, but one can very well inquire about the appropriateness of the statement (a judgment which will rest partly on whether the speaker has evidence for believing his statement is true, and so on).

For sentences like 2.141 we may therefore postulate that there is an underlying performative of the type *I say to you, I declare to you that.* Such an analysis makes it possible to treat all sentences alike, since it postulates that all have the underlying structure of:[17]

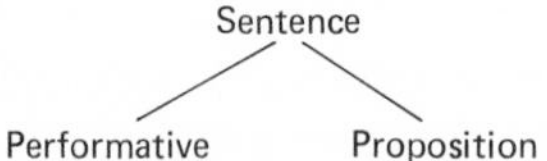

In addition it also explains some rather interesting properties of sentence structure. In an article proposing that the underlying structure of declarative sentences is, very abstractly:

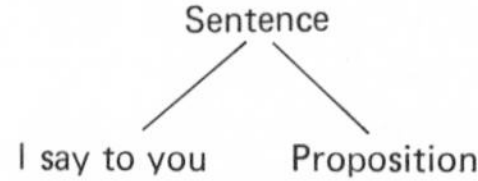

John R. Ross (1970) shows that if an underlying *I* and *you* are postulated, then we can readily account for the *myself* and *yourself* forms in such sentences as:

2.145 Physicists like { myself / yourself / *himself / him } don't often make mistakes.

[17] Some types of discourse, however, such as third person narratives, linguistic treatises, descriptions of machines, and the like, in which the speaker's (or writer's) performance act is minimized, suggest that perhaps the performative dominates the whole discourse rather than the individual sentence. How such problems are to be handled must await more detailed study of discourse than has yet been carried out.

Normally, "reflexive" pronouns with *-self* have antecedents, as in *I hit myself, You like yourself too well, He admired himself.* There is no overt antecedent in 2.145. However, if we postulate an underlying *I* and *you,* then there are underlying antecedents for *myself* and *yourself;* the performative does not include a third person, so *himself* is naturally ungrammatical.

Abstract though the performative is, it may be thought of as containing at least the following elements: a first person (*I*), an addressee (*you*), one of the special class of performative verbs (or the abstract structures underlying them), and nonpast tense. If an overt performative verb is present but either the tense or the person conditions are violated, we get a *description* of a speech act; in such a sentence the verb does not have performative force. Consider, for example:

2.146 I pronounced you man and wife.
2.147 You permitted me to go.

Unlike 2.135, 2.146 does not constitute a marriage, only a description of one. Similarly, 2.147 constitutes the description of a permission, or the claim that permission was granted, but it does not constitute an act of permission itself, as 2.136 does. Furthermore, an underlying performative can have the force of an action only when it is associated with the highest ranking underlying sentence in an utterance. When one sentence is subordinated to another, the subordinate sentence cannot have performative force. Consider, for example:

2.148 Bill says he promises to go.
2.149 Bill says, "I promise to go."

My saying either of these sentences would not constitute an act of promising; it could only constitute a report of such an act. We will therefore need to distinguish between underlying performatives that can never function as acts (for example, when subordinated) and those that can function as acts, given a speaker.

Only a very small number of performatives have been selected here for detailed discussion. They are all performatives that can be manifested as auxiliaries or as nothing at all, and they have been selected largely because the manner in which they could be overtly expressed has changed in interesting ways in the history of English. The performatives will be given notations like "saying" or "promising" simply as a shorthand device for naming highly abstract elements (including first person, second person, nonpast tense, and so on).

Saying

As we saw above, saying usually has no overt surface form at all. When this is the case, performative and proposition together form what is traditionally called a declarative sentence, as for example, 2.141 and:

2.150 One hundred of the allies were killed today.
2.151 They did not approve of the referendum.

Predicting

Predicting has two main forms: *I predict* and the auxiliary *will*. For example, we find as paraphrases of each other:

2.152 I predict his going.
2.153 He will go.

It has been customary to say of sentences like 2.153 that they are statements involving "future tense." It certainly is true that, if I say *He will come,* his coming will occur in the future, and that *will* often translates a "future tense" inflection in languages like Latin and French (for example, Latin *ibit* "go-future-he"; French *il ira* "he go-future"). But English has no special future inflectional tense marker. Furthermore, if we want to express the idea of futurity we have all kinds of ways open to us, of which *will* is only one (if the commonest). We have already considered some of these ways for expressing futurity in connection with nonpast tense (see p. 43). Another point to consider is that *will* often does not imply futurity, as in:

2.154 He is waiting for me; he will be wondering why I am taking so long.
2.155 Oil will float on water.

In these sentences *will* can hardly be future. Each of the sentences 2.153–2.155 have one thing in common – they are predictions. Prediction is normally interpreted as foretelling what is to happen in the future; but given certain circumstances, one can also predict what is happening simultaneously to one's prediction, or one can predict the general behavior characteristic of certain classes of objects. So, I can predict that at the same time as I am talking he is wondering what I am doing, and I can predict that the members of the class of liquids called oil characteristically float on water, implying not only that oil will do so, but also that it has in the past and presumably does so right now.

For some dialects, *will* is in a special relationship with *shall*. *Shall* is used for the first person predictive, *will* for the second and third persons. Some people to whom such a relationship is not natural have nevertheless been taught it and use it with more or less ease. Most American speakers, however, use *will* for all persons, except in questions with action verbs, as in:

2.156 Shall I be going to Denver again this summer?

However, this use of *shall* carries with it certain assumptions, such as asking for approval, and is rarely purely predictive.

Promising

Promising is realized by *I promise,* or by *will,* or by *I/we will, you/he/she/it/they shall; will* and *shall* alternate mainly in those dialects which express prediction by *I shall, you will.*

"Promise" is here used in its broadest sense. The concept involved is in many contexts more readily interpretable as 'I take it upon myself/resolve that . . .'. Consider, for example:

2.157 He shall go to college.

The sentence means, 'I shall see to it that he goes to college' or 'I take it upon myself/resolve that he shall go to college'.

It is important to distinguish the *will* of promises from the non-predictive, nonperformative *will* involving volition, which is a variant of *I desire/wish/want.* In OE *will* was used almost exclusively in the volitional sense meaning *I want;* nowadays, however, *will* is rarely a variant of *want,* except in phrases like:

2.158 Whether you *will* or no.
2.159 If you *will* be a nuisance, I'll have to punish you.

and in negative sentences like 2.1.

Permitting

The performative for permitting may be realized as *I permit/allow you to . . .* or as the auxiliaries *may* or *can.* The following four sentences are therefore paraphrases of each other:

2.160 I permit you to go.
2.161 I allow you to go.
2.162 You may go.
2.163 You can go.

While 2.160–2.161 are unambiguous, 2.162–2.163 are ambiguous. In addition to having the sense 'I permit you to go', 2.162 is also a paraphrase of:

2.164 I say to you maybe (it is possible that) you will go.

May meaning "maybe" can obviously not have performative force. *Can* also has a nonperformative use, hence 2.163 is a paraphrase not only of 2.160–2.162 but also of:

2.165 I say to you, you have the ability to go.

Can is used unambiguously as a nonperformative in such a sentence as:

2.166 Get yourself a good mask so that you can go to the Halloween party.

and unambiguously as a performative in:

2.167 You can go to the party provided you don't go in drag.

One can only permit someone to *do* something, not to *be* something; therefore, only propositions with Agents and verbs designating actions can occur in acts of permitting. Consider, for example:

2.168 He may be sad.
2.169 He may like it.

Unlike 2.162, these sentences are unambiguous; both contain nonperformative *may* meaning 'maybe'. Both contain *he* functioning not as the Agent of acts of sadness or liking, but as the Experiencer of states of sadness or liking. Hence the lack of ambiguity in these sentences.

Commanding

If I can permit somebody to do something, I can also command him to do it; normally, however, I cannot permit or command him to have an inner experience. Hence I can say:

2.170 Enjoy the evening.

but not:

2.171 *Like the evening.

(The bumper sticker, *America, like it or leave it,* is a threat, not a command. *Be friendly* is a command to act in a friendly way, not to feel friendliness.)

The number of ways in which I can express commands is quite extensive, varying from extreme politeness and circumlocution, as in:

2.172 How would you like to go?

to a polite request such as:

2.173 Would you please water the roses?

to an abrupt "imperative" such as:

2.174 Water the roses!

The imperative force of the speech act remains the same, however, and the constraint that what is commanded must be an action remains constant. For example:

2.175 Would you like to be pretty?

is not a command to you to be pretty, but a question.

Imperative structures in English form a special class of commands which are characterized by having no overt subject and no overt tense, as in 2.174. If the object of the verb is a second person pronoun, then reflexivization must take place, as in:

2.176 Look at yourself in the mirror.

The same kind of argument as was used to explain the *-self* forms in 2.145 is used to support the hypothesis that the underlying structure of commanding involves at least *I command you that you . . .* in some very abstract form. Further support is given by the tag-form of the command, as in:

2.177 Do it, will $\left\{\begin{array}{l}\text{you!} \\ \text{*I!} \\ \text{*these men!}\end{array}\right\}$

To go back to 2.175, while it cannot be interpreted as a command to be pretty, 2.175 does nevertheless have the force of a different kind of command—a command to tell me something. Similarly, 2.172 is interpretable not only as a polite command to go but alternately as a question, or rather a command to tell me about your feelings (you'd like to go for a week, not at all, or whatever), or a command to tell me in what manner you would like to go (fly, drive, and so on). Questions are commands to reply and form a special subset of commanding. They have their own grammatical characteristics that differentiate them on the surface from imperatives. For one, they have overt subjects; some have special question words and special word orders.

There are two main types of questions. For one, I may ask for a *yes* or *no* reply to a whole proposition. Consider, for example:

2.178 Is that apple ripe?
2.179 Did he like it?

Questions of this type are not surprisingly often called "yes–no questions." Alternatively, they may be called "truth questions," as they ask for the truth-value of the proposition.

Instead of asking for a *yes* or *no* answer, I may also ask for specification of some incompletely specified part of the proposition, as in:

2.180 Who went?

This sentence presupposes I know someone went, but not his name, identity, and so forth, and I want you to fill in the details. So *Oh, some fellow* is not really a well-formed answer (though it may be partly well-formed insofar as it adds some specification, in this case that the someone was male). A truly well-formed answer would have to be something like *John* or *The Director of the museum* since in these examples no part of the specification is left indefinite, as it is in the answer *some fellow*.

I can question different parts of the proposition, not only those expressed by nouns. To question the verb, for example, we use the form:

2.181 What did he do?

A well-formed answer might be *He fell down* or *He ran away*. As the verb *do* suggests, only action verbs can be used in reply to questions of this type. *He liked the wine* is not an answer to 2.181, nor, in fact, is it an answer to any kind of question other than *How did he react?*

Since the element in question is marked by a *wh-*, questions which contain such elements are sometimes called *wh-* questions. Another name is "content question"; the latter term will be used here.

If we now turn back to the yes–no questions and consider that besides 2.179 there is the subordinated "indirect question" form with *whether*,

2.182 I asked *whether* he liked it.

we can see that it is possible to hypothesize that all questions have an underlying element marked on the surface by *wh-*. In the case of yes–no questions, this element is *either . . . or;* when *wh-* is attached to *either* it is expressed as *whether*. In NE *whether* can be used only when a yes–no question is subordinated; in earlier English, however, it could also occur in nonsubordinated "direct" questions like 2.179 (see pp. 73 and 119), a fact which gives support to the hypothesis that yes–no questions have an underlying *either . . . or*. The full underlying structure of yes–no questions is, according to such an analysis, something like *I command you to reply and specify which one is true: either he liked it or he didn't like it*.

The same elements of the sentence that are affected by negation are often also affected by commands to reply. In other words, questions often introduce suppletive indefinite quantifiers and adverbs, and so on. In negations, *some–any* suppletion is the norm (see p. 47). In questions it is favored, but not obligatory. The exact conditions under which the *any* form is preferred are not fully clear. There does, however, seem to be in yes–no questions a strong correlation between the *some* form and the assumption that the answer will be *yes;* with the *any* form the assumption is that the answer will be *no,* or else no assumption is made about the answer.[18] In content questions, *some* usually correlates with positive expectations, *any* with negative expectations or else with absence of expectations. Consider:

2.183 Would you like some milk? (Expected answer: *yes*)
2.184 Would you like any milk? (Either the expected answer is *no* or there is no real expectation)
2.185 Who wants some mustard? (Expectation that some want it)
2.186 Who wants any mustard? (Either no expectation or perhaps the speaker assumes that as he does not want any, no one else will or should)

E. THE FORMATION OF COMPLEX SENTENCES

It was pointed out in the first chapter that an essential property of natural languages is that the language user can construct an infinite set of sentences. The primary mechanism that permits us to do this is often called "recursion"; it is the device for constructing complex sentences from several simple underlying sentences.

The simplest case of recursion is illustrated by "coordination," or the conjoining of sentences by *and,* as in:

2.187 John danced and Bill sang.

Schematically, the structure of such sentences is:

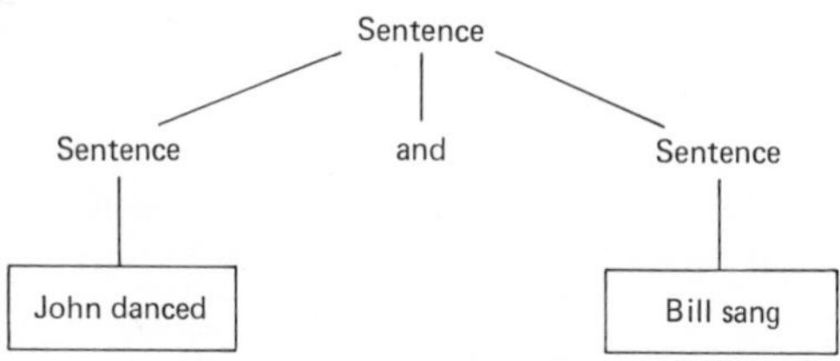

Each coordinated sentence has the same rank as its neighbor; there is no limit on the number of possible sentences that can be coordinated to each other, though, as we shall see, there are limits on the types of sentences that can be coordinated.

More complex are so-called "embeddings," where one or more sentences are conceptually and grammatically subordinated to a higher

[18] Some languages have overt markers specifically designed to signal such assumptions in questions, for example, Latin *num* (assumes the answer will be negative) and *nonne* (assumes the answer will be positive).

sentence (often called the "main clause"). Schematically, this kind of recursion looks like this:

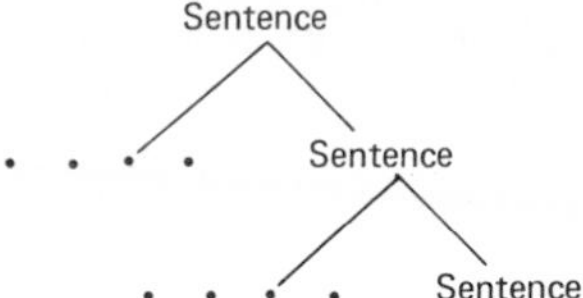

Again, there are no limits on the number of sentences subordinated, though there are considerable limitations on the structures of sentences that may be subordinated and on the surface forms they take. Of the various types of subordination, two will concern us here: "complementation" and "relativization." Complementation involves a whole sentence rather than an NP functioning as one of the arguments of a proposition (usually the Patient). For example, in:

2.188 I expect that he will go.

(that) he will go is a sentence in its underlying structure; it functions as the Patient in the proposition of the higher sentence *I (Experiencer) expect X (Patient).*

Relativization involves the subordination of a sentence to a noun; the sentence then functions as a modifier of that noun, delimiting it in various ways: Consider:

2.189 I enjoyed the play that bored you.

where *that bored you* is in its underlying structure a sentence modifying the noun *play.*

Coordination

Any two or more sentences with the same performative can be coordinated by *and;* consider 2.187 where two sayings are coordinated, and:

2.190 He will be there tomorrow and will do everything you want.

where two predictions are coordinated. There are, however, constraints on combinations of sentences with different performatives. While saying and predicting may be coordinated, as in:

2.191 He has been abroad and will go again.

saying and commanding may not:

2.192 *He saw her and go!
2.193 *He saw her and how did he behave?

There are various rules for reducing coordinate sentences; they all operate on surface structures. One of the simplest of these rules is that if the subject is the same in the coordinated sentences, it may be deleted in any of the sentences other than the first. So we find, besides:

2.194 He saw her and he went up to her.

the reduced (and more usual) form:

2.195 He saw her and went up to her.

If the verb and objects are the same then a similar collapsing rule applies. Besides:

2.196 Harry saw Jane and Bill saw Jane.

we have the reduced (and again more usual) form:

2.197 Harry and Bill saw Jane.

In NE coordination reduction always results in the surface structure juxtaposition of two subjects, two objects, and the like. In earlier English, however, the coordinated elements were often split (see p. 97).

Complements

"Complement" is the name given to a sentence usually functioning as the Patient of a proposition. There are a great number of complement types in English, depending on the verb, to which they function as an argument; to treat them adequately is impossible in a book of this length, so I have selected for discussion only a very small representative group that happen to have undergone significant changes in the history of English. The structures to be discussed may be illustrated by:

2.198 It is significant that he likes Bruce.
2.199 I resent it that he is always drunk.
2.200 It is true that he ran away.
2.201 I believed that he liked her.

Sentences 2.198 and 2.199 contain "factive" complements. This means that the proposition of the embedded sentence is assumed to be true.[19] Notice that if I negate the higher sentence, as in:

2.202 It isn't significant that he likes Bruce.
2.203 I don't resent it that he is always drunk.

---

[19] For a very important discussion of the group of complements considered here, see Kiparsky and Kiparsky (1970).

the negative has no bearing on the truth-value of the complement; it is still assumed to be a fact that he likes Bruce, is always drunk, or the like. On the other hand, 2.200 and 2.201 involve no such assumptions and are called "nonfactive." If I negate the main proposition of these sentences, as in:

2.204 It isn't true that he ran away.
2.205 I didn't believe that he liked her.

then no assumption is made concerning the complement in isolation from the main clause about whether he did or did not run away, whether he did or did not like her.

Some further examples of verbs allowing factive complements are: *be relevant, be tragic, matter, suffice, amuse, regret, comprehend.* Further examples of nonfactives include: *be likely, be true, seem, appear, suppose, conclude, think, doubt.* Some verbs may allow either kind of complement, such as *remember* (note that *I remembered that he went* is factive, while *I remembered to go* is not, as the negative versions of these sentences demonstrate).

The criterion I have given for distinguishing factives from nonfactives is primarily a semantic one; there are, however, many syntactic reasons for distinguishing factives from nonfactives. Among them is that in 2.198 *it* can be replaced by *the fact:*

2.206 The fact that he likes Bruce is significant.

whereas in 2.200 it cannot:

2.207 *The fact that he ran away is true.

This suggests that *it* in 2.198 is a true subject, while in 2.200 *it* is only a meaningless place-holder or "pseudo-subject" that occurs in subject position simply because modern English (though not earlier English) requires NP in that position.

A further difference between factives and nonfactives is that verbs which allow factive complements also allow "gerund" subjects or objects (depending on the verb):

2.208 His liking Bruce is significant.
2.209 I resent his going.

but nonfactives do not:

2.210 *His seeing her is true.
2.211 *I thought his telling a story.

Yet another difference is that most nonfactives allow what some linguists have called "subject-raising," while no factives do. When subject-raising occurs, the subject of the complement sentence is raised to the subject position of the main sentence. Beside:

2.212 It appears that he likes judo.

there is a subject-raised form:

2.213 He appears to like judo.

but beside the factive:

2.214 It is obvious that he likes judo.

there is no:

2.215 *He is obvious to like judo.

Of particular interest is that if a factive is embedded to a proposition with past tense, then the factive complement can be past or nonpast:

2.216 It was obvious that the world was/is round.

But if a nonfactive is embedded to a higher sentence with past, then the complement must be past too:

2.217 It appeared that the world was/*is round.

In languages that have subjunctive versus indicative verb inflections, such as German, French, Latin, and earlier English, factives are normally indicative, nonfactives may be indicative or subjunctive. The use of indicative versus subjunctive will be of particular interest to us in the following chapters.

There are certain verbs like *doubt, forbid, be difficult, be hard* that allow nonfactive complements and that behave syntactically rather like negatives. For example, they allow (but do not require) *some–any* suppletion in the complement. We find, for example, such positive–negative pairs as:

2.218 I believe that he saw $\left\{\begin{array}{l}\text{someone}\\ \text{*anyone}\end{array}\right\}$.

I doubt that he saw $\left\{\begin{array}{l}\text{someone}\\ \text{anyone}\end{array}\right\}$.

2.219 It will be easy to find $\left\{\begin{array}{l}\text{some}\\ \text{*any}\end{array}\right\}$ witnesses.

It will be hard to find $\left\{\begin{array}{l}\text{some}\\ \text{any}\end{array}\right\}$ witnesses.

In some dialects of present-day English and also at earlier stages of the language, the grammatically negative characteristics of verbs like *doubt* are even clearer, since the complements may allow not only suppletion but also negative-incorporation. In such dialects, for example, *I doubt that he saw anyone* can or must be expressed as *I doubt that he saw no one* (see pp. 96, 151).

Relative Clauses

Relative clauses modify a noun. Each of the two sentences that result in a main clause and relative clause must have an NP with the same reference as an NP in the other sentence. The noun in the main clause is called the "head." The noun in the subordinate clause is pronominalized by *who* if it is animate, *which* if it is inanimate, or *that,* provided the relative is contrastive (see below). Sentence 2.189 therefore has the structure *I enjoyed the play* (head); *The play bored you.*

There are two types of relative clauses: those that are contrastive or "restrictive," as in:

2.220 The horse *that is black* finished third.

and those that are noncontrastive, parenthetical, or "appositive," as in:

2.221 The horse, *which is black,* finished third.

Appositive, but not restrictive, relatives are marked off from their heads by commas in writing, by an intonation break in speech.

The assumptions behind the two types of relative clause are quite different; in 2.220 it is assumed that there are many horses of which only one is black, but in 2.221 no assumptions are made about the other horses' colors. Sentence 2.220 contrasts the one black horse to all those that are not black while 2.221 makes no such contrast.

Restrictive relatives, being contrastive, cannot modify nouns with unique reference, such as proper nouns or superlatives:

2.222 *John that is a piano-player might be a good person to invite to the rap session.
2.223 *My youngest sister that you met yesterday is a Jesus freak.

They can, however, modify any other noun.

Appositive relatives, being noncontrastive, may modify nouns with unique reference; they cannot, however, modify generic nouns of the type *any X:*

2.224 *Anyone, who likes linguistics, is a fool.

Appositive relatives are fairly common in the written language, but they tend not to be used much in speech; instead a coordination or two separate sentences is preferred. This will not concern us further here.

Reduced Relatives

It has been a characteristic of English right from the earliest days that the relative pronoun of restrictive relatives can be deleted under certain conditions. In NE we can say:

2.225 I have brought the book that you asked for.

and also (colloquially probably far more commonly):

2.226 I have brought the book you asked for.

If we go through all the theoretically possible kinds of relative clause reductions we will find that relative markers functioning as the objects in the relative clause can be deleted as in the example above; so can those relatives functioning as subjects provided that the verb on the surface is: (i) *be* + *Adjective;* (ii) *be* + adverb of place; (iii) passive auxiliary (*be* + *PP*) + verb. If the relative pronoun is deleted in such clauses, *be* must be too. Besides:

2.227 The painter *who is good at landscapes* is here.
2.228 The linguist *who is from New York* is a loud-mouth.
2.229 The judge *who was kidnapped yesterday* is now free.

we find:

2.230 The painter *good at landscapes* is here.
2.231 The linguist *from New York* is a loud-mouth.
2.232 The judge *kidnapped yesterday* is now free.

However, besides:

2.233 The linguist who is a transformationalist is speaking.

we do not find:

2.234 *The linguist a transformationalist is speaking.

A further constraint on relative clause reduction is that for some relatives, if the tense in the main clause is past, that in the relative may be past or nonpast; for example:

2.235 I knew the girl with a broken tooth.

is ambiguous between:

2.236 I knew the girl at the time that she had a broken tooth (She may or may not have a broken tooth now).

and

2.237 I knew the girl who has a broken tooth (She has one now; she may or may not have had one when I knew her).

If, however, the tense in the main clause is nonpast, then that in the relative must be too:

2.238 I know the girl with a broken tooth.

derives unambiguously from:

2.239 I know the girl who has a broken tooth.

If the adjective in the reduced relative clause is simple—that is, not followed by a complement—then it is preposed to the noun. Thus the reduced form of:

2.240 the man who is old

is not:

2.241 the man old

but:

2.242 the old man.

There are several reasons why it is useful to consider at least certain prenominal adjectives as derived from relative clauses. For one, *the old man* and *the man who Tense be old* mean the same thing.[20] For another, in NE restrictive relatives do not occur with proper nouns as antecedents, so neither 2.222 nor:

2.243 *John that is old is a fraud.

is grammatical. If we consider the adjectives that can precede proper nouns, we will notice heavy restrictions on the lexical items available and also special semantic properties. How many adjectives can you put before

---

[20] Like 2.233 above, such a sentence as *The old man was a student at Harvard* is ambiguous between *The man who is old now was (in his youth) a student at Harvard* and *The man who was already old was a student at Harvard;* however, a sentence like *The old man is a student at Harvard* is unambiguous.

John? Try *bald, fat, lovable.* If possible at all they are epithets – that is, words which have come to form part of a person's name, as in *blue-eyed Athena.* Try *poor.* This certainly occurs; so does *old.* But *poor John* is unlikely to be equivalent to *John who is poor,* nor is *old John* likely to be *John who is old. Poor, old, little,* and the like form a small set of adjectives that can occur preposed to proper nouns but they all occur in the "affective," "emotional" sense; *poor,* for example, means 'pitiful' not 'indigent'. If we did not claim that prenominal adjectives which mean the same as they do in relative clauses are derived from relative clauses, we could hardly account for the fact that they are synonymous with and also share the same restrictions as the relative clauses. Affective prenominal adjectives, on the other hand, do not share the same characteristics as relative clauses and are therefore not derived from them.

3 OLD ENGLISH

When anyone turns for the first time from Modern English to English as it was recorded over a thousand years ago, he is invariably struck by the feeling that Old English is really a totally different language. The vocabulary is very different, the syntax looks more like German than English, and the spelling conventions have little resemblance to ours. Yet he is told that this language is after all English, the English of a thousand years ago, but still English. Once the reader becomes familiar enough with the structure of the language, the reasons become fairly obvious. This is not only a language spoken in the geographical location England, but there is also a clear continuity of language development from OE on; most importantly from the syntactic point of view, most of the differences, like the use of inflection and a variety of word order patterns, turn out to be chiefly surface differences. The basic structure is very similar to that of NE—in fact, identical in most cases. Even relics of many of the surface structures can be found in one form or another and in one dialect or another in NE.

As was pointed out in the first chapter, most of our data for prose syntax are to be found in biblical, homiletic, and philosophical works, histories and geographies; much of it is translated from Latin or at least inspired by Latin models. Nevertheless, countless studies have shown that in all but a few literal translations such as interlinear glosses, most writers were actually remarkably little influenced by Latin in the basic syntax they used. Possibly the most Latinate of the well-known writers was Ælfric (ca. 1000) who developed in his *Lives of the Saints* and *Homilies* a highly elegant style, clearly inspired in many ways by Latin rhetorical devices, especially those used in periodic sentence structure. The underlying structure itself is, however, typical of Old English and shows little direct evidence of borrowing from Latin; if anything, Ælfric's style is in fact much closer to Germanic alliterative verse than to Latin narrative, and parts are practically indistinguishable from the Anglo-Saxon poetic conventions of the time.

Since Ælfric was very clearly a highly conscious stylist, he probably does not represent most accurately the "informal educated" language of the time. I have therefore chosen to illustrate the description of OE syntax with materials from rather less conscious rhetoricians, the author or authors of the works attributed to Alfred. Especially useful is the passage in *Orosius* describing Ohthere and Wulfstan's voyages since it is apparently a report of their firsthand account to King Alfred. Also useful are the prefaces to the *Cura Pastoralis* and the *Boethius* since they are probably not translations; another invaluable source is the Anglo-Saxon *Chronicle* recording the annual events in Anglo-Saxon history.[1] The *Orosius, Cura Pastoralis, Boethius,* and the major part of the version of the *Chronicle* known as the *Parker Chronicle* all date from about A.D. 880–890 when, as far as we can tell, there was no tradition for prose style and possibly the gaps between spoken and written forms of the language were not as great as they came to be later.

Many of the illustrative quotations will be taken from the specific passages mentioned above. Since the passages are short, they do not contain examples of all the constructions under consideration. Sometimes they contain an example so complex as to confuse rather than clarify the issue. I have therefore also used passages from the main body of the texts, especially the *Orosius*.

The Alfredian works are expository and narrative, so imperative and interrogative structures are hardly attested at all. To fill the gap, I have selected some quotations from Ælfric's *Colloquy* (a short Latin dialogue between teacher and pupil, with OE interlinear glosses) despite the more than one hundred years' time lag and the difference in style. As far as we can tell from the sparse Alfredian evidence, Ælfric's use of imperative and interrogative structures was not significantly different from that of earlier writers. His *Grammar,*[2] with Latin and Old English side by side, provides many useful insights into a great number of structures discussed in this chapter, especially those involving performatives, tense, and aspect; so reference is occasionally made to this work too.

A. THE PERFORMATIVE

In OE auxiliary verbs are rarely used to express performatives; instead other forms of expression are favored, for example, main verbs, adverbs, subjunctive inflections, and the like; or there may be no surface

---

[1] For the editions of all primary texts, see Bibliography B, Primary Texts. References are to page and number. Rather than reflect the inconsistency between various editorial practices demonstrated by the cited texts, I have chosen not to mark vowel length in grammatical citation forms, although such procedure is customary; in a study of syntax the length-marks are irrelevant.

[2] Quotations from this text have been normalized insofar as ȝ has been replaced by *g*, and γ by *w;* this normalization is in keeping with the editorial practices of the other texts used.

expression of the performative at all. The broad principles of the use in OE of verbs cognate with our modern auxiliaries are fairly well agreed on, but there is sometimes disagreement about particular examples. Even when a form like *will-* is present that looks as if it may be exactly equivalent to our performative *will,* we can sometimes not be certain in precisely what sense the verb is being used: whether it retains its original sense as a main verb (as a main verb *will-* means 'intend, want') or whether it is being used as the realization of predicting. This means that there is a lot of ambiguity in the surface structures of sentences that resemble, and are indeed the etymological ancestors of, our modern auxiliaries *will, shall, must,* and so on. The larger context of the discourse often disambiguates a sentence that is ambiguous when taken on its own; sometimes the Latin source may do so too, but since translations of Latin tend to be fairly free, such sources are not very reliable. The modern reader is also always in danger of reading a modern interpretation into an older passage. Quotations in the sections on performatives should therefore be considered with a caution even beyond that normally required by any example from a text, particularly a text of a language no longer spoken; they are likely, rather than certain, examples of the structure at issue.

Saying

As in NE and indeed most languages, saying is characteristically not expressed at all. If it is, it takes the form of such main verbs as *secg-* 'say' and *tell-* 'tell, state that'. As in NE, there is no realization by an auxiliary.

Predicting

Typically, predictions are not realized by an auxiliary in OE and can be distinguished from sayings only by context, such as *if*-clauses:

3.1 Ælf. Coll. 37.194 [The cook speaks] gif ge me ut adrifaþ . . . ge *etaþ* wyrta eowre grene 'if you me out drive . . . you eat herbs your green = if you drive me from your company, you will eat your vegetables raw' (*etaþ* translates the Latin future *manducabitis*).

Another context would be "adverbs of future time." In his *Grammar* Ælfric regularly translates a Latin future inflection by an OE nonpast and an adverb of time (typically time very close to the time of utterance). For example, Ælfric gives as the equivalent of Latin *stabo* 'I will stand' the OE:

3.2 Ælf. Gr. 123.17 ic *stande nu rihte oððe on sumne timan* 'I stand now straight away or in a certain time'.

An interesting distinction is often made for predicting versus saying in verbs that function like the modern verb *to be*. In OE there were three verbs that would now all be translated by *be,* whether as the main verb, the passive auxiliary, or the aspectual auxiliary. One was *beo-,* another *wes-,* and the third was *weorþ-*. *Beo-,* with its present tense forms *beo, bist, biþ, beoþ* 'I am, thou art, he is, we/you/they are', was frequently used to express *I predict X will be Y* and habitual occurrences (as in *She is usually late*); on the other hand *wes-* was preferred for *I say that I am X right now,* or for expressions of eternal truth (as in *There is a law that . . .*) or identity (as in *She is my mother*). *Weorþ-* basically means 'become' but in many contexts it is used instead of *beo-*.

An example of predictive *beo-* is:

3.3 Ælf. Coll. 37.200 [The cook speaks again] gif ge forþy me fram adryfaþ . . . þonne *beo* ge ealle þrælas 'if you therefore me away drive . . . then will-be you all thralls = if you drive me away for this reason . . . you will all be slaves'.

Beo- has no past tense of its own; in indirect speech, when a prediction or a comment on habitual conditions was quoted, the past tense form of *wes-* was used. By NE the two verbs *beo-* and *wes-* were completely collapsed in most dialects into our suppletive verb *be*. The decay of the distinction can readily be seen from earliest times since *wes-* is often used where *beo-* might be expected; although the reverse is also true to some extent, *wes-* was clearly the dominant form since we never find the identifying phrase *þæt is* in the form **þæt biþ* or **þæt weorþ*.

If an auxiliary is used at all to express prediction, the auxiliary is *will-* or *scul-* (cognate with our *shall*), whether the subject is first, second, or third person. When *will-* is used in OE it most often expresses the general prediction type that we find in *Oil will float on water:*

3.4 Or. 230.26 elpendes hyd *wile* drincan wætan 'elephant's hide will drink wet = elephant's hide will absorb water'.

Otherwise most instances of *will-* and *scul-* when used predictively occur only embedded in other sentences.

The predictive use of *will-* and *scul-* is rare in OE, however. Both verbs were originally main verbs, and it is as main verbs that they are most commonly found. *Will-* basically means 'intend, want' and as such is the direct ancestor of the now recessive NE "volitional will":

3.5 Or. 17.7 he æt sumum cirre *wolde* fandian hu . . . 'he at one time wanted to discover how . . .'.

A good example of both volitional and predictive *will-* side by side is found in:

3.6 Or. 128.5 Þa Darius geseah þæt he oferwunnen beon *wolde* (predictive), þa *wolde* (volitional) he hiene selfne . . . forspillan 'When Darius saw that he overcome be would, then wanted he him self . . . to-kill'.

As a main verb, *scul-* basically expresses obligation, necessity, or compulsion (like our *must, ought to*):[3]

3.7 Or. 18.19 Æghwilc gylt be hys gebyrdum. Se byrdesta *sceall* gyldan fiftyne mearðes fell 'Each pays (tribute) according-to his means. The richest has to-give fifteen martens' skins'.

Rather less common, and almost entirely restricted to biblical materials, is the use of *scul-* in the sense 'to owe', as in *He him sceolde tyn þusenda punda* 'He owed him ten thousand pounds', and from this seems to have developed the sense 'be of value' (that for which something is owed is something of value):

3.8 Ælf. Coll. 31.129 Canst þu temian hig? . . . Hwæt *sceoldon* hig me buton ic cuþe temian hig? 'Know you to-tame them? . . . What value-were they to-me unless I knew to-tame them?'

We may postulate that perhaps one of the conditions for the extension of the *scul-* of obligation to predicting was its use in sentences like:

3.9 Or. 218.20 Ic *sceal* eac niede þara monegena gewinna geswigian þe on eastlondum gewurdon 'I shall/must also of-necessity of-those many fights be-silent that in eastlands come-to-be'.

where *niede* carries the weight of the meaning 'necessity' so that *scul-* can be interpreted primarily as a signal of prediction (if I ought to do something, the obligation is now; but presumably I am not doing it, I shall do it). Other contexts, such as the prediction of what must inevitably (of necessity) happen, whether by royal, judicial, or divine ordinance, may also have contributed to the extension of *scul-* to predicting:

3.10 Or. 84.34 Uton nu brucan þisses undernmetes swa þa

---

[3] As such *scul-* translates Latin *debēre* 'to have to'. Even when a Latin original is available, however, there are problems of interpretation since *debēre* itself came to be used in late Latin as the signal primarily of prediction rather than obligation. The often-quoted passage in Bede's story of Cædmon (*The Old English Version of Bede's Ecclesiastical History of the English People,* ed. Thomas Miller, E.E.T.S. No. 96, London: Trübner [1891]), Be. 344.2 *Hwæt sceal ic singan?* provides a good example of some of the difficulties in interpretation. The OE sentence translates the Latin *Quid debeo cantare?* As Bede was writing in the late sixth century A.D. he was not using Classical Latin (in which *debēre* unambiguously means 'to have to') and therefore the Latin original is as ambiguous as the OE, and can mean either 'What shall I sing?' or 'What should I sing?'

sculon þe hiora æfengifl on helle gefeccean *sculon* 'Let-us now enjoy of-this breakfast as they shall/must who their supper in hell get must'.

In any event, we must be cautious not to interpret any instance of OE *scul-* too easily as the realization simply of predicting, without any sense of obligation.

Promising

Promising, like predicting, is usually manifested simply by the nonpast tense. Like prediction, it tends to select *beo-*, rather than *wes-*, if a *be* verb is involved:

3.11 CP 7.25 ond to ælcum biscepstole on minum rice wille ane onsendan; 7 on ælcre *bið* an æstel se *bið* on fiftegum mancessa 'and to each bishopric in my kingdom I-intend one (copy of CP) to-send; and in each shall-be one bookmark which shall-be of (worth) fifty of-mancuses'.[4]

There is some evidence that *scul-* was used occasionally in later OE to express promising, see *The Battle of Maldon* 54, feallan *sceolon* hæþene æt hilde 'Fall shall heathens in battle', and *Genesis* 2.17, Ðu *scealt* deaðe sweltan 'Thou shalt death die'. In these instances we may posit an underlying performative since in each case the speaker (Byrhtnoþ in the first, God in the second) seems to be not so much reporting what fortune, the gods, almighty power, or the like will bring about, but rather taking it upon himself to see that the heathen shall fall and that you shall die. In both instances the expectation is very strong—therefore more than a prediction. All promises carry with them a sense of necessity, but necessity evolving from one's own actions rather than those of others. It is therefore only a small step from the nonperformative use of *scul-* (I say there is necessity that) to the performative (I take it upon myself that).

Permitting

Permitting was expressed either by the main verb *alyf-* 'permit' or by the auxiliary *mot-*. *Mot-* is used chiefly in reports of permissions, as follows:

3.12 Or. 21.4 7 þonne rideð ælc hys weges mid ðan feo, 7 hyt *motan* habban eall 'and then rides each his way with the

[4] A *mancus* was a coin worth thirty OE pennies. The "sigil" 7 is the OE equivalent of the ampersand—shorthand for *and/ond* 'and'.

money and it may/are-permitted[5] to-have all = and then each goes his own way with the money and can keep all of it'.

In many reports of permission, *mot-* approaches the neutral meaning 'be able' rather than 'be permitted'. *Mot-* (replaced by its past tense form *must*) is no longer used in NE as the expression of either permission or ability; it is now used mainly as the expression of necessity. The modern use of *must* can be traced back to OE times; as it did not develop fully until ME, however, it will not be discussed until the next chapter (p. 118).

Occasionally *mag-* may be interpreted as the manifestation of permitting. By far the greatest number of instances of *mag-*, however, illustrate its basic nonperformative sense 'prevail against, have the physical power to', hence 'be able to':[6]

3.13 Or. 24.29 ælc wiht *mæg* bet wyð cyle þonne wið hæte 'each creature prevails better against cold than against heat'.
3.14 Or. 19.19 seo is bradre þonne ænig man ofer seon *mæge* 'which is broader than any man over to-see is-able = which is too broad for any man to see across'.

Mag- is never used in the modern sense of *maybe, possibly.*

The ancestor of *can, cunn-* is never used in OE for permission. It means 'know (how to)' or 'be intellectually able to'.

Commanding

The main verbs expressing command are typically *bidd-, beod-,* and *hat-*. As in NE, commands could be expressed in a wide variety of ways depending on the attitude of the speaker to the hearer. The typical "imperative" structure, equivalent in function to the bald *Go!, Look it up!,* and the like, is expressed in OE as in NE by a subjectless sentence; the verb, however, is marked by an imperative inflection which is *-a* or *-e* (depending on the verb class) for the singular, and *-aþ* for the plural, as in:

3.15 Ælf. Coll. 31.132 *Syle* me ænne hafoc 'Give me a hawk'.
3.16 Ælf. Coll. 48.310 *Gaþ* þeawlice þonne ge gehyran cyricean bellan 'Go devoutly when you hear of-church bells'.

The subset of commands which are questions have the same under-

---

[5] Such switches from singular to plural are common with collectives, indefinites, and so on. For another example, see 3.43.

[6] *Might* "strength" is in fact a nominal form of the old verb *mag-* just as *height* is the nominal form of the adjectival verb *be high*.

lying characteristics as they do in NE; the surface realizations are rather different, however. Most striking is the absence of *do*. In OE we find structures of the type *Came he?,* but not **Did he come?; What said he,* not **What did he say?* The OE rule is that if an auxiliary is present, it occurs to the left of the subject; otherwise the main verb occurs in this position:

Auxiliary Subject Verb . . .
Verb Subject . . .

In content-questions the *wh*-attached element occurs to the left of the verb again. Hence we find sentences of the type: *Whom saw you?* (*wh*-object, verb, subject). Some excellent examples are to be found in Ælfric's *Grammar* and *Colloquy:*

3.17 Ælf. Gr. 226.4 "fecisti hoc?" *dydest ðis?* "non feci" *ic ne dyde*. "uis hoc?" *wylt ðu ðis?* "non" *nese*. 'Did-you this? I not did. Want-you this? No'. . . . "manducasti hodie?" æt ðu to dæg? "etiam, feci" *gea, ic dyde*. 'Ate you today? Yes, I did'.

3.18 Ælf. Coll. 21.28 *Hæfst þu ænigne geferan?* 'Have you any companion?'

3.19 Ælf. Coll. 20.22 *Hwæt sægest þu yrþlingc? Hu begæst þu weorc þin?* 'What say you, ploughman? How carry-out you work your? = How do you carry out your work?'

Another way in which the surface form of OE questions differs from that of NE questions is that in OE direct yes–no questions may be introduced by *hwæþer* (= *hw-ægþer* 'Which of two, whether'). The number of instances are few, but they represent a clearly established pattern that persisted through ME and, in slightly different form, into ENE and even into NE. Indirect (subordinated) yes–no questions are regularly introduced in OE by *hwæþer* 'whether' as, indeed, they still are (though *whether* is being supplanted by *if*). In both direct and indirect questions introduced by *hwæþer,* the word order typical of statements is used:

3.20 Bo. 73.24 Hwæðer ge nu secan gold on treowum? 'Whether you now seek gold in trees? = Do you now seek gold in trees?'

While direct questions with *hwæþer* alternate with direct questions without it, *hwæþer* seems to be favored when the speaker anticipates a negative answer, when he wishes to emphasize the doubt in his mind, or even his incredulity, as if there were an underlying *Is it really true that. . . ?* In these cases the verb is usually marked by the subjunctive (see 3.87 below).

In most other respects, OE questions are like NE ones. This means that the optional suppletion of quantifiers like *some* by *any,* which was noted for NE, also occurs in OE. Examples are not plentiful, partly because questions are relatively uncommon in the largely narrative OE prose texts, partly because not all the suppletion sets existed in OE (for example, *already* → *yet* as in *He has already arrived, Has he arrived yet?,* which does not appear until ENE). Nevertheless they are sufficient for us to know that at least the sets *sum* → *ænig, an* → *ænig* were well established in questions by OE times, as in 3.18 above.

B. THE PROPOSITION

In OE nominal expressions can have exactly the same functions as in NE. Our concern here will be with the rules that give NPs in these functions a surface representation. Frequently the relationship between the underlying structure and the actual sentence is less complex, or more transparent, that in NE. We have already found this to be the case with such structures as yes–no questions introduced by *hwæþer.* We will find a close correlation between underlying and surface structures again when we consider relative clauses; but this correlation is most noticeable in the proposition partly because subjectivalization obscures the underlying form considerably less often than in NE.

The Verb and Associated Arguments

The Verb

Verbal subcategories are presumably the same in OE as in NE. In the absence of a native speaker we cannot verify the assumption that action versus nonaction verbs existed; however, there is no evidence to the contrary. The criteria by which we categorize certain classes in NE do not, of course, always hold for earlier stages of the language; we cannot, for example, use presence or absence of *be* + *PrP* in the expression of progressives as a criterion for action verbs in OE since overt progressives were used only rarely and the OE equivalent to NE *be* + *PrP* was used more freely than *be* + *PrP* is in NE. On the other hand, other criteria are as available as in NE, for example, substitutability of action verbs but not of nonaction verbs by the substitute verb *do-* (often called a "pro-verb") as in:

3.21 Or. 98.17 ondrædende þæt Læcedemonie ofer hie *ricsian* mehten swa hie ær *dydon* 'dreading that Laecedemonians over them rule might as they before did = dreading that the Laecedemonians might rule over them as they had done in the past'.

Action verbs in OE (as in NE) can be further subcategorized into causative and noncausative. Consider, for example, *The water boiled* versus *She boiled the water* (caused the water to boil), *The sauce hardened in the freezer* (became hard) versus *She hardened the sauce in the freezer* (caused it to become hard), and also *She died* versus *He killed her* (caused her to die). In NE causative versions of noncausatives are either identical in appearance with the noncausative (for example, *boil, harden, walk,* and so on), or else suppletive (for example, *set* versus *sit, kill* versus *die*). In early Germanic there was a device that was highly "productive" (see p. 15) for forming causatives: an *-i-* had been added to the singular past tense base to form a new verb as in *sit-* (nonpast tense base), *sat-* (past tense base), *sat-i-* (causative base). From this device we get *set* versus *sit, fell* versus *fall, lay* versus *lie.*[7] Various sound changes have operated to partially obscure the relationship between the causative and noncausative forms of these verbs.

The device for forming causatives with *-i-* was already unproductive in OE. When causative verbs such as *sett-* 'set' had not been inherited from earlier Germanic, the causative was usually formed by the main verb *lǣt-* 'cause, make, let' or *gemac-* 'cause, make' and a sentence complement.

OE provides a particularly good example of the close interrelationship of verb and adjective. Especially noticeable is the fact that in OE we find a great number of verbs which have been replaced by adjectives, especially those with Experiencer (for example, *Him hyngreþ* 'Him hungers', now not just *He hungers* with subjectivalization of the Experiencer, but also *He is hungry,* with adjectivalization of the verb). During discussion of the perfect and passive auxiliaries we will find even closer connections between adjective and verb. It is examples like this that, in the absence of significant counter-evidence, justify on a historical basis the conclusion one can draw independently without reference to history that adjectives are a subcategory of verbs. The fact that adjectives agree with nouns in number, case, and gender (for discussion of these terms see below) is a surface phenomenon, a manifestation associated with the subcategory adjective.

Nominal Expressions

The functions of nominal expressions

CASE AND UNDERLYING FUNCTIONS. It is impossible to discuss the realization of underlying functions in OE without discussing "case" as well.[8] "Cases" are inflections that mark the surface relationship of

---

[7] In OE there was also a pair *cwel-* 'die', *cwell-* 'kill'; in the latter form the double *ll* is the direct result of various phonological changes associated with the loss of the *-i-* derivative formative. In NE we have replaced the nonaction verb by the Scandinavian word *die,* but we still have the causative *kill.*

[8] In the theory of "case grammar" that lies behind this book the underlying functions as well as the traditional surface cases are sometimes called cases (see especially Fillmore, 1968). This is because, as we shall see, there is a marked correlation between underlying functions and surface case. I use the term "case" for surface case only in order to avoid possible confusion.

nouns to each other and to the verb. They also mark the surface relationship called "agreement" (see p. 84) of demonstratives, numerals, adjectives, and the like to nouns.

In OE several distinctions could be made between cases. In NE we have only relics of the earlier system. For nouns we have one overt case marker, the *-s* or "genitive," as in the *cat's tail,* the *children's toys.* This *-s* genitive is the surface marker of, among other things, the relationship called Possessor in possessive constructions. As is true of all case inflections, the *-s* genitive inflection is not the only marker of the underlying function involved: I could equally well speak of the *tail of the cat,* in which case *of* would signal possession; *of,* however, is an independent word, not an inflection, and is not a case marker. Just as inflection is not the sole marker of any one underlying function, so too no one underlying function is always marked by the same case inflection.

While nouns in NE are marked for only one case, certain pronouns in most English dialects are marked for two. In standard English we differentiate not only between the marked genitive *his* and the unmarked *he,* but also between these two and *him.* This kind of contrast exists for the personal pronouns *I, we, he, she, they* (but not for *you, it* which, like nouns, have only one marked case, the genitive), and for the relative and the interrogative *who.* In OE, however, the system was considerably more complicated.

OE is characterized by a case system with five potentially contrastable inflections. This is a relatively simple system compared to later Proto-Indo-European or to Modern Russian with eight cases, but is roughly comparable to Modern German which has four cases used largely in the same way as the OE cases. While never more than four, and rarely more than three, different overt inflections are available for any noun, we speak of five cases and simply say that two or more have the same realization so that we can generalize about the surface functions of all nouns and about the ways in which all demonstratives (*this, that*), adjectives, and so forth agree with the nouns they modify. Demonstratives have five overt distinctions for the masculine singular. As it is the noun function which determines case in the demonstrative, we could not account for these five unless we postulated five cases for the nouns.

The OE case markers, like most case markers in Indo-European, are in their phonological realization simultaneously markers for gender and number. Number, gender, and case must, however, be treated separately because they have different grammatical functions (for number and gender see pp. 84 and 85 respectively). Details of the particular manifestations of nominal inflections will be found in any grammar of OE or history of English in the section on "accidence" or "morphology" and will not detain us here. Sample paradigms of typical *Demonstrative + Noun* combinations, and of the third person pronoun are, however, provided for ease of reference in Appendix D.

What particular case is selected in an OE sentence is, as in most other languages with more than a vestigial case system, a function of various different phenomena. For one, there is case selection by subjectivalization. Subject is signaled by "nominative," a case which frequently has no phonological manifestation at all. Since almost any function can be subjectivalized, nominative is the case that obscures the greatest number of underlying functions. As subjectivalization is optional in many structures in OE, not every sentence has a nominative; this and other problems are discussed below after case-assignment to nonsubjectivalized nouns.

If a noun is not subjectivalized, the following case-assignments generally operate: (a) "genitive" for Possessor in the special kind of configuration illustrated by *the man's hand;* (b) "dative" for Experiencer and Goal, and also for adverbs of place-in-which; (c) "accusative" for Patients, Sources, and also adverbs of direction and time-during-which; (d) "instrumental" for Instrument, and also adverbs of time-at-which and manner. As we shall see below, however, constraints may be imposed by particular prepositions and verbs that override the grammatical properties described here. The resultant complexity in case-assignment provided just the kind of situation that might be susceptible to simplification by successive generations. The complexity, however, was clearly not a cause for the change since other languages, notably Old High German, had similar systems, but no comparable extensive loss of case markings occurred. Certain languages like Russian with fundamentally similar systems have in fact increased the complexity of their systems.

GENITIVE. The genitive in NE is associated in the surface structure with the Possessor in possessive constructions and with many different underlying functions. In OE, the genitive seems particularly common as it not only occurs in constructions now characterized by the genitive but also in many others where we would prefer the preposition *of,* or no overt inflection or preposition at all. In OE prepositional alternatives to the genitive were virtually not used; *of* at this date meant 'from' and is a preposition typically associated with the Source function. We therefore find the genitive inflection used regularly for possessive constructions as in 3.4 and in such phrases as *Norþmanna land* 'Northmen's land', *hwæles hyd* 'whale's hide', and so on. It also regularly occurs in "subjective genitive" constructions (those in which the genitive is, in the underlying structure, the Agent of the action expressed in the nominalized verb), as in:

3.22 Or. 1.20 ymbe *monegra oþerra folca* gewinn 'about of-many other peoples' battles = about the battles of many other peoples' (the peoples battled).

The genitive is still usual in NE in these constructions. While it is also still available for "objective genitives" (see p. 39), it is no longer as usual as the prepositional form; in OE only the genitive form occurs, however:

3.23 Or. 2.11 for *hiora mægdena* offrunga 'because-of their maidens' sacrifices = because of the sacrifice of their maidens' (they sacrificed their maidens).

Among other uses of the genitive inflection in OE are the "partitive genitive" and the "genitive of measure." Partitive genitive is the name given to such constructions as *part of X, half of X:*

3.24 Chron. 90.26 (897) þa gefengon hie *þara þreora scipa* tu 'then captured they of-those three ships two'.

In NE *of* has almost completely replaced the genitive inflections in this construction, but the very fact that we use *of* suggests that there is a direct line of descent from the OE usage. In fact, this is the one construction in OE which does sometimes allow alternation of the inflection with a preposition:

3.25 Or. 84.29 þæt wæs nigon X hund þusenda *of Persa* 'that was nineteen hundred thousand of Persians'.

but the sense of "from among" may still be very strong in this use of *of.*

Closely related to this construction is the genitive of measure as in 3.11 (*fiftegum mancessa* [genitive]) and in:

3.26 Or. 18.32 hit mihte beon *þreora mila* brad 'it might be of-three miles broad'.

In these constructions an adjective of measure such as *long, broad, high,* has a genitive phrase as its complement. A relic of this genitive can be found in, for example, a *three-foot pole* where the form *foot* is derived from the genitive plural *fota.*[9] Like most relics, constructions like *three-foot pole* occur only in a very few contexts; specifically, only in prenominal expressions of measure: **A pole three foot long* is not grammatical. Phrasal expressions with *of* have not replaced the genitive inflection in phrases of measure; in general, then, this construction has had quite a different history from the partitive genitive.

There are several other uses of the genitive, but they tend to be more specialized than those discussed above. Indeed, in certain instances they occur so sporadically or in phrases so fixed as to seem wholly idiomatic. For example, we find a "genitive of duration" in

[9] The forms of the plural are: nominative and accusative *fet,* genitive *fota,* dative *fotum.*

dæges and nihtes 'night and day', but not **monþes* 'month'.[10] Possibly *He works nights* is a descendant of the genitive construction here, though it may also reflect the accusative of extent in time (see p. 80); certainly *nights* is thought of as a plural, not a genitive singular in NE. The expression *He works of a night,* however, is a direct replacement for the OE genitive of duration associated with the lexical items *dæg* and *niht.*

DATIVE. The dative is typically used to mark nonsubjectivalized Experiencer and Goal:

> 3.27 CP 7.6 Forðy *me* (Experiencer) ðyncð betre 'For-this to-me seems better'.
>
> 3.28 Or. 18.1 þa teð hie brohton sume *þæm cyninge* (Goal) 'those teeth they brought some to-that king'.

and also for many adverbial expressions, especially those involving place-in-which.

INSTRUMENTAL. Instrumental and dative are never distinguished in the inflectional endings of nouns in OE. They are, however, distinguished for adjectives and demonstratives in the masculine singular, although the dative can be used wherever the instrumental case is expected, that is, dative is the dominant form. In earliest OE instrumental case alone is associated with the nonsubjectivalized underlying Instrument function: in practically every text after *Beowulf* (ca. 720?), however, Instrument was also associated with the preposition *mid,* not by the case alone (see p. 80). The instrumental case inflection is also associated with the underlying function of concomitance ('together with') as in:

> 3.29 Chron. 76.2 (878) þæs on Eastron worhte Ælfred cyning *lytle* (instrumental) *werede* geweorc æt Æþelinga eigge 'then at Easter built Alfred king with-little troop stronghold at Athelney = then at Easter King Alfred built a fort at Athelney with a small troop'.

It is also used in comparisons (*þy ma þy* . . . 'the more the . . .'), in fixed phrases, many of them causal subordinates, for example, *for þy þæt* 'because', and in expressions of time-at-which, for example, *þy ilcan dæge* 'on that same day'.

The underlying functions of Instrument and concomitance remain in NE, but now they are signaled exclusively by prepositions (usually *with*), and not by an inflection.

---

[10] The *-es* of *nihtes* is itself idiomatic and presumably patterned on the *-es* inflection of *dæg; niht* is feminine and in other constructions carries the genitive inflection *-e.*

ACCUSATIVE. The accusative is the case marker normally attached to a nonsubjectivalized Patient as in *hine seah* 'him saw', *hæfde hine gebundenne* 'had him in-a-state-of-being-bound'; it is also the case normally used for nonsubjectivalized Source (although dative also occurs):

3.30 Or. 96.22 Persa cyning benom *þone* (accusative) *ealdormon* his scire 'Persians' king deprived that chief of-his shire'.

Accusative is also typically used to mark adverbs of extent in space and time, for example, *ealne weg* 'all the way', *ealle þa hwile* 'all the time'.

PREPOSITIONS AND CASE. Surface nominal function is primarily indicated by case in OE. Other factors are, however, also important, notably word order and the use of prepositions. Just as certain underlying structures are associated with certain cases, they are also associated with certain prepositions. Typically they are: *þurh* and *fram* (also spelled *from*) for Agents, *mid* for Instrumentals, *to* for Goal, *of* and *fram* for inanimate Source, *æt* for animate Source, and a large array of prepositions used for adverbial expressions of time, duration, place, and direction. In some instances a preposition is obligatory, for instance, if the Agent is overtly expressed in a passive sentence it must be realized by a prepositional phrase. In others it is usual, for example, Source and Instrumental; in others a prepositional phrase is practically never available—for instance, the functions of Possessor and Experiencer are hardly ever found in prepositional phrases at all. For the most part, however, a prepositional phrase may be optionally selected as an alternate to simple *Noun + Case*. Introductory grammars frequently give the impression that prepositions are rare in OE; it is true they occur considerably less often than in NE, but they are certainly not rare.

Prepositions themselves select case on the noun with which they are in construction. Sometimes the case they select is the same as that determined by the functions discussed above. For example, the prepositional expression of Goal with *to* selects dative in:

3.31 Chron. 86.26 (894) his suna twegen mon brohte *to þæm cyninge* 'his sons two one brought to that king'.

just as the nonprepositional expression of Goal selects dative in 3.28. But sometimes the case selected by a preposition is not the same as that selected by the underlying functions; this is particularly clear when more than one preposition is available for the same underlying function and the prepositions require different cases. Both *þurh* and *fram,* for example, function as the agentive "by" in passives, but the first requires the accusative and the second the dative:

3.32 Or. 108.30 ær þon hit *þurh ænne þeowne mon* (accusative) geypped wearð 'before it by a serving man revealed was'.

3.33 Or. 282.5 he þær beswicen wearð *from his agnum monnum* (dative) 'he there betrayed was by his own men'.

CONSTRAINTS ON CASE IMPOSED BY VERBS. The difference between (a) cases required by prepositions with the same function (like *þurh* and *mid*), (b) cases required by prepositions, and (c) those required in the absence of prepositions, may well have been a factor contributing to the breakdown of the case system in late OE. A further factor was probably the way in which certain verbs could overrule both sets of case-assignment rules discussed above and impose their own case selections. For example, *hyngr-* 'hunger' allows the regular assignment of dative to the Experiencer (*him hyngrede* 'to-him hungered'), or it may overrule this and assign accusative (*hine hyngrede* 'him hungered'). *Onfon* 'receive' selects genitive or dative on the Patient, as well as the expected accusative:

3.34 Chron. 76.18 (878) 7 *his* (genitive, Patient) se cyning þær onfeng æt fulwihte 'and him the king there received at the-baptismal-ceremony'.

Certain verbs like *bruc-* 'enjoy', *hreows-* 'respect', *fægn-* 'rejoice' typically select genitive on the nonAgent or nonExperiencer, as in *He þæs bruceþ* 'He enjoys of-this'. The genitive has in some cases been replaced by one of the prepositions as in *He is ashamed of her,* in others it has been totally lost (see p. 123).

SUBJECTIVALIZATION. Subjectivalization in OE is a grammatical process by which one NP is assigned nominative case; it then determines the number in the verb. As we saw in Chapter 2, in NE subjectivalization is a grammatical process by which one NP is assigned a particular position (usually the left-most NP slot in the sentence) and then determines the number of the verb. The difference in the two characterizations is the result of changes in the case system and in word order that have occurred between OE and NE.

Absence of Subjectivalization. While the number of verbs that permit or require subjectivalization not to occur is small in NE, the number in OE is considerably greater. Most verbs which can have Experiencer as their only argument either rarely or never allow subjectivalization to occur, as far as we can tell from the available texts; expressions like *Mec longade* 'Me longed', *Him þyrstede* 'To-him thirsted', *Him speow* 'To-him succeeded', all of them without subjects, are typical of OE. They are usually called "impersonal" constructions. If Patient is realized by a sentence, the Patient is also usually not subjectivalized; it never is if it has the form *þæt + Sentence* (for further discussion of this point, see p. 102). If a verb has two or more arguments, of which none is Agent, then subjectivalization is usually optional; if subjectivalization does occur, the Experiencer is usually chosen as subject.

Passive. It was pointed out on page 36 that in NE the passive can be considered a special kind of subjectivalization: one in which (typically) the Patient or Goal is subjectivalized and the Agent is not. In NE such a construction is automatically marked by the "passive auxiliary" *be* + *PP* and by the prepositional phrase *by* + *Agent.* In OE, however, passivization is more complex. It involves subjectivalization of a Patient or Goal if the Patient or Goal would receive the accusative case marker in a nonpassive ("active") sentence. If, however, they would receive a nonaccusative marker, they are not subjectivalized. In OE the passive is therefore a construction in which the Agent is introduced by the preposition *fram* or *þurh* (that is, is nonsubjectivalized) and in which one of the passive auxiliaries *beo-* + *PP, wes-* + *PP,* or *weorþ* + *PP* is present. An example of a nonsubjectivalized ("impersonal") passive is:

3.35 CP. 123.8 eft ðurh ðone witgan wæs gecid hierdum (dative) 'after by that wise-man was rebuked to-shepherds = afterwards the shepherds were rebuked by that wise man'.

Such nonsubjectivalized passives are typical of early Indo-European. Similar constructions can still be found in modern languages like German: *Dir sei dafür herzlich gedankt* 'To-you be for-it heartily thanked'.

The passive has an interesting history. For one, it did not always require a *be* auxiliary in Germanic. Gothic had a passive verbal inflection, not a *be* auxiliary. In OE a relic of the inflection is to be found in one verb, *hatte,* a "passive" verb meaning 'is/was called'. Regularly OE required the segmentalized form with a *be* auxiliary. We do, however, also find a construction without, as in *Þas þing sind to donne* 'Those things are to do' and:

3.36 Or. 290.9 Firmus wearð gefangen, 7 forþgelæded *to sleanne* 'Firmus was captured and led-forth to slay (= to be slain)'.

In NE relics of this construction can still be found in, for example, *This house is to let,* but it is idiomatic and nonproductive (we would hardly say *This kit is to build*). A further construction without an auxiliary and with the subject *man* "one" is always mentioned in the handbooks:

3.37 Or. 240.1 bæd þæt him mon brohte þone triumphan ongean 'commanded that him one brought that triumphal-procession toward'.

It is used extensively in translation of Latin passives but as the Agent is subjectivalized and there are no grammatical passive features, this construction is not syntactically a passive.

The segmental passive with an auxiliary is well established by earliest OE. As in other constructions with a *be* verb, all three forms, *beo-, wes-, weorþ-* are used; *beo-* is used to express prediction or intermittent generality while *wes-* expresses permanent generality or present action, and *weorþ-* stresses the activity and the event. Sometimes the sense of 'becoming' is still so strong in *weorþ- + PP* that it seems to approximate our use of *get* as in *It got stolen* versus *It was stolen*. In his *Grammar,* Ælfric uses only *wes- + PP* and *beo- + PP* for the passive, but in his *Lives* and *Homilies* he uses *weorþ- + PP* even more than does Alfred (and Alfred used *weorþ + PP* quite extensively). It has been speculated that *weorþ- + PP* is less formal than the other two and therefore was not used in the *Grammar*.

The *be* verb form of the passive seems to have originated as a restructuring (see p. 11) of adjectival phrases. In NE we find: *The windows were broken, The door was shut,* both of which are ambiguous. In one meaning they are passive (the windows were broken by someone); in another they express state (the windows were in a state of brokenness). In NE only the context disambiguates these two meanings; the context may be extralinguistic or linguistic (such as the disambiguating force of *by the students, were being* versus *for three days*). In OE the "stative" form was further distinguishable by adjectival inflections. The following sentences referring to the same event show the contrast between the adjectival and the passive forms quite clearly:

3.38 Or. 44.24 On þære ilcan tide wurdon twegen æþelingas *afliemde* (adj. ending) of Sciþþian 'At that same time were two princes put-to-flight from Scythia' (stative).

3.39 Or. 1.25 hu II æþelingas wurdon *afliemed* (no inflection) of Sciþþium 'how two princes were put-to-flight from Scythia' (passive).

However, some cases typically had no surface manifestation, notably nominative masculine singular and nominative and accusative neuter singular. Hence uninflected participles and adjectival participles were sometimes ambiguous, as *afliemed* would be in *An æþeling wurde afliemed of Sciþþian* 'One prince was put-to-flight from Scythia'.

It was constructions of the latter kind that presumably provided one of the conditions for the restructuring of the adjectival patterns; this was particularly easy as the adjectival expression refers to a state that can only have been reached after something has been done, that is, a window can only be in a state of brokenness if it has been broken. Both the passive and the stative-result constructions have remained side-by-side; in some instances the adjectival form has developed its own independent word, as in *The windows were open* (stative) versus *The windows were opened* (passive).

Perhaps because of the relative novelty in OE of all auxiliaries, passive auxiliaries never occur with aspectual auxiliaries and only very rarely with such auxiliaries as *mag-, scul-, will-*. We have already met one of the rare examples of a passive auxiliary together with *will-* in 3.6.

Passives with perfective meaning were simply expressed by the passive auxiliary with past tense; those with progressive meaning were expressed by the passive auxiliary with the nonpast tense.

Deletion of the Subject. In successive sentences, whether subordinate, coordinate, or independent, the subject is quite frequently deleted. Usually it must be in identity with the subject in the first of the succession of sentences:

3.40 Chron. 25.6 (626) Her com Eomer fram Cwichelme West Seaxna cyninge. Þohte þæt he wolde ofstingan Eadwine cininge 'In-this-year came Eomer from Cwichwelm, West-Saxons' king. Thought that he would kill Eadwine king'.

This kind of subject-deletion is common in languages with extensive inflections and does not represent the kind of "telegraphic style" with which we associate subject-deletion in NE.

AGREEMENT. Demonstratives, quantifiers, numerals, and those adjectives that modify a noun after relative clause reduction (as in *these fine buildings*) "agree" with the noun in OE—that is, they have the same case (and gender and number) specifications as the noun. So if the noun is marked for genitive, then the demonstratives, numerals, adjectives, and so forth modifying it will also be marked for genitive.

If the verb is adjectival or nominal and the surface form of the sentence is *NP + be + Adjective* or *NP + be + NP,* then the adjective or predicate nominal agrees with the first NP; as the noun or pronoun of this first NP is the subject, the adjective or predicate nominal is also in the nominative case:

3.41 CP. 3.13 Swæ clæne hio (lar) wæs *oðfeallenu* 'So completely she (education) was decayed' (*-u* is the nominative feminine singular adjectival inflection agreeing with the nominative feminine singular subject *hio* 'she'; for nominal gender see the next section).

3.42 Or. 18.8 He wæs *swyðe spedig man* on þæm æhtum þe heora speda on beoð 'He was very wealthy man in those possessions that their riches in are = He was a man very wealthy in those possessions which count as their riches'.

The structure of nominal expressions

NOUN SUBCLASSES. As in NE, nouns are classified according to whether they are proper or not; if the latter, whether they are concrete or not. They are also subclassified according to whether they are animate or nonanimate, whether they can be pluralized, counted, and the like. The main difference in subclassification lies in the gender system.

Gender. The gender subclassifications are considerably different in OE from those in NE. In written and unemotional spoken NE only animate nouns are subclassifiable according to whether they are male (pronominalized by *he*), female (pronominalized by *she*), or neutral—that is, neither male nor female—(pronominalized by *it*); all other nouns are pronominalized by *it*. A system like this is called a "natural gender" system as it follows in general the semantic classification of entities. There is also a different "affective" system that can be used to indicate emotion in the spoken language; in this system *it* may be used for animates to express endearment (as of a baby) or disdain (of an adult); nonanimates may be pronominalized by *she* if a positive, *he* if a negative approach is implied.

In the written, unemotional style of OE and also many modern Indo-European languages including German, however, there is little correspondence between semantic sex and syntactic gender; all nouns, whatever their other subclassifications, are masculine, feminine, or neuter—terms used to designate syntactic as opposed to semantic gender. Such a system is called a "grammatical gender" system, which is quite distinct from "natural" and "affective" gender systems. Examples of the grammatical gender system can be found in OE *stan* 'stone', which is masculine and pronominalizable by *he* 'he', *wif* 'woman', which is neuter and pronominalizable by *hit* 'it', and *burg* 'city' which is feminine and pronominalizable by *heo* 'she'. The subclassifications are recognizable not only from the pronominalization but also from the number-case-gender inflections that may be attached to each noun, and also from the inflection of adjectives and determiners agreeing with the nouns.

Number. As in NE, most nouns can be either singular or plural, but certain ones must be subclassified according to whether they are one or the other (compare *frætwe* 'jewels, treasures', *gehyrstu* 'ornaments', which appear always to occur in the plural, and *þeowot* 'slavery', which is always singular). There is a further set, usually called collectives, that can take either the plural or the singular form of the verb depending on whether they are thought of as a group (a single unit) or as individuals, like *Congress, Parliament, people, team.* In NE we prefer to select one member and retain it throughout the sentence unless there is some particular reason for changing to plural. In OE, however, it was quite common to change number in the middle of the sentence, apparently without change of meaning:

3.43 Chron. 72.24 (874) Her *for* (sg) *se here* (sg) from Lindesse to Hreope-dune 7 þær winter setl *nam* (sg) 7 þone cyning Burgræd ofer sæ *adræfdon* (pl) 'In-this-year marched that enemy-army from Lindsey to Repton and there winter quarters took and that king Burgræd over sea drove'.

DETERMINERS: DEFINITE AND INDEFINITE. One of the most striking things about the NP in OE is the almost complete absence of anything directly corresponding to our *a* and *the*.

In NE a noun marked as "new information" will normally be preceded by *a* if it is a count noun, but by nothing at all if it is mass, for example, *I need a dollar,* but *I need love.* In OE neither count nouns nor mass nouns had overt markers for "new information," in other words, the OE equivalent of *I need a dollar* would be *I need dollar,* compare 3.29. Nevertheless, the NE *a* is derived from an unstressed version of the numeral *one* (OE *an*) and still shares many characteristics with *one.* For example, when an NP of the type *a* + *Noun* is pronominalized, the pronoun form is *one:*

> I looked for a sea-urchin and I found *a sea-urchin* →
> I looked for a sea-urchin and found *one.*

A is also used only in the singular (the plural of *a book* is *books* or *some books*) and only with nouns that can be counted, just as the numeral *one* is. It is therefore not inappropriate to ask whether traces can be found in OE of the development of the article *a.* And indeed we do find a few instances of OE *an* which are difficult to interpret as the numeral, for example:

> 3.44 Or. 102.7 ac *an wind* com of Calabria wealde 'but one/a wind [a blast of wind?] came from Calabria forest'.

It was nevertheless many centuries before it came to be used as in NE.

If NE *a* derives from OE *an, the* derives from the OE *þ-* element that occurs in most forms of the demonstratives *this* and *that. Þes, þeos, þis* 'this' is used specifically as a pointer (or "deictic"); *se, seo, þæt* 'that' may be either a pointer or more often an element that singles out a specific noun from the general class, hence its frequent use in the heads of relative clauses, as in:

> 3.45 CP. 7.10 eall *sio giogup* þe nu . . . 'all that youth which now . . . = all the specific youth that now . . .'

It is this kind of singling out that we get in constructions of the type *se* + *Proper Noun:*

> 3.46 Chron. 80.2 (895) 7 hie wæron Hloþwiges suna, *se Hloþwig* was *þæs aldan Carles* sunu, *se Carl* was Pippenes sunu and they were Hlothwig's sons, that Hlothwig was of-that old Charles (Charlemagne) son, that Charles was Pepin's son'.

where *se* specifies the particular Hlothwig and Charles, and separates them from others of the same name. In addition *se* also seems to indicate "aforementioned" in this sentence. *The* grew directly out of such uses of *se, seo, þæt.* While *the* does not occur in OE, there are instances of *se, seo, þæt* (but not of *þes*) used in a way that suggests weakening of the dual sense "specific" and "aforementioned" to simply "aforementioned." For example, we find names of peoples regularly associated with *se: þa Beormas* 'those Permians', *þara Terfinna land* 'of-those White-Sea-Finns land = the land of the White-Sea-Finns', where the demonstrative indicates a known rather than a specific member of a set and certainly does not point. The demonstrative is also used to express the notion "culturally known" as in *seo sunne* 'that/the sun', *seo heofon* 'that/the heaven'.

Since the surface form of the demonstrative carries more information about number, gender, and case than that of practically any other nominal expression in OE, it is naturally the demonstrative that we turn to in trying to determine the number, case, and gender of a particular NP in a particular sentence. One of the characteristics of the Germanic languages is that when an adjective follows a demonstrative it is marked on the surface with what is known as the "definite" (or "weak") inflection—this is typically *-an* and provides minimal information concerning number, case, and gender, for example, *þæs godan monnes* 'of-that good man', *þæm godan menn* 'to-that good man', *þy godan menn* 'with-that good man' (instrumental). In the absence of a demonstrative, the adjective carries the "indefinite" (or "strong") inflectional forms which provide maximal information concerning number, gender, and case: *godes monnes* 'of-good man', *godum menn* 'to-good man', *gode menn* 'with good man'.

Because of the agreement of determiners with the nouns they modify, there is none of the ambiguity in possessives that we find in, for instance, *the man's hand* in NE where we may not on first thought be sure whether *the* modifies *man* or *hand.* In OE it is quite clear that in constructions of this type the determiner modifies the Possessor, for example, *þæs monnes hand* 'the man's hand' where both the determiner and *man* are in the genitive.

PRONOUNS. The OE pronominal system is particularly interesting in terms of the history of the language as it has undergone many changes. The relative pronoun system will be discussed in the section on relatives below. Here we will restrict ourselves to certain facets of the personal pronouns.

In the section above, we observed that nouns could be either masculine, feminine, or neuter, regardless of whether they were animate or inanimate. While nouns had only one gender subclassification, the pronominal forms had two; the one followed the noun classification; the other followed the same kind of natural gender system as we have in NE. The same kind of double pronominal system operates in Modern German.

In general, if a noun is pronominalized, the further away the pronoun is from the noun with which it is in identity, the more likely it is to carry natural gender. The dual classification is to be found in the following:

3.47 CP. 5.3 ðæt ðu *ðone wisdom* (masc.) ðe ðe God sealde ðær ðær ðu *hiene* (masc.) befæstan mæge . . . befæste. Geðenc hwelc witu us ða becomon for ðisse worulde ða ða we *hit* (neuter) . . . ne lufodon 'that you that wisdom that to-you God gave there where you him (= it) apply may . . . apply. Think what-kind-of torments to-us then came in-respect-of this world then when we it . . . not loved'.

Personal pronouns in NE reflect the singular–plural distinction in *I* versus *we, he* versus *they,* but have neutralized it for the second person (*you* is semantically ambiguous as a surface form between singular and plural, but is grammatically plural as a surface form insofar as it requires the plural, never the singular, form of the verb in standard English, such as *You, Jean, are to go, *You, Jean, is to go*). In OE no such neutralization took place and *þu* 'thou' is regularly used for the singular, *ge* 'you' for the plural.

In addition to these distinctions, earlier OE also made distinctions between dual and plural for the first and second persons, for example, *wit* 'we two' versus *we* 'we', *git* 'you two' versus *ge* 'you'. For first and second person pronouns, then, plural strictly means 'more than two'; *we* and *ge* are, however, often extended in meaning to cover "two or more'.

While OE makes certain pronominal contrasts that are no longer current, there are in NE some surface contrasts that do not occur in OE. On page 42 it was pointed out that in NE we distinguish between *John saw him* and *John saw himself.* In OE, however, the "reflexivization" of a pronoun in identity with a preceding noun that occurs in the same proposition typically does not take place:

3.48 Or. 230.16 hu hi *hi* behealdan sceolden 'how they them (selves) direct should'.

Sometimes a form *self-* is optionally present. When it occurs, it is usually emphatic and retains its original sense of 'self' or 'person' as in the NE emphatic, nonreflexive *He himself left.* It is likely, for example, that in:

3.49 Or. 294.4 þa adrencte he *hiene selfne* 'then drowned he him self'.

hiene selfne is emphatic, closer to the meaning 'He drowned his own self' than we might expect from NE, where the *self* form is obligatory.

As we saw on page 36, certain verbs that in NE are associated with two underlying NPs in identity functioning as Agent or Experiencer and Patient, or the like allow only one surface NP with a double function: for example, the *I* in *I went, I rose* functions both as Agent and as Patient. In OE such verbs allowed the optional realization of both functions; the second function, if expressed, is always in its pronominal form, but although it is in identity with the Agent or Experiencer, reflexivization never occurs. Hence we have *He him hamweard ferde,* not **He him selfne hamweard ferde* in:

3.50 Or. 74.32 he *him* hamweard ferde to his agnum rice 'he him homeward went to his own kingdom = he went (betook himself) home to his own kingdom'.

Most verbs occurring in OE in this construction semantically denote movement (for example, *gewit-* 'go', *sitt-* 'sit down') or occasionally state of mind (for example, *ondræd-* 'fear'); the rather archaic *I fear me she has left* that we sometimes hear in NE, usually in jocular speech, is a direct descendant of this construction.

Tense

As in NE, and in fact all Germanic languages, there are only two grammatical tenses in OE: past and nonpast. Inflectionally, there are far more different forms than in NE: first, second, and third person singular are distinguishable from plural in both past and nonpast; all the standard handbooks on OE or on the history of English give a list of the major inflections, so they will not be repeated here.

Aspect

Distributive Habitual

Just as in NE, habitual activities, whether distributive or not, normally have no special overt verbal form such as an auxiliary:

3.51 Or. 20.16 7 se cyning 7 þa ricostan men *drincað* myran meolc 'and that king and those richest men *drink* mare's milk'.

If the preposition involves a main *be* verb and habitual aspect, especially distributive habitual, then *beo-* is preferred over *wes-* or *weorþ-;* see 3.42 for a nondistributive habitual, and for the distributive habitual:

3.52 Or. 20.19 þær is (always) mid Estum ðeaw, þonne þær *bið* (whenever there is) man dead 'there is among Estonians custom, when there is man dead = there is a custom among the Estonians that whenever a man dies'.

Progressive

Typically this aspect too has no overt form in OE. As a result there can be ambiguities between habitual and progressive aspect, although usually the context makes the aspect clear. If progressive has an overt form, it is a *be* verb (*beo-, wes-, weorþ-*) requiring *-ende* as the PrP on the main verb, as in:

3.53 Or. 19.33 þæt scip *wæs* ealne weg *yrnende* under segle
'that ship was all way running under sail'.

Wes- is favored over *beo-* as the expression of nonpast progressive, except in predictions, when *beo-* is favored. *Weorþ-* hardly occurs at all in Alfredian writings and is very scarce even in Ælfric's writings despite the great number of instances of *weorþ-* as a passive and as a perfect auxiliary; this is probably because *weorþ-* was still associated with inception and change rather than action simultaneous with the time of utterance even after the full sense of 'become' had been lost.

In his detailed study of the progressive in Germanic, Mossé (1938) points out that of all the early Germanic languages, OE uses the overt progressive most. In Gothic the form is very rare and seems to occur only as the literal translation of a Greek progressive. In OE, too, the progressive form may have been influenced by a foreign language, this time Latin, since it occurs most extensively in translations of Latin; it does, however, also occur in a poem as old as *Beowulf* and on occasion in the Ohthere and Wulfstan passage of *Orosius* (for example, 3.53 above) and in the *Chronicle*. It seems therefore that it may have been a genuine OE construction, though it undoubtedly owed much for the expansion of its use to Latin models. Certainly it is in keeping with the segmentalization processes that occurred in the expression of, for example, the perfect. Even when it occurs in translations, it is most commonly found, according to Mossé, with verbs denoting movement, especially those associated with warfare, for instance, *winn-* 'fight', *feoht-* 'fight', *herg-* 'harry', *slea-* 'slay', *far-* 'go', *iern-* 'run'. Right from the start, then, it has been primarily associated with action verbs.

Sometimes the *beo-/wes- + PrP* auxiliary is used in constructions where we would not use it. Consider, for instance:

3.54 Or. 8.14 of Danai þære ie, seo *is irnende* of norþdæle
'from Danai that river which is running (= which runs) from northern-part'.

3.55 Or. 12.35 þæt seo ea *bið flowende* ofer eal Ægypta land
'that this river is flowing over (= floods) all Egyptians' land'.

In NE we would prefer the simple nonpast since a generality that always holds true is being described in the first instance and distributive habitual in the second; neither expresses an action in process in the immediate present. In some instances, then, we find the *beo-/wes-* + *PrP* construction extended in OE from its basic progressive to nonprogressive use.

Perfect

If overt distinctions between progressive and nonprogressive were not made consistently, there was also a failure to distinguish regularly between perfective and nonperfective in the surface structure. Often the simple past tense marker sufficed where we would give overt realization to perfect as in the confession of the Prodigal Son, Luke 15:21 *Fæder, ic syngode* 'Father, I sinned' (in the Vulgate the verb is marked for perfect: *peccavi* 'I have sinned'), and in:

3.56 CP. 3.2 ðe cyðan hate ðæt me *com* swiðe oft on gemynd hwelce wiotan iu wæron giond Angelcynn 'to-you tell command that to-me came very often to mind what wise-men before were throughout England = let it be known to you that it has very often come to my mind what . . .'

In older Germanic the prefix *ga-* (OE *ge-*) had been used to signify, among other things, perfective aspect. The sense of completion involved in the perfect gave rise to the use of *ga-* as a word-formative signaling "entirely, completely," even "achieve by"; hence we find such verb pairs as OE *bind-* 'tie', *gebind-* 'tie up', and *ærn-* 'run', *geærn-* 'get by running'. The result was that such a sentence as *He hit geband* was ambiguous between 'He has tied it' and 'He tied it up'; indeed, as the perfective *ge-* was not attachable to the word-formative *ge-* (there are no instances of **He hit gegeband*), there was another possible interpretation: 'He has tied it up'. From earliest OE times, and probably even earlier Germanic, *ge-* was therefore not a very efficient realization of perfect, and other forms were found to express it. One possibility was to use adverbs, as does Ælfric in giving the OE equivalents of Latin perfects:

3.57 Ælf. Gr. 130.13 "amabam" ic lufode . . . "amaui" ic lufode *fulfremedlice* 'I loved . . . I loved fully/to-completion = I have loved'.

Another possibility was to do what was being done elsewhere, as in the performative and passive systems: to extend the use of certain main verbs and use them as auxiliaries in segmentalized verbal phrases. This does not mean that the development of the segmentalized form was the result of deliberate planning; nothing could in fact be further from the truth. Rather, the construction developed as a probably quite unconscious restructuring of existing patterns along lines typical of the Germanic languages.[11]

The segmentalized phrases for perfective are of two types:

(1) A *be* verb requiring PP on the following verb (the *be* verbs are *beo-, wes-, weorþ-,* and they carry the same distinctions as elsewhere). Such perfects are used only with verbs denoting some kind of change, for example, *cum-* 'come', *far-* 'go, travel' (involving change of place), and *geweorþ-* 'become' (involving change of status). The name "mutative verb" is sometimes given to this type of verb.

(2) *Habb-* + *PP* (the ancestor of our *have* + *PP*) which is used with other verbs.

Some examples are:

3.58 Chron. 86.16 (894) *wæs* Hæsten þa þær *cumen* mid his herge . . . *hæfde* Hæsten ær *geworht* þæt geweorc æt Beamfleote 7 *wæs* þa ut *afaren* on hergaþ 'was Hæsten then there come with his enemy-army . . . had Hæsten before built that stronghold at Benfleet and was then gone out on pillaging = Hæsten had arrived there with his army . . . Hæsten had previously built the stronghold at Benfleet and had then gone out on a foraging expedition'.

3.59 Or. 222.8 on þæm swicdome *wearþ* Numantia duguð *gefeallen* 'through that treachery was of-Numantia flower fallen'.

Habb- + *PP* was dominant from earliest times, so we find occasional instances of it with mutative verbs like *far-* 'go' which normally occur with the *be* perfect, but such structures are rare until ME.

Both sets of perfective auxiliaries were genuine OE constructions that go back to our earliest records. They coexist with, and in certain

[11] Indeed, the phenomenon seems to have been areal and to have occurred at various times all over Europe in different language families, including late Latin and Romance, Modern Greek, and the Germanic languages. The possessive structures with *have* are themselves relatively late (though they do, of course, precede the development of the *have* perfect by several generations at least). In Chapter 2, note 6, it was pointed out that the same underlying functions are to be found in *The book is mine, I have the book;* in the first the Patient is subject, in the second the Possessor. In the history of various languages like Latin and Germanic, the *be* construction with Patient as subject is earlier than the *have* construction with Possessor as subject (see Lyons 1968:391–397). Since both Latin and OE reflect similar developments through the *be* to the *have* possessive and from the *have* possessive to the perfect, it has been suggested that Latin influenced Germanic and that the *have* forms were borrowed at successive stages. Considering the frequency with which the *have* perfect occurs in OE, considering that not only the verb *habb-* but also *ag-* 'have, possess' was used as a perfective, and considering that the development of perfective phrases with *habēre* in Latin is largely restricted to mental experiences (for instance, *I have it understood*) but to actions in OE (for instance, *I have him bound*), it is unlikely that the OE perfect is borrowed directly from Latin. It is very likely, however, to have been reinforced by Latin, so much so that the alternate auxiliary *ag-* was almost completely lost by Alfredian times as a perfective.

cases are ambiguous with, two rather different constructions from which they were derived.

The origin of the segmentalized *be* perfects, like that of the segmentalized *be* passive (p. 83), is to be found in adjectival constructions (this time, however, there is no underlying passive-resultative structure), for example, *we wæron gecumene* "we were (in the state of having) come," where *gecumene* is an adjectival form of the verb *cum-*, agreeing in number, case, and gender with the subject *we*. Relics of this construction are to be found in, for instance, *The cookies are all gone* (in a state of goneness), but whereas in OE this type of construction was fully productive, it is now available only to a small number of verbs and those that do occur in it are often used metaphorically: the leaves may be fallen, but I can hardly be fallen except in the metaphorical sense.

The conditions for restructuring the *be* + adjectival participial construction were presumably the same as those that resulted in the development of a segmentalized passive: some of the adjectival inflections had no overt form—for example, when the adjective agrees in number, gender, and case with masculine or neuter nominative singular. So we find *He wæs gecumen* 'He was in the state of having come' with no overt signal of nominative masculine singular. Having no overt inflection, the participial verb could be interpreted as having no inflection at all, not even an underlying one. This meant that the adjectival, stative character of the participial verb could be ignored; what was left was the completive sense always present in structures of the type *He was in a state of having come,* and the construction was open to reinterpretation as the expression of perfect, which is never inflected.

The new perfective phrase was generalized to other contexts such as masculine plurals so that there resulted a contrast between (i) the adjectival *We wæron cumene,* as in:

3.60 Or. 224.5 Craccuse wæron monege cyningas . . . to fultume *cumene* (adjective) 'to-Craccus were many kings . . . as help come'.

and (ii) the perfective *We wæron cumen,* as in:

3.61 Or. 82.13 Hie wæron *cumen* (past participle) Leoniðan to fultume 'they were come to-Leonitha as help = they had come to help Leonitha'.

The development of the other perfect auxiliary, *habb-* + *PP,* is more complex, but also involves adjectival participials. As might be suspected from the form *have,* structures with Possessors like *I have a book* were also originally involved.

In earliest OE we do not find *habb-* + *PP* in perfective constructions, only in possessive ones like *Ic hæfde hine gebundenne* 'I had him in-a-state-of-being-bound', where *gebundenne* is an adjectival form of the verb with the accusative masculine singular adjectival inflection *-ne* agreeing with *hine*. Consider also:

3.62 Chron. 85.8 (894) Ac hie *hæfdon* þa heora stemn *gesetenne* 7 hiora mete *genotudne* 'But they had then their period-of-service in-a-state-of-being-sat-through and their food in-a-state-of-being-used-up'.

As this quotation from the *Chronicle* shows, the possessive construction continued in use. By the eighth century, however, the perfective had developed from it and coexisted with it.

Just as the *He wæs gecumen* construction split into two giving an adjectival and a perfective construction, so the sentence type *Ic hæfde hine gebundenne* split into two. *Habb-* was reinterpreted as a marker of perfectiveness and the adjectival nature of the participial was lost. As in the case of the *be* perfects this restructuring was facilitated by the fact that the adjectival ending was not always overtly marked, for example, *Ic hæfde hit gebunden* 'I had it in-a-state-of-being-bound'. As a result, we find such perfective constructions as

3.63 CP. 5.19 wiotona ðe . . . ða bec eallæ befullan *geliornod* (perfect participle, no inflection) *hæfdon* 'of-wise-men who . . . those books completely learned had'.

besides the adjectival possessive

3.64 Bo. 1.8 ða (he) þas boc *hæfde geleornode* (adjective, inflected) 'when (he) those books had in-a-state-of-learnedness'.

From constructions with original Possessors, the perfective *habb-* was generalized to others without Possessors, such as

3.65 Or. 88.28 ic *hæbbe* nu *gesæd* hiora ingewinn 'I have now told their intestine-struggles'.

The absence of sentences with groups of auxiliaries like *He may have seen her* is a noticeable feature of OE. They did not develop until ME (see p. 145).

Negation

Negation is expressed by a negative adverb. In NE this is typically *not;* in OE it is typically *ne*. *Ne* in OE is an independent word, invariably occurring (in the meaning 'not') before the auxiliary if there is one, otherwise before the main verb:

3.66 Or. 264.13 þæt he na siþþan geboren *ne* wurde (passive auxiliary) 'that he never after born not would-be = that he (Christ) should never be born after that'.
3.67 Or. 17.28 ac hie *ne* dorston (main verb) þær on cuman 'but they not dared there on come = but they dared not land there'.

Ne can be attached to a small set of verbs like *habb-* 'have', *ag-* 'have', *wes-* 'be', *wit-* 'know', *will-* 'will' to form *nabb-, nag-, nes-, nyt-, nyll-,* respectively (a relic of the latter is to be found in *will ic nill ic* → *willy nilly*). It can also be attached to some indefinite quantifiers and adverbs such as *a* 'ever', to form *na* 'never'. Although it no longer occurs as an independent unit, and can no longer be attached to verbs, *ne* has relics in the suppletive "negative-incorporated" forms of indefinite quantifiers and adverbs like *no* (negative + *any* → *no*), *never* (negative + *ever* → *never*), and so on (see p. 47).

Nowadays, in Standard English at least, the occurrence of a negative-incorporated form such as *no* and of *not* in the same sentence is taboo, so a sentence like *I don't want no milk* is considered "substandard" or ungrammatical. The taboo against multiple negation is of fairly recent origin. In earlier forms of English it was totally acceptable, often, although by no means exclusively, for emphasis. In OE multiple negation is very common indeed and any element that permitted negative-incorporation could have *n-* attached to it. Multiple negation was, however, not obligatory in most constructions. We find, for example:

3.68 Or. 178.20 cwæð þæt hit *na* geweorþan sceolde þæt . . . 'said that it never come-to-pass ought that . . . = said that it ought never to happen that . . .'

with negative-incorporation of the adverb *a* 'ever', but no *ne* before *sceolde,* side by side with the multiple negatives of:

3.69 Or. 42.4 þæt hit *na* buton gewinne *næs* '(so) that it never without battle not-was = so that it was never without war'.
3.70 Or. 20.18 *ne* bið ðær *nænig* ealo gebrowen mid Estum 'not is there not-any ale brewed among Estonians = no ale is brewed among the Estonians'.

The only construction in which multiple negation was obligatory was in negative coordination (see p. 96).

The particular set of elements that allow negative-incorporation is quite similar to that in NE: the suppletive quantifier *ænig* 'any' (→ *nænig* 'not-any, no'), the numeral *an* 'one' (→ *nan* 'not-one, no'),[12] adverbs like *a* 'ever' (→ *na* 'not-ever'), *æfre* 'ever' (→ *næfre* 'not-ever'), pro-

[12] The surface contrast between *nænig* and *nan* was lost in early ME, and *nan* (later *no*) came to serve for both underlying structures.

nouns like *a-wiht* 'anything' (→ *na-wiht, nauht* 'not-anything, not at all'), *ægþer* 'either, both' (→ *nægþer* 'not-either, not-both'), and so forth.

In NE, negation causes suppletion not only in the proposition of which it is a constituent, but also in the sentence complement subordinated to that proposition (p. 48). While suppletion spreads under the influence of negation into the complement sentence, negative-incorporation does not. In OE, however, some instances of negative-incorporation as well as suppletion in the complement do occur:

3.71 CP. 5.20 ðæt hie *hiora* ða *nænne dæl* noldon *on hiora agen geðiode wendan* 'that they of-them then not-one part not-wished into their own language to-turn = that they then did not wish to turn any part of them into their own language'.

Like multiple negation, negative-incorporation in the complement was optional in OE. In certain later forms of English, notably some Black dialects, both have become obligatory (see p. 194).

Suppletion in the complement may result not only from the presence of a negative constituent in the higher sentence but also from the presence of a grammatically negative verb like *doubt* (p. 61). Such verbs in OE include *tweo-* 'doubt', *forbeod-* 'forbid', *forber-* 'refrain from', *geswic-* 'stop', and *wiðcweð-* 'refuse'. These verbs allow suppletion of *an* → *ænig,* and the like in the complement, as in NE; they also allow negative-incorporation in the complement. Hence we find besides:

3.72 Or. 254.8 *forbead* þæt hiene mon god *hete* 'forbade that him one God called'.

the negative-incorporated form:

3.73 Or. 262.22 *forbead* þæt mon na ðær eft *ne* timbrede 'forbade that one not-ever there after not built = forbade anyone to build there afterwards'.

C. THE FORMATION OF COMPLEX SENTENCES

Coordination

The chief coordinating conjunction in OE affirmative sentences was *and/ond* (often graphically symbolized by the "sigil" 7). A complex emphatic coordinator *ægþer ge . . . ge* 'both . . . and' is also found. *And* is regularly used to coordinate two or more sentences if the first is affirmative, as in 3.11, 3.12, and so on. When two or more negative sentences or phrases are coordinated, however, the coordinating conjunction is *ne* (or occasionally the complex emphatic coordinator *naþer ne . . . ne*):

3.74 Or. 156.8 swelcne hie ær ne gesawon *ne* secgan ne hirdon 'such-as they before not saw and-not say not heard = such as they had neither seen nor heard tell of before'.

As in NE, coordinate sentences which differ only in their subjects may be reduced, resulting in structures of the type *Hengest and Æsc fengon to rice* 'Hengest and Æsc succeeded to the kingdom'. We also find another construction, however, in which the identical parts of the underlying sentence structures are deleted in all but the first of the coordinated sentences, but the subjects of subsequent coordinate sentences are not moved into the first sentence. Such constructions are particularly common in early and middle OE:

3.75 Chron. 12.20 (455) æfter þam Hengest feng to rice *7 Æsc his sunu* 'after that Hengest succeeded to kingdom and Æsc his son = and after that Hengest and his son Æsc succeeded to the kingdom'.

but may also be found in very late OE:

3.76 Chron. 265.10 (1137) Xpist slep *7 his halechen* 'Christ slept and his apostles = Christ and his apostles slept'.

In NE these sentences would either require the conjoining suggested in the loose translation or else would require some such alternative realization as 'after that Hengest succeeded to the kingdom and his son Æsc did so too'.

The OE construction under discussion is often called the "split coordinate" since the coordinate elements are separated from each other. It has been suggested that these constructions are favored in OE because complex sentence elements were ordered, within specific limitations, according to their length and functional load rather than according to their syntactic groupings: the longer and the more complex the construction, the more likely it was to be split and part put at the end of the sentence.[13] The treatment of relative clauses bears out such an assumption well. By ME we find far greater tolerance for the stacking of phrases and clauses at the beginning of the sentence; from ME on, ordering is based chiefly on syntactic groupings rather than the size and functional load of a constituent, and by the twelfth century conjoined constructions of the type *Christ and his apostles slept* are preferred over the type illustrated by 3.75 and 3.76.

---

[13] For a detailed discussion of the constraints on various types of splits in OE and for some hypotheses on why they occurred see especially Reskiewicz (1966).

Complements

Indicative versus Subjunctive

The distinction between factive and nonfactive complements is probably clearer in a language like OE, where a contrast between "indicative" and "subjunctive" mood is fully developed, than in a language like NE where the distinction has fewer or more diverse overt markings.

"Subjunctive" is a verbal inflection associated with such properties as potentiality, contingency, hypothesis, conjecture, unreality, exhortation, prohibition, wishing, desiring. Strictly speaking, it signals the attitude of the speaker, but in languages like OE its use is generalized to other contexts as well by convention (certain verbs and certain syntactic structures favor subjunctive complements). On the other hand, it is sometimes not used where it is expected, especially if there is present in the surface form of the sentence a word that itself makes the attitude overt, such as if a verb like *doubt* is present. Like other inflections, subjunctive has no necessary one-to-one correspondence with underlying properties of the sentence. In some languages like Greek, an "optative" inflection is used for wishes, and the subjunctive (frequently called conjunctive) is used for hypotheses and the like. In other languages, like NE, auxiliaries such as *should, would, may,* serve the same kinds of function as the subjunctive.

The "indicative," in contrast to the subjunctive, is a verbal inflection associated with facts that have occurred, are occurring, or are sure to occur. Indicative is therefore typical of factive complements, whereas the subjunctive is typical of many nonfactives.[14]

Indicative also alternates with subjunctive (especially when an overt attitudinal expression like *I doubt* is present), and as such is the dominant form which neutralizes the contrast in "mood" or attitude.[15] The direction of neutralization, that is, *Subjunctive* and *Indicative* → *Indicative*, is not just a property of English, but of many languages; in fact it may well be universal for all languages that have subjunctive versus indicative inflections.

We will here look at a few selected instances of nonfactive comple-

---

[14] Subjunctive factives may, however, occur, as in Or. 116.6 *him gelicade þæt hie þær mehten* (subjunctive) *betst frið binnan habban* 'to-them pleased that they there might best peace within have = they were pleased with the idea that they would most easily find peace there'. In this sentence the structure of the complement is complex: the fact that there was a possibility pleased them; that they were going to have peace is not an established fact (as Orosius goes on to show, the idea that they would have peace was only a pipe-dream). The function of the subjunctive in such a sentence is to cast doubt on the assertion *They were going to have peace* and as such is the surface expression of *There was a possibility that.*

[15] There are, however, a few instances of the spread of subjunctive from a higher to a lower clause in which the subjunctive would normally not be expected, for example, from a subjunctive head clause to a relative. This involves a kind of agreement across verbs and is not a significant counter-example to the general tendency for the indicative to dominate.

ments with subjunctives.[16] Subjunctive is regular if only the complement is present and the higher sentence has not been given overt form as is common in the expression of wishes and exhortations. When the higher sentence is present, however, the subjunctive may be replaced by an indicative or occasionally by some phrasal auxiliary expression involving *scul-/will-* + *Main Verb* (the latter kind of construction is discussed beginning on p. 148 in the next chapter).

Wishes by definition make no assumption that what is wished for will come true; they often involve the assumption that the wish will *not* be realized or is unrealizable. They may often not even assume an addressee —wishes can be expressed aloud although nobody is around (this is never true of well-formed commands or statements). In OE, wishes are often expressed without an overt verb of wishing; the subjunctive is then the prime signal of the wish:

3.77 CP. 3.18 Gode ælmihtegum *sie* (subjunctive) ðonc ðætte . . . 'to-God almighty be thanks that . . .'

There is a special auxiliary verb *uton* "let us" that is used for first person plural exhortation (see example 3.10). *Uton* may derive from the past tense subjunctive of *wit-* 'go' in early Germanic, but in OE it seems to be a fixed form, no longer with any clear relationship to the *wit-* verb. The following passage illustrates well the use of *uton* for the first person plural, and the subjunctive for others:

3.78 Ælf. Coll. 41.234 *uton* towurpon hwætlicor þas geflitu, 7 *sy* (subjunctive) sibb 7 geþwærnyss betweoh us 'let-us stop speedily these arguments, and let-there-be peace and concord between us'.

Overt verbs of wishing also occur; typically they introduce a subjunctive complement (though a neutralized indicative form is also possible):

3.79 CP. 9.5 forðy ic *wolde* ðætte hie ealneg æt ðære stowe *wæren* (subjunctive) 'for-this-reason I wished that they always at that place were (= would be)'.

Exhortations have stronger assumptions than wishes—they assume

[16] Other constructions in which the subjunctive is often used in OE include "conditional" sentences with either overt or implied *gif* 'if', provided that a "contrary-to-fact" condition is expressed. It is in constructions of this type that some speakers still make a distinction between indicative and subjunctive: *If he were* (subjunctive) *here, we could go* (he is not here; the condition is contrary-to-fact); *If he is here, we can go* (whether he is or is not, is open to question). In other constructions we have largely replaced the subjunctive by a segmentalized auxiliary or else make no overt signal of the doubt (for details, see pp. 148 and 179). So-called "concessive" sentences of the type beginning with *þeah* 'although' are also typically subjunctive; so too are "purposive" clauses introduced by *for þæm þæt* 'so that, in order that', and certain temporal clauses introduced by *ær* 'before', and so on.

at least an addressee and that what is exhorted is realizable, and probably will be realized. They do not have quite the same assumptions as commands, however, since they do not assume the action commanded will be performed.

Sometimes commands are expressed as exhortations, however, especially when "polite commands" are given; in such cases the assumptions are those of commands, but the surface forms are those of exhortations. Exhortations assume that the addressee has some freedom of choice, whereas commands do not; hence exhortations are typically addressed to God, or to superiors. They are also preferred to commands for laws and other types of admonitions addressed to a large group of people either present or not, living or not yet alive:

> 3.80 CP. 9.2 ic *bebiode* on Godes naman ðæt nan mon ðone æstel from ðære bec ne *do* (subjunctive) 'I request in God's name that no man that book-mark from that book not take'.

although exhortations can also be made in the immediate presence of the speaker. By convention, the subjunctive is used in complements of both command and exhortation verbs in reported speech:

> 3.81 Or. 238.8 Þa *het* Pompeius þæt mon þæt fæsten *bræce* (subjunctive) 'Then commanded Pompey that one that stronghold should-destroy'.

In fact, reported speech is usually expressed in the subjunctive. Originally, the subjunctive was used in reported speech when the speaker wished to cast doubt on the truth of what was reportedly said. A much-cited example of such a use of the subjunctive is to be found in Ælfric's *Homilies:*

> 3.82 Ælf. Hom. I.16.19 Nu *cwædon* gedwolmen þæt deofol *gesceope* (subjunctive) sume gesceafta ac hi leogað 'now said heretics that Devil created some creatures but they lie'.

Instead of the subjunctive we sometimes find *scul-* + *past tense* used to indicate 'was said to', as in:

> 3.82 Bo. 98.26 ic wat þæt ðu geherdest oft reccan on ealdum leasum spellum þætte Iob Saturnes sunu *sceolde bion* se hehsta god . . . 7 *sceolden* gigantes *bion* eorðan suna 'I know that you heard often say in ancient lying tales that Jove Saturn's son should be the highest god . . . and should giants be of-earth sons = I know that you often heard tell in ancient stories that Job, the son of Saturn, was supposedly the highest god . . . and that the giants were supposedly the sons of earth'.

This use of *scul-* is one of the few indisputable instances of an auxiliary and verb having the function of the subjunctive (in most of the others the force of obligation or volition is still very marked).

The subjunctive was also generalized to indicate that the speaker did not commit himself to the truth of what was reportedly said; hence it was generalized to all reported speech. For example, when it is reported that:

3.84 Or. 17.2 He cwæð þæt he *bude* (subjunctive) on ðæm lande norþweardum wiþ þa Westsæ. He sæde þeah þæt þæt land *sie* (subjunctive) swiþe lang norþ þonan 'He said that he lived in that land northwards toward the West-Sea. He said, however, that that land extended very far north from-there'.

there is probably little or no doubt in the speaker's mind of the truth of Ohthere's statement; he is simply not committing himself to a value-judgment.

Verbs of thinking like *wen-* 'think', *þync-* 'think' often have subjunctive complements. Again, the subjunctive presumably originally emphasized the difference between the personal, subjective quality of thinking as opposed to the objective quality of knowing (which introduces factives), but in many instances the use of the subjunctive seems conventional rather than functional.

When the thought concerns a negative, the complement is regularly subjunctive:

3.85 CP. 3.16 ic wene ðætte noht monige begiondan Humbre *næren* (subjunctive) 'I think that not many beyond the-Humber not-were'.

Indeed, a negative environment almost always triggers a subjunctive in nonfactives. The complement may be negative as in 3.85; or the higher sentence may be negative as in:

3.86 Or. 86.3 þeh ne geortriewe ic na Gode þæt he us ne *mæge* (subjunctive) gescildan 'although not shall-distrust I never to-God, that he us not can shield = although I shall never distrust God so much as to think he cannot shield us'.

If the verb of the higher sentence is grammatically negative, but no overt negative occurs, the subjunctive is still the expected inflection in the complement, as in 3.21 (*mehten* is subjunctive) and 3.72 (*hete* is subjunctive).

How strongly subjunctive is associated with negatives can be seen in yes–no questions introduced by *hwæþer* (see p. 73). Such questions are favored when the speaker wishes to emphasize the doubt in his mind, and especially when he expects a *no* answer (they frequently translate Latin yes–no questions with *num*, the signal that a negative answer is expected). When this is the case, these questions typically occur in the subjunctive:

3.87 Or. 220.8 Hwæþer Romane hit *witen* (subjunctive) nu ænegum men to secganne . . . 'Whether the Romans it dare now to-any men to say . . . = Do the Romans now really dare to tell anyone that . . .'

Subject and Object Complement

As far as subjectivalization of factive and nonfactive complements is concerned, the most important thing to note is that no complement of the form *þæt + Sentence* occurs in subject position; that is, a construction like *That he came is obvious* is apparently ungrammatical in OE. Nonfactives can in NE still not occur in that position, but since the nineteenth century factives have been available.

Another important point is that, as might be expected from the comments on subjectivalization (p. 81), it was possible for nothing at all to occupy the subject position. A pronominal *hit* or *þæt* may occupy this position if the complement is factive, or a pseudo-subject *hit* or *þæt* if the complement is nonfactive, but they were strictly optional. If the complement is embedded to an "impersonal verb" like *þenc-* 'seem', *geweorþ-* 'happen', the presence of a pseudo-subject is in fact very rare:

3.88 Chron. 90.19 (897) swa him selfum *ðuhte* þæt hie nytwyrðoste beon *meahten* (subjunctive) 'according-as to-him self seemed that they most-useful be might = according as it seemed to him that they would be most useful'.

Unquestionable instances of subject-raising with verbs like *þync-* 'seem' are hard to find. Their rarity appears to be more than chance textual skewing as translators clearly had difficulty with finding the correct OE form to correspond with Latin subject-raised structures. Of the few sentences likely to involve subject-raising, most can be interpreted as having surface complements rather than subjects, as, for example:

3.89 Or. 94.30 Ne geþyncð þe *swelc gewin* noht lustbære 'Not seems to-you such battle not-at-all agreeable'.

It is possible that we have here a construction without the subordinator *þæt* and without the *be* verb of the complement, but nevertheless a surface complement since the following types of construction also exist:

3.90 Or. 120.10 Þonne þuhte (singular) eow *þas tida* (plural) beteran 'Then seemed to-you those times better'.

If *þas tida* were the subject, then we would expect number agreement in the verb. It is only in ME that subject-raising seems to have occurred more than sporadically.

Objectivalized complements, whether factive or not, are often characterized by an anticipatory *þæt,* especially if the complement is separated from its main verb:

3.91 Or. 172.2 *Þæt* gefremede Diulius hiora consul þæt þæt angin wearð tidlice þurhtogen 'That arranged Diulius their consul that that beginning was in-time achieved = Their consul Diulius arranged it that it was started in time'.

The anticipatory *þæt* is typical of the Germanic languages, and continues down to the present day in conversational English; it is highly disfavored in "elegant" written English, however.

Relative Clauses

It is reasonable to suppose that the contrasts between appositive and restrictive relatives existed from the earliest times since the distinction is in essence that of fundamental semantic relationships. There is no evidence, however, that the two constructions were overtly differentiated, that is, the surface structures for both are the same. It is actually only in NE that sharp distinctions in usage arise, with *that* used for restrictive relatives but not for appositives.

Full Clauses

There are two main types of relative pronoun in OE; one is the indeclinable *þe,* a form which dropped out completely during the ME period, and the other is the declinable *se, seo, þæt,* identical in form with the demonstrative 'that'.[17] Both types of relative pronoun are used for restrictive and appositive clauses, though a tendency has been noted for *þe* to occur more often with unambiguous restrictives and for *se, seo, þæt* to occur with unambiguous appositives. Some other tendencies have been observed; for example, in poetry *þe* is favored when the head noun is preceded by a demonstrative (as in *se man þe* 'that man who'); if *se, seo, þæt* does occur with heads with determiners, it occurs most often after neuter singular nouns, so the type *þæt hus þæt*

[17] There is a third very rare relative: *seþe, seoþe, þætþe* (*þætte*) in which the two forms are combined: Or. 260.4 *oðsace nu . . . se seþe* (relative) *wille oþþe se þe dyrre þæt . . .* 'deny now . . . he who will or he who dare that = let him who will or dares now deny that. . . .' A fourth relative: *se þe, seo þe, þæt þe* is sometimes cited in the literature; the *se* part has the case of the head, not of the pronominalized noun in the relative clause, however, and therefore can better be called an emphatic demonstrative followed by the indeclinable *þe* than a fourth type of relative. Some very clear examples of the *seþe* versus the *se þe* constructions are to be found in *Beowulf* 1296 and 3002, respectively; they are cited and discussed in Mitchell (1965:75).

'that house that' is much commoner than *se mann se*. Stress conditions have sometimes been adduced to account for these tendencies, but the circumstances for the different choices are far from clear.

Although unlike NE *that* in form, *þe* shares many of its characteristics. If we assume that relativization operates on surface structures, then relativization by both *þe* and *that* results in moving the noun they pronominalize to the left of the clause, leaving any preposition in construction with that noun in its original position. Hence we find in NE *This is the room that he works in,* but not **This is the room in that he works;* and, in OE:

3.92 Or. 19.9 Ohthere sæde þæt sio scir hatte Halgoland *þe* he *on* bude 'Ohthere said that that shire was-called Heligoland that he in lived'.

3.93 *Ohthere sæde þæt sio scir hatte Halgoland on þe he bude.

Since *þe* is invariable, it is not marked for number, case, or gender. Most commonly it functions as the pronominal replacement of a noun that would carry either nominative or accusative case, but it is also used where the case would be genitive, dative, or instrumental. For example, in 3.92 the case of the relativized noun would be dative.

Sometimes *þe* will occur in its usual place at the beginning of the subordinate clause while the underlying noun is given surface realization as a personal pronoun:

3.94 Or. 102.24 7 ic gehwam wille þærto tæcan *þe hiene* his lyst ma to witanne 'and I whomever shall also teach *wh-* him of-it would-please more to know = and I shall also teach whomever it would please to know more about it'.

While it is not possible to predict exactly when this *þe . . . Pronoun* construction will occur, it is clearly used at least in some instances to avoid possible ambiguity. It may also be used for emphasis; especially in poetry it may also be used for rhythmic effect rather than for grammatical reasons. This kind of construction is quite common in the languages of the world.

The other relative, *se, seo, þæt* is declined for number, gender, and case. Unlike *þe,* it appears not to occur with the personal pronoun form of the relativized underlying noun. If the relativized noun has a preposition associated with it, the preposition is moved along with the relative pronoun to the beginning of the subordinate clause. In this respect *se, seo, þæt* relatives behave rather like *who, which* in NE as in *The city in which we lived* (though we have the alternative possibility of retaining the preposition in its original place, an alternative not open to OE speakers).

3.95 Or. 74.17 ymbutan þone weall is se mæsta dic *on þæm* is iernende se ungefoglecesta stream 'round that wall is that hugest ditch in which is flowing that most-enormous current'.

3.96 *dic *þæm* se ungefoglecesta stream is iernende *on.*

Such constructions as 3.95 are, however, rare; *þe* is clearly preferred if the underlying NP is associated with a preposition.

Most relatives immediately follow their heads, but this rule does not always apply, in accordance with the principles already alluded to in the previous section on coordination: that long groupings are preferred at the end of the sentence:

3.97 Or. 260.11 sealde þæm munucum (head) corn genog *þe wæron æt Hierusalem* 'gave those monks grain enough who were at Jerusalem'.

If an NP functions adverbially, for example as a time adverb, other relatives are available than those already mentioned. These are the adverbial relatives, identical in form with the "basic" adverbs of the category—that is, *þær* for relative adverbs of place, *þonne* for relative adverbs of time. Special forms for the relative adverbs did not develop until ENE when *wh-* was generalized from the personal pronoun relatives *who* and *which* to adverbial relatives (*where, when*):

3.98 Or. 10.15 Þæt sint India gemæro þær *þær* Caucasus se beorg is be norþan 'that (those) are India's boundaries there where Caucasus the mountain is in the-north'.

Reduced Relatives

In OE there were more restrictions on the reduction of relative clauses than today, as far as we can tell. Relatives with the structure . . . *be + Adjective* were readily reduced. Otherwise, few instances of relative clause reduction can be found; those that occur indicate that the *be* verb did not have to be deleted along with the relative marker:

3.99 Or. 288.13 Ualens wæs gelæred from anum Arrianiscan biscepe *Eudoxius wæs haten* 'Valens was taught by one Aryan bishop Eudoxius was called (= called Eudoxius)'.

The only constructions in which deletion of the relative pronoun occurred at all frequently (other than those with . . . *be + Adjective* in the relative clause) were those with *(ge)haten* 'called', as in 3.99, and those with demonstrative *þæt* as head (presumably because of the identity in sound between the antecedent *þæt* and the relative pronoun *þæt*):

3.100 Or. 78.3 gedyde þæt (head) nan hæþen cyning ær gedon ne dorste 'he-did that no-one heathen king before do not dared = he did what no heathen king had dared do before'.

When relative clauses are reduced, the adjective in early OE texts, especially poetry, tends to occur after the noun. In later OE prose, however, it is normally prenominal, unless it is coordinated; in the latter case it is usually split, as in *His good men and true*.

There is some evidence that descriptive rank titles such as "king," "queen," and the like are derived from relative clauses. In NE, they regularly precede the name, unless a demonstrative is present (we say *King Henry,* but *Henry, the King*). In OE certain rank titles regularly occur after rather than before a person's name; these titles include *cyning* 'king', *biscop* 'bishop', *ealdormann* 'alderman, chief', *mæsse-preost* 'priest (who could say mass)':

3.101 CP. 3.1 *Ælfred kyning* hateð gretan *Wærferð biscep* his wordum luflice 'Alfred king bids greet Werferth bishop with-his words with-good-will = King Alfred bids Bishop Werferth be greeted with words full of good will'.

Rank titles which are primarily biblical, for example, *heahfædere* 'patriarch' or are late borrowings do not occur after the noun. This suggests that the *Alfred cyning* construction had become fixed or "fossilized" in earlier OE. New terms that came into use in later OE occurred before the noun on the model of adjectives and also possibly on the model of biblical Latin phrases such as *Dominus Christ* 'Lord Christ'.[18]

D. WORD ORDER

This section presents an outline of some of the major tendencies of OE word order. Some have already been explicitly touched on; others have been exemplified in quotations but have not been discussed.[19]

It is often said that OE word order was much less constrained than that of NE. Recent scholars have shown, however, that word order is by no means free in OE; the problem is to determine what the constraining factors are and what other factors override them. In a contemporary language paraphrases and pitch and stress can be referred to when we are in doubt about the particular kind of emphasis signaled by some word order pattern, but when we have no access to the spoken language it is naturally very hard to determine such matters. Extensive studies of discourse have, however, brought to light many of the constraints on word order exercised by such elements as old versus new

[18] Classical pre-Christian Latin favored the same type of rank titles as earlier OE, for example, *Scipio consul* rather than *consul Scipio*.

[19] Only three orders are given here. All possible arrangements of *Subject + Verb + Object* are, however, evidenced in OE.

information, position at the beginning of a discourse versus position in the middle of one, and so on.

For nonemphatic discourse the following generalizations apply (parentheses indicate the element does not have to be present; X is a cover term for various adverbs, interrogatives, pronouns, and so on):

(1) In most main clauses or the first of a set of coordinates, if the underlying sentence is a saying, promise, or prediction, and if the proposition is affirmative, the order is:
Subject (Auxiliary) Verb (Object) . . .

(2) In main clauses if the underlying sentence is a command to answer (interrogative), or if the proposition is negative, or certain adverbs of time and place occur, the order is:
(X) {Verb / Auxiliary} Subject . . .

(3) In subordinate clauses or any coordinated clause except the first, the order is:
Subject (Object) . . . Verb (Auxiliary)

Type 1 Word Order

Type 1 word order is the same as the usual NE order, except that certain regular operations override it, as, for example, the obligatory shift of pronoun objects to preverbal position and the splitting of auxiliaries (see below). Clear examples of Type 1 are to be found in 3.4, 3.7, 3.65.

Type 2 Word Order

As in NE, questions are of Type 2 order (except those questions introduced by *hwæþer;* these are of Type 1, as in 3.20): see 3.8, 3.17–3.19. Apart from nonsubject interrogative pronouns, only a few elements can occur if the X position is filled. These elements are, typically, the negative *ne* 'not' and certain adverbs of time and place like *þa* 'then' and *þær* 'there'.

In OE negative sentences with the negative particle *ne, ne* always precedes the verb, whatever word order characterizes the rest of the sentence; most often this order is Type 2 in main clauses, as in 3.70 and 3.86.

The adverb *þa* 'then', which occurs so frequently in OE narrative prose, especially in the *Chronicles,* nearly always initiates Type 2 order, as in 3.24, 3.49 and 3.81. It is contrasted with the subordinating *þa* 'when' which also occurs clause-initially, but is accompanied by regular subordinate order (Type 3), as in 3.6 and:

3.102 CP. 5.8 *Đa* ic ða ðis eall gemunde (Type 3) *ða* gemunde ic eac hu ic geseah (Type 2) . . . 'When I then this all remembered, then remembered I also how I saw . . .'

Other time adverbs that occur sentence-initially, such as *þonne* 'then', *her* 'in this year', *siþþan* 'afterward' (see 3.12, 3.40, 3.43, and also 3.38), and place adverbs such as *þider* 'thither', *þær* 'there', often share the same word order as sentences with *þa* 'then'; Type 2 order is not consistent with them, however, and it is possible to rank the frequency with which the formula *Adverb + Verb + Subject* occurs from author to author and period to period. By late OE (for example, the later parts of the *Peterborough Chronicle*) *þa* 'then' still typically occurs with Type 2 order but the others rarely do so.

Very few noninterrogative structures have retained Type 2 word order in NE except for sentences introduced by negative adverbs like *scarcely* and *hardly* (for example, *Scarcely had he said that when . . .*) and concessive constructions (like *Had I left sooner, I would not have seen the fire*).

Type 3 Word Order

"Subordinate order" is most characteristic of complements and adverbial clauses of time, place, and manner other than those mentioned above, less so of coordinates other than the first, and least of relative clauses. However, in Alfredian prose it seems to be the basic order for all three constructions. Examples are: for complements, 3.21, 3.47, 3.48, and 3.80; for relative clauses, 3.10, 3.47, and 3.63; and for coordinates:

3.103 Or. 238.18 Æfter þæm þe he hie oferwunnen hæfde (adverbial clause of time, Type 3), he for on Bretanie þæt iglond (main clause, Type 1), 7 wið þa Brettas gefeaht (coordinate, Type 3), 7 gefliemed wearð (coordinate, Type 3) 'After that that he them overcome had, he went to Britain that island and against those Britons fought and put-to-flight was'.

When more than one auxiliary is present, the usual order is:

$$\ldots \text{ Main Verb } \left\{\begin{array}{l}\text{Progressive}\\ \text{Passive}\end{array}\right\} \text{ Modal}$$

as in 3.6. While the construction may sometimes be split so that the modal occurs before the main verb, the orders **Main Verb + Modal + Progressive* and **Main Verb + Modal + Passive* never occur.

Type 3 order became recessive in later OE and was lost by later ME.

Rules Overriding Types 1, 2, and 3

Overriding these general rules are some others of which only a few are mentioned here.

Most importantly, an object which is a pronoun precedes the verb, whether or not a main clause is involved, as in 3.50. In fact, most pronouns occur before the verb; only those with prepositions tend to follow the verb. This kind of situation is fairly typical of those languages of the world that have Type 3 order.

Sometimes an object noun occurs before the verb in main clauses, probably on the pattern of the pronoun (usually emphasis is involved when nouns occur in this position, but that is not always the case). An object noun or pronoun is often placed between an auxiliary and a main verb in main clauses, as in 3.9. This is hardly surprising, in view of the fact that the modal and perfect auxiliaries were originally main verbs that introduced subordinate clauses, and those subordinate clauses would be in Type 3 order; *Ic sceal his geswigian,* in other words, had as its origin the structure *Ic sceal Complement.* Another force that may account for the splitting of auxiliary and main verb by an object, whether pronominal or not, was the tendency we have already observed in coordinations and relative clauses to divide constructions into two according to the length of the construction and the relative functional load of its parts (see pp. 97 and 105).

Most other rules concern the position of individual subclasses of adverbs or even individual words. For example, *mon* "one," the indefinite pronoun, never occurs sentence-initially, whatever its function in the sentence: see 3.31, 3.37, and 3.72.

Where these rules do not apply or where Types 1, 2, and 3 are overridden in other ways, we may often adduce emphasis. A very characteristic emphatic order is *Object + Subject + Verb,* an order that could be used quite unambiguously provided that the nouns or pronouns had clearly differentiated inflectional markings as in 3.34, or if the context was unambiguous as in 3.28. In some instances where the conditions for the word order patterns are not so clear, we may speculate that there has been influence from poetry (where the word order rules applied less rigidly). Primarily, however, we may speculate that the kind of variability we discussed in Chapter 1 was at work, a variability which led to the eventual dominance in later OE of Type 1 over Type 3, and during ME the loss of Type 3.

4 MIDDLE AND EARLY MODERN ENGLISH

The most obvious difference between Old English and Middle English is that in ME there are far fewer inflections and that the word order is closer to that of Modern English. Subjectivalization is also generalized. The processes by which these changes came about were largely completed by the mid-thirteenth century, although the older system is still to be found in the fourteenth century in some areas, especially the Southeast. Syntactically, the language of the main literary and cultural areas of England, especially London, remained much the same from the late thirteenth to the early eighteenth century, and so ME and Early Modern English will be treated together in this chapter.

It is usually said that OE is largely "synthetic," but that from about 1250 on English is largely "analytic." A synthetic language is one which is characterized by a great number of inflections; for example, mood (indicative versus subjunctive), number, case, and gender are given surface form as inflections. Also inflections are often realizations of two or more syntactic properties simultaneously; for example, the OE nominal inflections combine number, case, and gender, and the verbal inflections combine number, tense, and mood. By contrast, an analytic language is one in which elements of this type are either not given overt form at all or are expressed by separate words. Neither OE nor NE is completely synthetic or analytic. NE still has some inflections and, as we have seen, OE already showed tendencies toward analytic expressions – the development of the segmentalized aspectual auxiliaries is a case in point; so too is the tendency toward more and more extensive use of prepositions in later OE. Both segmentalized aspect and prepositions are to be found in earliest OE; what we find in ME and later English is not innovation toward analytic structure but rather extensive generalization of an already operative system.

Many scholars have argued that the loss of inflections and the resultant preponderance of analytic structures were caused by phonological changes. In particular, they attribute inflectional loss to the collapse of contrasts between final unstressed syllables, for example, between *-e, -a, -u* and between *-es* and *-as* (all unstressed vowels were collapsed as [ə]). It is, however, hard to see how these distinctions could have been lost if they had been fully functional; if they were, then with their loss we could expect loss of communication. It is more plausible to assume that the collapse of unstressed vowel contrasts was made possible precisely because they were not fully functional, that is, because they were redundant with or overridden by other grammatical elements. There is in fact considerable evidence to support this hypothesis. For example, already in late OE adjective endings were collapsed or else lost entirely when the adjective occurred in the structure *Noun + be + Adjective,* but not when it occurred before the noun; had the loss of adjectival endings been entirely due to phonological processes, we would expect the endings to be reduced everywhere equally. Similarly, as was mentioned in Chapter 1, although most inflections of the type *-en* dropped out toward the end of ME, *-en* did not do so when it had the grammatical function of past participle (as in *ridden, hidden, seen*); and some functional inflections, like the noun plurals, remained. One of the preconditions for the loss of case inflection may have been the counterpoint between cases automatically assignable from the underlying functions and cases selected by verbs and prepositions; this counterpoint demonstrates the relative noninformativeness of case inflections. Noninformative elements are generally simplified in a language, so it is not surprising that the case system (among other inflectional systems) was reduced. All the same, many inflectional losses could not have occurred if word order had been as variable as it was in OE, since the overt relationships between elements in the sentence would be insufficiently marked for satisfactory communication to take place in the absence of both case inflections and heavy word order restrictions. It was at those points where the structure of the sentence was most unambiguous that inflections could be reduced or restructured. In turn, as inflections became less distinct, word order became more constrained. So we can postulate a kind of cyclical development with some word order patterns allowing the partial collapsing of inflectional distinctions, this collapsing itself becoming a condition for further restrictions of word order, and these restrictions in turn allowing for more collapsings of inflections, and so on. The process of inflectional reduction is clearly not yet complete and is less far-reaching in Standard English than in some other dialects, as we shall see in the discussion of NE in the next chapter.

If phonological change has often been suggested as a major cause of inflectional loss, so has the influence of foreign languages, especially French. French had no nominal and very few pronominal case inflections; it had a two-way instead of a three-way gender distinction, and so forth. While it is likely that French contributed to the loss of inflections insofar as it speeded it up, it certainly did not cause it, since the change was clearly in progress by 1000, before French came to have any significant influence in England. Even Alfredian works show sporadic signs of it, especially "reverse spellings" of *-a* and *-e,* indicating that the two were no longer fully contrastive.

How extensive the influence of French was on English syntax will probably never be known exactly. There is no doubt that French lent support to many changes that had their beginnings in OE, but there seem to have been very few major syntactic structures borrowed directly. In fact, it is doubtful whether syntactic structures completely foreign to a language are ever borrowed; only those which can be readily absorbed within the system are taken into it. Nevertheless, the power of French must not be underestimated.[1] In later OE times (ca. 1000 on), Norman French was a prestige language, at least for those who aligned themselves with King Æthelred and his son, Edward the Confessor. From the time of the Norman Conquest until the mid-fourteenth century, French (first Norman, later Central French) was the language of the court, of law, and of education; it was spoken not only by Frenchmen at court and in the church, but also by those relatively few Englishmen who were members of the upper class. The beginning of the thirteenth century, when Normandy was lost to the English, saw the beginning of the hostility to France that was to grow into the Hundred Years' War and a new sense of nationalism; with it developed inevitably a greater respect for English over French. Yet it was not until after the mid-fourteenth century, partly with the rise of the middle class, that English came to be used instead of French as the language of the law (1362) and of Parliament (also 1362) and as a medium for teaching grammar in the schools. Under such circumstances it is inevitable that French must have influenced at least the educated sector of native English society in a very significant way. The number of loanwords in everyday English attests to this.

In the later ME period, writers like Chaucer clearly still thought of French as the prestige language. Chaucer himself spent much time in France and translated many French works; even he, however, seems to have borrowed little in the way of syntactic structures from French. From the fifteenth century on the influence of French declined, until political and cultural events in the late seventeenth century once more brought it high prestige.

During the Renaissance it was Latin, and to a far lesser extent Greek, that was the most influential language. Latin had been very important from OE times on as the language of the Church and of philosophy; in the Renaissance, interest in the classics gave Latin renewed importance. Yet at the same time the sense of individualism fostered by the Renaissance gave English a prestige it had never enjoyed before. Grammarians like Richard Mulcaster in the mid-sixteenth century hotly defended English as a worthy medium for serious dis-

[1] See Baugh (1957), Chapters 5 and 6, for extensive discussion of the rise and decline of French culture in England.

course, and by the end of the century English came to be the medium for all genres of writing. From that time on concern with the development of an elegant, well-proportioned style increased until it became a major issue in the eighteenth century. In the meantime, immediate contact with foreign languages in a bilingual or quasi-bilingual context became the privilege of individuals rather than of the educated upper class as a whole, and therefore the direct linguistic influence of other languages decreased.

Where appropriate, brief mention is made in the following pages of possible syntactic loans from Latin, French, and also Scandinavian. The loans from Scandinavian must all have entered English before the mid-eleventh century, since most direct Scandinavian influence ceased with the death of King Canute in 1042; nevertheless, they are largely not attested until the twelfth century. The time lag between when the borrowings must have occurred and when they are first found in the extant manuscripts presents an important reminder of the time lag between the occurrence of changes in the spoken language and their use in the written records available to us.

Illustrations of ME syntax are taken from Chaucer's *Tale of Melibee* and from the *Paston Letters*. While *Melibee* is a translation from French, it is nevertheless written in a fairly informal style and illustrates well the type of sentence structures found in most texts of the time. Since Chaucer is probably more familiar to readers of this book than other writers of the time, it seemed unreasonable not to give quotations from his work, despite the translation problem. The *Paston Letters* are an invaluable source of information on late ME. A large collection of documents ranging in date from 1422 to 1509, they are mainly by middle-class people without courtly or literary pretensions. For the most part they concern household and business matters, written in haste to members of the same family, and as such constitute the first major collection of writings in informal "conversational" style. More Northeasterly in dialect though they are than Chaucer's English, they represent the dialect which later had the greatest influence on London English, and therefore may be considered well within the mainstream of the development of English.

It is not until the late sixteenth century that we find an extensive body of what appears to be language consciously made to equate with the spoken idiom. I have chosen to illustrate this kind of language mainly from Shakespeare's plays, especially from the *Henry IV* plays and the *Merry Wives of Windsor,* a large part of which are devoted to scenes of "bourgeois" life, as portrayed by Falstaff and his cronies. Supporting examples from Deloney's bourgeois tales and Nashe's picaresque stories show how typical of the "language of everyday" the Falstaff scenes are.[2]

[2] For those who wish to study late sixteenth-century style, Nashe's *Unfortunate Traveller* is well worth careful analysis since it includes an excellent parody of the Euphuistic style, particularly as developed by Sir Philip Sidney, that contrasts markedly with Nashe's own "bourgeois," "colloquial" style.

One source of colloquial English, the conversation books that have been so popular from the sixteenth century on, has not been used for various reasons.[3] First of all, they are of little literary or social interest; furthermore, they are not particularly likely to be known to readers of this study; but most importantly they are not very reliable. They are primarily concerned with giving fairly literal translations of phrases into French, German, Italian, and so on, or from those languages into English, and suffer from the constraints of translation and of discourses taken out of context. The modern Berlitz phrase books may give an exaggerated picture of the problems involved; nevertheless, such a picture is not entirely irrelevant for estimating the reliability of data from phrase books of earlier centuries.

A. THE PERFORMATIVE

Saying

Of prime interest is the use, especially in sixteenth and seventeenth century biblical and religious language of an overt performative *say,* as in *I say unto you, Verily I say unto you* (with stress on the truth of the assertion). This formula may be a borrowing from Hebrew, or at least from the Hebrew of the testaments. In any event, it never gained wide currency, and in most other stylistic contexts saying had no overt form.

Predicting

During ME and ENE, predicting came to be expressed less and less frequently by the simple nonpast tense, unless an adverb designating future time was also present. Instead, *shall* and *will* came to be the regular realizations of prediction.[4]

Most ME authors prefer *shall* to *will* for all persons, perhaps because the strong volitional quality of *will* was still deeply felt. Chaucer seems to have been one of the first to prefer *shall* for the first person, *will* for the other persons.

During ENE, *will* came to be used more and more for the second and third person predictive, but very rarely for the first. This means that in the early part of the period *shall* was used for all three persons,

---

[3] For some examples, see *Florio his Firste Fruites* (1578), *Florios Second Frutes* (1591), J. Eliot, *Orthoepia Gallica* (1593), and C. Holyband, *French Schoole-Maister* (1606).

[4] Mustanoja (1960:490) claims that in earlier ME *will* occurs mainly in the South and in "popular works" like songs, *shall* mainly in formal prose.

Some useful, partly statistical, studies on the use of *shall* and *will* during ENE can be found in Fridén (1948) and Ehrman (1966: Appendix A). Unfortunately Ehrman does not differentiate clearly in her tabulations between first and nonfirst person use of *shall* and *will*. All statistical studies are partly subjective – one simply cannot recapture the full nuances in many instances – nevertheless, they are useful as indicators of tendencies and point up the differences in terms of frequency between uses of auxiliaries at different periods.

will mainly for the second and third. But by the end of the sixteenth century, *shall* was recessive in second and third person predictions about the future, and in general we find first person *shall,* second and third *will.* This is on the whole what we find in Shakespeare, though instances of first person *will* and second and third *shall* are found (for instance, *Othello* V.ii.197: Perchance, Iago, I *will* ne'er go home. *Richard III* V.iii.232: And if I die, no soule *shall* pittie me).

Some typical ME and ENE examples are:

4.1 PL II.133.26 (1450) I kan not ben wel att ese in my hert, ner not *xal* ben tyl I here tydynges how ze don 'I can not be well at ease in my heart, nor not shall be till I hear news how you do'.
4.2 PL II.228.7 (1451) I suppose John Damme *shall* tell yow what he hath donn ther.
4.3 Sh. 1 Henry IV, II.iv.203 (Falstaff is telling Prince Hal a tall story about his deeds at Gadshill; Poins interrupts, and the Prince says) Prithee let him alone, we *shall* have more anon.
4.4 Sh. 1 Henry IV, I.ii.180 The virtue of this jest *will* be the incomprehensible lies that this same fat rogue *will* tell us.

Even if *shall* is recessive in ENE predictions about the future, it is still commoner than *will* in timeless predictive generalizations, as in:

4.5 Sh. MND I.ii.86 You can play no part but Pyramus: for Pyramus is a sweet-faced man; a proper man, as one *shall* see in a summer's day.

Shall is also more common in nonperformative expressions of prediction introduced by a temporal subordinator like *when,* a position in which neither *shall* nor *will* is permissible in standard NE:

4.6 Sh. Cor. IV.v.216 But *when* they *shall* see, sir, his crest up again . . . they will out of their burrows, like conies (= 'rabbits') after rain.

Another predictive (and sometimes also promissory) use of *shall* that is no longer available in standard NE is before *mowe* 'be able' (OE *mag-*), *cunne* 'can', or occasionally *will,* as in:

4.7 PL II.247.28 (1451) ye *shall mowe* have itt of Toppis "you will (be able to?) have it from Toppis."

Such constructions developed in late ME. They are often treated as instances of double predictive (or promissory) auxiliaries; another possibility is that *mowe, cunne,* and *will* were still being used in their main verb senses 'have the power to', 'know how to/be able to', and 'desire'. In

Southern literary English these constructions were short-lived, but in other dialects, especially Northern ones and now in Southern American, they have continued right up to the present day (see p. 192).

Predictive *will* tends to have mostly the same functions as in NE. Nevertheless, the immediate impression on a reader of early texts is that *will* is used rather differently. This is because *will* is more often used in its original volitional sense than in its predictive sense. For example, in her study of the use of *will* in sample Shakespearean texts, Ehrman (1966: Appendix A) finds that sixty percent of the instances of *will* are volitional in affirmative sentences or in statements. Hence the following examples of volitional *will* sound very different from NE:

4.8 PL III.253.1 (1461) hopyng alle thyng is and shalbe as they *wole* have it.
4.9 Nashe UT II.243.11 There is a little God called Loue, that *will* not bee worshipt of anie leaden braines.
4.10 Sh. MW of W II.ii.124 do what she *will,* say what she *will,* take all, pay all, go to bed when she list (= 'likes'), rise when she list, all is as she *will.*

Not all prediction involves nonpast tense or the auxiliaries *shall* and *will.* As we saw in the last chapter, if a *be* verb was involved in a predictive sentence in OE, then *beo-* (and sometimes *weorþ-*) was preferred over *wes-*. OE predictive *weorþ-* (ME *wurth, worth*) was lost in ME except in a few fixed phrases still found in ENE, such as *Woe worth the day. Beo-* and *wes-* had an interesting history. In Southern literary English, OE *sindon,* the third person nonpast plural of the *wes-* verb, was replaced by ME *beth, ben* as early as the mid-thirteenth century, so no contrast between the two verbs was retained in the plural, though some remained in the singular where *is* and *bith* remained side by side. In the sixteenth century the Northern form of the old *wes-* verb, *are,* in turn replaced *beth, be(n);* most Southern writers of the period used both forms, without significant contrast in meaning, as in:

4.11 Del. Jack of Newbury 37.26 wee *bee* as great foes, as the Foxe and the Snake *are* friends.

In other dialects, however, some contrast seems to have been maintained. There are traces of it in the *Paston Letters;* in Northerly texts *be* is typical for predictions throughout the ENE period, though *will/shall be* are also available. The *OED* (s.v. *be* A.1.3.a) cites the following example of predictive *be* in a sixteenth century Scottish text:

4.12 Stewart Cron. Scot. I.565 (1535) Traist weill . . . the feild this da *beis* ouris "Trust well . . . the field this day will-be ours."

(*He bes, they bes* are typical Scottish forms.)

Promising

In ME promising is usually expressed by *shall* for all persons; *will* is also used, but almost exclusively for the first person. Margaret Paston, for example, prefers *shall* for all promises, including ones involving first person:

4.13 PL II.266.14 (1452) he hath promysid that I *shall* (reported promise) have knowleche, and when he comyth I *shall* (performative promise) do your commawndement.

She does, however, occasionally use first person *will*, as in a letter mollifying her husband:

4.14 PL II.229.1 (1451?) I am sory therof, and *will* amend itt.

During ENE *will* is distinctly preferred over *shall* for first person, *shall* for second and third:

4.15 Sh. 1 Henry IV, I.ii.145 I *will* lay him down such reasons for this adventure that he *shall* go.

However, *I shall* as well as *I will* can be used promissorily. They are, for example, interchanged in:

4.16 Sh. AYLI III.ii.114 *Touch.* Truly, the tree yields bad fruit. *Ros. I'll* graff (= 'graft') it with you, and then I *shall* graff it with a medlar.

Even though *shall* and *will* could sometimes be interchanged, it is quite clear from such discourses as the following that a conscious distinction was usually made between *shall* and *will* in predictions and promises:

4.17 Sh. Henry V, V.ii.262 Nay, it *will* (predictive) please him well, Kate; it *shall* (promissory) please him, Kate.
4.18 Sh. Cor. III.i.85 *Sic.* It is a mind / That *shall* remain a poison where it is, / Not poison any further.
Cor. Shall remain! / . . . mark you / His absolute "*shall*"?

Verbs of motion after predictive and promising *will* and *shall* and after the *shall* that expresses necessity can be deleted if an adverb of direction is present. The construction was available in OE but did not become common until later:

4.19 Sh. 2 Henry IV, V.i.1 By cock and pie, sir, you *shall* not away tonight (= I take it upon myself that you won't go).

For an example with predictive *will*, see 4.6.

Exactly the same comments apply to the history of the OE preference for *beo-* over *wes-* in promises as for predictions (see p. 116).

Permitting

In OE the auxiliary most commonly used to express permitting was *mot-*. *Mot-* (and *most-,* originally a past tense form that came to be used interchangeably with *mot-*) continued to be used for permission up to about 1500:

4.20 PL II.266.30 (1452) I pray God that the trewth mote be knowyn.

In stock phrases like *So mote I thee* 'So may I prosper' it continued in use until the eighteenth century. During the ME period *mot-* was replaced by *mag-,* largely in the nonperformative sense of permission (in the sense 'I say there is absence of prohibiting conditions'). The full performative use of *may,* as in *You may go* 'I permit you to go', did not gain wide currency until the sixteenth century:

4.21 Sh. MND I.ii.51 You shall play it in a mask, and you *may* speak as small as you will.

In OE *mag-* meant primarily 'have the physical power to'. The use of *may* in this meaning declined during the seventeenth century when *may* was largely replaced by *can.* From the sense 'have the physical power to' there developed in ME the weaker sense 'there are no conditions to prevent *x*', a meaning still current; and then in ENE there developed the performative meaning 'I hereby permit (remove any obstacles if there are any)'.

The steps by which *mot-/must-* came to be the expression of the nonperformative 'there is necessity that' rather than of the performative 'I permit'' are somewhat obscure. If one is allowed by God, Fate, or other supernatural agency to do something, then maybe there is also the sense that one is required to do it (note also how we use *You may go now* as the "polite" form of the command *Go now!*). In any event, *mot-/must-* were recessive in the sense of permission in ME and came to be used first in the sense of obligation and then (from the later fourteenth century) also in the sense of inferred or presumed certainty, as in *He must have done it.* The latter use was not common until NE, however.

Can was still not used to express permitting at this time. For a discussion of the various uses of *can,* see Chapter 5.

Commanding

In ME and ENE it was quite common to express the command performative overtly, as in:

4.22 Del. Th. of Reading 313.18 Sirra, take my word, *I charge thee,* for this man, or else goodman butterfly, Ile make thee repent it.

Commands which are interrogatives have the same surface structure as in OE. This means that in yes–no questions without *whether* (OE *hwæþer*) the auxiliary occurs at the beginning of the sentence followed by the subject; in the absence of an auxiliary, the main verb occurs at the beginning. There are new auxiliaries in ME that were not used in OE, among them *do* (see p. 137), but this does not affect the general rule. So we find:

4.23 Sh. MW of W II.ii.16 thinkst thou I'll endanger my soul gratis?
4.24 Sh. MW of W II.i.174 Do you think there is truth in them?
4.25 Sh. MW of W III.v.4 Have I lived to be carried in a basket, like a barrow of butcher's offal?

Interrogatives of the type *whether + Subject + Verb* . . . were lost completely except in indirect questions, presumably because of the pressure of the interrogative word order (Type 2) in direct discourse. The force of this pressure is found in a new *whether*-construction which arose in ME with the order *whether + Verb + Subject* . . . or *whether + Auxiliary + Subject + Verb* . . . Consider, for example:

4.26 Ch. Knight A.1125 Wheither seistow (= 'say you') this in ernest or in pley?
4.27 Sh. MW of W III.ii.3 Whether had you rather lead mine eyes, or eye your master's heels?

In this construction *whether* presumably came to be felt as redundant with question word order and so was lost.

In ME and ENE the number of surface elements that could have interrogative *wh*-forms was greater than at any other period. In OE we find a system rather like ours: *wh*-attached forms of (i) the indefinite pronouns *hwa* 'who', *hwæt* 'what', *hwy* 'by/for what (why)'; (ii) the quantifier *hwæþer* 'which of two'; (iii) certain adverbs, such as *hwonne* 'when', *hwær* 'where'. In ME interrogative *wh-* came to be attached to more and more forms, giving us, for example, *wherein, wherefore, whereof, whereon, whereto.* One interrogative, *what,* is used very generally; it is particularly common where we would use *who* in asking a person's name, and where we would use *why:*

4.28 Sh. 2 Henry VI, I.ii.58 *Ch. Justice. What's* he that goes there?
Servant. Falstaff, and't please your lordship.
4.29 Nashe UT II.221.9 *what* neede the snaile care for eyes, when hee feeles the way with his two hornes?

B. THE PROPOSITION

The Verb and Associated Arguments

The Verb

The abstract properties of verbs have remained much the same from OE times on; for example, at all periods there have been verbs involving becoming, causing, and the like. The forms that these verbs can take have, however, changed for various reasons, some phonological, some because of borrowing, some because of restructuring.

It is often said that ME was a period when extensive "transitivization" took place—that is, many verbs that had not allowed objectivalization came to do so. For example, beside such earlier forms as *The spear stood at the door, The Republic decayed, The gun fell,* we find later *He stood the spear at the door, For fear of decaying the common good, Causing them to fall the gun.* Some examples from Shakespeare of verbs used "transitively" that are no longer used in this way are:[5]

4.30 Sh. 2 Henry VI, III.ii.98 Thy flinty heart . . . / Might in thy palace *perish* Margaret.
4.31 Sh. AYLI III.v.3 The common executioner . . . / *Falls* not the axe upon the humbled neck / But first begs pardon.

The view that transitivization is involved here—that is, that the verb itself underwent a change—derives from concentration on the surface structure. If one starts with a verb like *stand* and then sees how the contexts in which it can occur are extended over time, one inevitably also sees the verb as changing in a very radical way. If, however, one starts, as we have been doing, with the underlying structure and thinks of the form of a word simply as the manifestation of that underlying structure, then one can see that in many cases no new underlying structures have arisen, only new surface manifestations of already extant structures. Many of the instances of "transitivization" involve causatives, for example. *X stands: I stand X* have the relationship *X stands: I cause X to stand.* Before *I stand X* was available as a surface form, such expressions as *I cause X to stand* were available, either with an overt causative (see p. 121) or with some other causative marker. For example, in OE the noncausative *X stands* form involved *stand-* and the causative involved *ge-stand-*. In ME *ge-* was replaced by *y-* and was eventually lost so that the representations of the two constructions, one noncausative, the other causative, came to look the same. No underlying change had, however, taken place. Other phonological changes which resulted in the merger of formerly distinct

[5] Nearly all instances in Shakespeare of causatives that are no longer extant occur in his poetry; this supports the common thesis that there was greater freedom in the choice of words as realizations of underlying structures in poetry than in prose.

verb forms include the loss of phonologically double ("geminate") consonants, hence the merging of *cwel-* 'die' with *cwell-* 'cause to die, kill', *dwel-* 'err' with *dwell-* 'cause to err, lead astray'. The loss of contrast between *in* and *en* led to the merger of *sinc-* 'sink' with *senc-* 'cause to sink', and *stinc-* 'stink' with *stenc-* 'cause to stink'. As these examples indicate, words have often been borrowed to replace one or both members of an originally phonologically distinct pair; but again it is the surface forms of the verb that have changed, not its underlying abstract properties.

One of the most obvious examples of extensive surface change without underlying change can be found in the segmentalized causative. In OE it took forms such as *læt-, gemac-,* or occasionally in latest OE, *do-*. During ME *læt-* in its causative meaning became recessive; *gemac-* merged with *mac-,* and is still to be found in such expressions as *to make full. Do-* was used extensively as a causative in ME, as in *He did him die,* but was recessive by the end of the ME period (see p. 140). Several new verbs came to be used as causatives. One was *gar* which developed in the North around 1300 and continued there in general use until the seventeenth century. Another was *cause,* borrowed from French in later ME, but little used until ENE; yet another was *get* that came into use in the sixteenth century. And yet another was causative *have,* which came into use in ME but like *cause* did not gain wide currency until ENE. The special feature of *have* is that the underlying complement is always understood as a passive:

> 4.32 Sh. MW of W IV.ii.216 I'll *have* the cudgel *hallowed* and *hung* o'er the altar.

Like the segmentalized perfect *habb-* + *PP* of OE, this ME causative seems to have developed from reinterpretation of the resultative past participle that we find in such constructions as *He hæfde hine gebundenne* 'He had him in-a-state-of-boundness'. If the resultative, completive aspect of *He hæfde hine gebundenne* was the dominant feature that allowed restructuring in the case of the perfect, it was the implied passive that was the dominant feature that allowed restructuring in the case of the causative. The restructuring as both perfect and causative also involved the reinterpretation of an original Possessor (for example, *he* above) as Agent.

Nominal Expressions

The functions of nominal expressions

While the underlying functions which NPs could have, remained the same in ME and ENE as they were in OE, the surface realization of the different functions by case, prepositions, and the like underwent radical changes, mainly in ME.

CASE. For both nouns and pronouns genitive case has continued to be distinctly marked right up to the present day. All other case markings have been lost for nouns and considerably reduced for pronouns.

The first significant breakdown in noun inflection was between accusative and dative; where these originally differed, the dative form was generalized. Then the dative ending itself was lost, leaving a system in which nouns are marked for genitive case and otherwise unmarked.

The changes that took place in the pronominal and determiner systems were rather different. The instrumental and dative fell together early (the change was almost universally completed by 1200), leaving relics only in such forms as *why* (originally the instrumental of *hwa/hwæt* 'who/what'), in *the* in such phrases as *the more the merrier,* and in words such as *nevertheless* (the *the* part was originally *þy,* the instrumental demonstrative). Early too, but not quite so early as the loss of the instrumental, is the loss of the distinction between accusative and dative. The dative form was generalized for most pronouns: for example:

Accusative	Dative		
mec	*me*	⟶	*me*
hine	*him*	⟶	*him*
hie	*hire*	⟶	*hire/her*
hie	*him*	⟶	*him/hem*
hwone	*hwæm*	⟶	*whom*

This provides us with a three-way system at the surface level: genitive, "oblique" (the *me, him, her, hem, whom* forms), and nominative.

Only in one instance was the accusative generalized: *hit* (accusative), *him* (dative) → *(h)it;* as the accusative and nominative were the same, this meant that the neuter behaved like a noun with only genitive and unmarked forms. It may be that what we see is the operation of functional load. At a time when the "natural gender" system was beginning to predominate over the "grammatical gender" system, it was presumably felt that the contrast between male and neutral should be made as explicitly as possible in the pronominal system. The pressure of a male–neutral distinction was nevertheless not felt for the genitive form until much later than it was for the nominative, and *his* was used as the genitive for both genders until the NE period. *Its* is a new form (*OED* s.v. *its* A cites 1598 as the date of the first instance) derived from *it* and the *-s* genitive that had been generalized to all nouns. No instances of it are found in the Quarto edition of Shakespeare's plays, and only a few in the 1623 folio edition; instead we find the original *his,* the prepositional *of it* and occasionally the noninflected form *it,* as in *Hamlet* I.ii.216: It lifted up *it* head. Dissatisfaction with *his* as the genitive of *it* can be sensed in the attempt of the authors of the Authorized Version of the Bible to avoid it altogether; they use *of it, thereof,* and other prepositional forms almost exclusively. Their failure to use *its* can be attributed to their general conservatism and rejection of anything markedly innovative.

The function of cases was largely taken over by word order and prepositions. Only the genitive has remained fully functional as an inflection and even its function is more restricted than in OE. Where inflections remained, they functioned as indicated in the next few paragraphs.

GENITIVE. The genitive will be discussed first since it is not predictable; once genitive has been accounted for, the oblique and nominative forms of the pronouns can both be predicted.

To consider the function of the genitive first: inflectional genitive can on the whole occur where it was required in OE. In many instances, however, it is interchangeable with *of,* as in many constructions involving Possessors and subjective or objective genitive. When *of* and the genitive inflection are interchangeable, either *of* is the preferred form, as in the case of objective genitives, or else the inflectional genitive is, as in the case of subjective genitives. The development of *of* as an alternative to or replacement of some OE genitives, notably possessive, partitive, and "descriptive" genitives, will be discussed in the section on prepositions below. Occasionally genitive inflection has left no traces in either an inflection or a preposition. The OE genitive of measure, for example, has on the whole been replaced by expressions with neither the inflected genitive nor *of;* in particular, adjectives like *long* and *high* have from ME times on introduced noninflected, nonprepositional complements as in *three yards long, five inches high.*

As far as the form of those genitive constructions that persisted is concerned, during ME the *-es* genitive inflection (originally the masculine and neuter singular inflection of certain "strong" nouns) was generalized to all nouns in both the singular and the plural. The extension of *-es* to the plural occurred rather later than the extension of *-es* to the singular, as would be expected considering that the genitive plural in OE was never marked by *-es* while the genitive singular was often so marked. As was pointed out in Chapter 3, the original genitive plural marker *-a* has relics in certain restricted constructions in NE, for example, *a three-foot pole.* Some traces of the feminine singular *-e* and the "weak" *-an* genitive markers are also still to be found in such fossilized expressions as *Lady Chapel* (OE genitive singular *hlæfdige* 'lady'), and *Monday* (OE *monandæg* 'moon's day') as opposed to *Tuesday* with *-s-* from an original *-es* genitive (OE *Tiwesdæg* 'Tiw's day'). Chaucer frequently uses the *-e* genitive in fixed phrases like *his ladye grace;* but by ENE such relics were largely replaced by the regular *-es* forms.

With some nouns genitive was not overtly marked in OE. The original unmarked genitive was retained until late ME for kinship terms such as *mother, father, brother* as in *PL* III.288.2 (1461) *hyr broder advice,* although it was not invariably used. It was also extended to borrowed kinship terms such as *unkill* 'uncle' (a French word): *PL* II.230.18 (1451) *On of myn unkyll men,* and also to personal names and titles: *PL* II.97.18 (1449?) *the Byschope man.* These constructions, which originate in a genuine morphological phenomenon, may have contributed to the development of the noninflected, nonprepositional constructions that are historically derived from genitives, such as the genitive of measure discussed above, the ME "partitive genitive" of the type found in Ch. *Monk* B.3624 *no morsel breed* ("partitive genitives" of this type always involve mass nouns like *water, ale, bread*), and the "qualitative genitive" as in Ch. *Shipman* B.1239 *som manere honest thyng.* The latter construction was most common when the first noun was *kunn* 'kind, type', *mannere* 'kind', *mister* 'occupation'. Originally such constructions were expressed as *anes* (genitive) *kynnes* (genitive) *man* 'of-one kind man = man of one kind'; in ME the noninflected, nonprepositional form *an kyn man* developed and was by late ME reinterpreted as a partitive genitive: *a kind of man* (a subset of the larger class of man).

When the NP to which the genitive is attached is complex, the *-s* genitive may be used as a case marker on the last member of the group in NE, as in *the leader of the Senate Appropriations Committee's speech* (though when the group is as long as this, the *of* genitive is of course often preferred: *the speech of the leader of the SAC*). At earlier stages of English, especially OE and ME, however, the genitive was regularly attached to the head of the complex group, so we find not *our sovereign lord the king's* but *our sovereign lord's the king.* Furthermore, the Possessor in a possessive construction is positioned immediately after the head in OE and ME; so instead of *the Duke of Brittany's brother* we get *the Duke's brother of Brittany.* In late OE we find, for example:

4.33 Chron. 267.29 (1140) 7 nam þe kinges suster *of France* to wife 'and took the king's sister of France to wife'.

The group rather than the split genitive occurs first in Chaucer's poetry, for instance:

4.34 Ch. HF 1489 The grete *god of Loves* name.

but the split genitive is still far more common. By Shakespeare's time we find the reverse: the group genitive has come to be used regularly in prose, while the split construction occurs only occasionally, and then in poetry:

4.35 Sh. 1 Henry IV, III.ii.119 The *Archbishop's* Grace *of York.*

The split construction illustrates, as do the split relative and the split coordination already discussed in the previous chapter, the preference in earlier English for grouping and splitting complex constructions according to their length rather than according to their syntactic unity.

A final note on the surface representation of genitive: in later ME a construction which had its origins in OE came to be very popular—genitive expressed by an uninflected personal or human noun and third person pronoun marked for genitive, as in:

4.36 PL II.102.16 (1449?) the *child is gwnys* (= 'gowns, clothes').
4.37 Sh. 1 Henry VI, IV.vi.3 And left us to the rage of *France his sword.*

In OE the construction only occurred with foreign names, as in:

4.38 Or. 12.19 Nilus seo ea hire æwielme 'Nile that river her flood'.

This suggests that the pronoun was used to substitute for a foreign inflection. In ME the genitive *his* was preferred, regardless of the gender of the modifier:

4.39 PL V.38.6 (1469) My moder *ys* sake.

Only in ENE were attempts made to mark gender. Wyld (1936:316) quotes Lyly, *Euphues* 86 *Juno hir bedde.* The pronoun form dropped out partly perhaps because of the antipathy of most stylists from the sixteenth century on to "pleonastic" or repetitive pronouns, but probably even more because in the spoken language an unstressed *his* (usually with loss of *h*) sounded identical with the genitive *-es*. The syllabic *-es* genitive (with a vowel) that, as poetic rhythm shows, survived long after the unstressed vowel in the *-es* plural was lost, itself probably owes much to the interchange between the genitive inflection and the pronoun form.[6]

NOMINATIVE AND OBLIQUE. The contrast between nominative and oblique case forms is to be found only in the relative, interrogative, and third person pronouns. As a gross generalization, case is determined by surface function (such as subject, predicate nominal) or by position in the sentence. In the educated literary English favored by the schoolbooks, the subject pronoun and the predicate nominal pronoun are nominative, as in *I came, It is I;* other pronouns are oblique, as in *Whom did you see?, He saw her*. Spoken standard English, however, is characterized by a system in which pronouns preceding the verb are nominative, those following it are oblique: *I came, It is me, Who did you see?* There are also nonstandard dialects where even coordinate subjects are oblique in form: *Him and me left.*

While the system favored by schoolbooks is the one that first developed in ME, a shift toward the system now actually used started very early. For example, *It's me* is attested in the sixteenth century; so are *Who did you see?* and *Who did you give it to?* Only the nominative

[6] It is interesting to note how strong an impression the use of a pronoun in this position left on later generations. As late as the mid-eighteenth century when the construction was virtually lost, Dr. Johnson still sees fit to criticize "the opinion long received" that the *'s* is a contraction of *his*, as in *the soldier's valour,* for *the soldier his valour* (in the Grammar prefaced to his *Dictionary,* no page, section entitled "Of Nouns Substantives").

instead of the oblique relative, as in *I saw the man who you told me about,* is an NE phenomenon.

The history of *It's me* is an interesting one as it involves much more than a change in the case marking of the first person pronoun. In OE and ME it took the form *Ic hit eom* 'I it am' = 'I am the one'. In the fourteenth century, *hit* came to be positioned at the beginning of the sentence; the verb, however, still agreed with *I,* hence we get *(H)it am I.* When a third person singular personal pronoun was involved, as in *(H)it is he, is* presumably agreed with *he,* not with *(H)it,* on the same principle as the *(H)it am I* construction. However, since the leftmost NP in a sentence is usually the subject, *(H)it is he* was reinterpretable as involving agreement of *is* with *(H)it.* Generalization of this structure led to the development by the end of the fifteenth century to *(H)it is I.* Finally, toward the end of the sixteenth century we find *It is me* with *me* rather than *I,* presumably under the pressure of the postverbal position where oblique pronoun forms usually occurred, as in *He saw me.* Although Shakespeare prefers the older type, *That's I, It was I,* he does sometimes use the oblique form:[7]

4.40 Sh. Twelfth Night II.v.84 *Mal.* Besides, you waste the treasure of your time with a foolish knight.
Sir And. That's *me.*

The generalization of the oblique form to pronouns following all verbs including *be* can occasionally be found as early as OE times; in the later part of the *Peterborough Chronicle,* for example, we find:

4.41 Chron. 207.16 (1070) 7 eall þæt þider com þæt wæs *þone hæcce* (assusative instead of expected nominative *se hæcce*) 'and all that thither came (arrived) that was that crosier'.

It is therefore unlikely that *It's me* and parallel forms are directly borrowed from the French *C'est moi,* as some have suggested, though the French model may well have supported a native development.

Even such structures as *Him and me went* can be found very early. Mustanoja (1960:129-130) cites as an example:

4.42 Caxton. Aymon 78 all the foure brethern, and all *theym* of theyr companye arayed themselfe.

It has been suggested that this kind of usage was emphatic; whatever its function it has never been fully accepted as polite written usage.

While the personal pronouns have throughout English shown a ten-

---

[7] Visser (I:239) points out that Shakespeare used *It's me, That's him* in the speech of people of all ranks and apparently did not consider it uneducated. He may, however, have considered it "conversational."

dency to generalize the oblique form, the interrogative and relative *who-* forms have shown a tendency to generalize the nominative form. As early as 1500, the oblique interrogative *whom* was frequently leveled to the nominative *who* except when preceded by a preposition. A study of Wycherley's plays, written at the beginning of the NE period, shows an absolutely consistent use of interrogative *whom* after prepositions and *who* everywhere else. Shakespeare's plays are not quite so consistent, but the following passages are quite typical:

4.43 Sh. AYLI III.ii.304 *who* doth he [Time] trot withal?
4.44 Sh. LLL II.i.2 Consider *who* the king your father sends,/ To *whom* he sends.

The identical sounding *who* of relative clauses did not share the same characteristics; for example, *whom* is regularly used for a relative in functions other than subject or predicate nominal whether a preposition precedes or not, in exactly the same texts as favor interrogative *whom* exclusively after prepositions. Here is just one more instance to indicate that inflectional changes are in many instances subject to syntactic rather than phonological conditions.

PREPOSITIONS. The prepositional constructions already available in OE came to be used far more extensively in ME. In some instances they were generalized considerably further than they are now and many prepositional uses that developed in ME and ENE dropped out again later. The following relationships between underlying functions and prepositions apply in ME and ENE, though—as in NE—there are exceptions, usually imposed by certain verbs.

From earliest OE the nonsubjectivalized Agent in passives had been introduced by an obligatory preposition, usually either *þurh* or *fram*. Both were lost by the fifteenth century. Three other prepositions were extended during ME to Agentive use and replaced *þurh* and *fram:* (i) *of,* which became the most popular Agentive until ca. 1600; this use of *of* is an extension of its use expressing source or origin; (ii) *be* (from which *by* is descended), also an extension of its use expressing source or origin; (iii) *wiþ,* which replaced OE *mid* and was originally used for Instrumentals, but was later extended from inanimate Instrumentals to animate Agents. The following passage from Chaucer illustrates all three new Agentive prepositions:

4.45 Ch. Mel. B.2526 yet be they nat worth a stree (= 'straw'), but if (= 'unless') they be defended *by* trewe freendes . . . that he be biloved *with* hys subgetz . . . that is a lord to be biloved *of* his citezeins and *of* his peple.[8]

[8] *Biloued with his subgetz* could mean 'beloved among his subjects'; the context of the other Agents, however, suggests that the agentive is better than the concomitative interpretation.

It is the forms *with* and *by* that are most productive in ENE:

4.46 Sh. Much Ado II.i.56 Would it not grieve a woman to be overmastered *with* a piece of valiant dust?

Of was distinctly recessive but can still be found in Shakespeare:

4.47 Sh. AYLI III.ii.330 I have been told so *of* many.

The OE instrumental preposition *mid* was lost by the end of the ME period and replaced by *with. Wiþ* in OE had meant 'against', as it still does in *withstand* and in one meaning of *to fight with the Russians.* It was presumably in structures of the latter type that *with* came to express concomitance (as in *to fight alongside the Russians*). We may speculate further that concomitant *with* (found already in OE) was extended to use with inanimates as in *fight with a spear* and so came to be used for the Instrumental. Influence from the Old Norse instrumental preposition *viþ* doubtless played a considerable part in the development of *with* as the Instrumental, especially as *with* seems to have supplanted *mid* in this function first (ca. 1200) in the Northeast, which was the area where Scandinavian was most powerful. It was only a simple step to extend the use of *with* to the Agent.

Patient is normally objectivalized or subjectivalized (in passive sentences), and so normally no preposition is associated with it. When a preposition is available, from ME times on it is usually *of,* as in *admit of X, like well of X. Of,* and also *fram/from,* are the two prepositions typically associated with Source; *æt* was recessive in early ME as the preposition associated with animate Source (as in *Ask it at her*). *To* is usually associated with Goal. As we saw in the previous chapter, *to* was occasionally used with Goal already in OE; by ME it was used extensively, perhaps under the influence of French *à.* The French form *à* itself was doubtless the model for the development in ME of constructions like *Give it at her* (Goal), though Latin *ad* and Scandinavian *att* were probably also influential. In addition to being used with Goal, *to* also came to be used with Possessors:

4.48 Sh. M for M I.iv.19 the fair sister / *To* her unhappy brother Claudio.

To never gained much popularity in possessives, however, and now is recessive except in titles, such as *secretary to the president.* The regular preposition that came to be associated with Possessor was *of.*

In OE *of* was used mainly to signal "out of, originating from," or part-to-whole relationship. Probably strongly supported by the influence of French *de, of* spread from the partitive use to possessive constructions and to many others that had involved the genitive marker.

The partitive genitive, which we saw from 3.25 could already in

OE be expressed by a preposition rather than a genitive, came in ME to be expressed almost exclusively by *of,* as in *parts of the country;* during ME numerals often introduced prepositional phrases even when the NP was indefinite (they still do when the NP is definite), as in Ch. *Wife of Bath,* D.992: *of ladyes foure and twenty.* During ENE the modern system became more or less established: *twenty-four of the ladies,* but *twenty-four ladies.*

The prepositional form of the partitive genitive came toward the ME period to be generalized to an emphatic construction that developed in very late OE. This construction is typified by *one the best man* where *one* is followed by a definite article, superlative adjective, and a singular noun: Ch. *TC* I.1081: *and oon the beste knyght, / That in his tyme was or myghte be.* According to Mustanoja (1960:298) Spenser and Shakespeare were among the last to use this expression. By the seventeenth century it was totally replaced by *one of the best men* on the model of the partitive construction. The influence of the partitive can be seen as early as Chaucer's time. An intermediary stage is evidenced by such sentences as Ch. *Nun's Priest* B.4174: *Oon of the gretteste auctour (author) that men rede,* where *oon* has been reinterpreted as a numeral rather than an emphatic, but the partitive construction has not yet been extended to *auctour* which is still singular. Expressions like this provide an excellent example of the kinds of blend that result from innovations before they are fully integrated into the linguistic system.

In OE a "genitive of definition" occasionally occurred of the type *Egypta folc* 'of-Egypt people'. In early ME this construction became quite common, especially the form with *of;* the latter continues in use until the present day: *the city of San Francisco.* This construction may well have been influenced by French where *de* is usual, as in *la ville de Paris* 'the city of Paris'.

A double genitive construction, with both the inflection and the preposition, that is quite frequently found today originated in the ME period. From the first it has been limited to constructions with indefinite heads:

> 4.49 PL II.250.21 (1451) seyd that she wold nowgth that *no* (negative-incorporated indefinite) *servaunte of herys* shuld reporte no thyng that . . .

It exemplifies very well the way two alternative surface forms, one inflectional, the other segmental, may be combined.

SUBJECTIVALIZATION AND OBJECTIVALIZATION. For objectivalization see the discussion of transitivization on pages 120–121.

The Spread of Subjectivalization. ME saw not only the simplification of the inflectional case system, but also the reduction of the available choices between subjectivalization and nonsubjectivalization. The so-called "impersonal" sentences continued in currency throughout ME, but subjectivalization or at least pseudo-subjectivalization came to be required by more and more verbs; by NE the construction was almost totally lost except for a few fixed expressions like *Methinks that* (but not **Him thinks that*).

Various factors operated to bring about this change. For one, as the inflectional contrast between nominative, accusative, and dative broke down in the noun, the difference between subjectivalized and nonsubjectivalized nouns was minimized and eventually lost. Where in OE there was a contrast in the nouns according to whether they occurred in constructions like *Cyningas hie lǽddon* 'The-kings them led' or like *Cyningum hyngrede* 'To-the-kings hungered', none was to be found by late ME. In the past tense, the verbal distinctions between singular and plural were also lost with the result that the late ME and ENE equivalents of the sentences above were: *The kings led them, The kings hungered* (the differences in word order and the use of the article are unimportant for this particular discussion). In the present tense, however, a contrast was still observable as in *The men walk, The men thinketh* where the plural (with no overt inflection) agrees with *men* in the first sentence but the singular (signaled by *-eth*) fails to agree with *men* in the second.

The pressure of indistinguishable noun forms, coupled with that of position (the left-most NP of a sentence was usually the subject) led to the generalization of two sentence types: (i) the subjectivalized sentence type in which the Experiencer is subjectivalized, as in *The man liketh to hunt;* (ii) the sentence type with *(h)it,* as *It liketh the man that* where *it* is a dummy place-holder, the function of which is to fill the positional subject slot and so provide a pseudo-subject.[9]

The pressure of these forms also influenced sentences with pronouns even though nominative and oblique were distinct, so that by ENE instead of *Him liketh that* we find either the subjectivalized *He liketh to* or the pseudo-subjectivalized *Hit liketh him that.* Chaucer and the Pastons still use the earlier forms regularly with certain verbs like *need, think, seem:*

4.50 Ch. Mel. B.2309 of swich thyng as *yow* (pl., oblique) *thynketh* (third person singular) *that is best for youre profit.*

4.51 PL V.11.9 (1469) *me semyth you may wel excuse you be the money.*

By ENE, however, they were rarely used. Visser (I:35) states that Sir Thomas More is one of the last early sixteenth-century writers to use these constructions regularly. In the later sixteenth century it is found

[9] Until ca. 1325 *like* (OE *lic-*) was used whether the Experiencer or the Patient was the subject. From ca. 1325 on *please* was often preferred if the Patient was subject; it has completely superseded *like* under this condition since ca. 1850.

as one of Spenser's conscious archaisms. With other late sixteenth-century authors, like Shakespeare, it is almost completely restricted to the idiomatic expression *methinks* and *me had rather.*

In the examples above, the Experiencer precedes the verb. This position is typical for nonsubjectivalized pronouns in OE and still in ME. In ENE, however, surface objects, whether pronouns or nouns, typically follow the verb as in NE. The fact that in impersonal constructions they still precede the verb reflects the fossilized nature of the construction. At the same time, the position doubtless contributed to the generalization of the subjectivalized form.

Passive. As might be expected, subjectivalization of formerly "impersonal" passives followed the pattern of subjectivalization of actives. In the case of impersonal passives, the pressure of the pattern *Subject + Auxiliary + Verb . . .* was particularly strong since so very few verbs actually allowed the impersonal passive construction. Furthermore, impersonal passives occurred only when Experiencer or Goal was realized as dative or genitive in the active, not as accusative. With the collapse of the distinction between accusative and dative, this restriction no longer applied. The loss of impersonal passives occurred relatively early though some later examples are to be found:

4.52 Ch. Wife of Bath D.9 *me was toold.*

and, with a pseudo-subject:

4.53 PL II.211.17 (1451) *it shuld be thanked alle tho* (= 'those') that labored a yens (= 'against') hem.

For the development of perfective passives with overt *have + PP,* as in *He has been robbed,* see p. 145; for structures of the type *The meat was bringing in,* which are often called passives, see p. 144.

Deletion of the Subject. In OE, a pronoun subject in identity with some noun in the previous sentence was omissible provided ambiguity did not arise. At no point was subject deletion common except in coordinates with identical subjects, and it came to be used less and less frequently during later OE and ME. It is very rare by later ENE and tends to be poetic.

The second person pronoun *thou* was often omitted, whether or not it was in identity with *thou* from the preceding sentence, again usually in poetry: Sh. *Cymbeline* V.v.110: *Knows't* him thou look'st on? speak, / *Wilt* have him live? The omission of *thou* can perhaps be explained on the grounds that the second person singular verb inflection *-est* is very distinctive; also, direct address to a second person is characteristic of spoken, conversational, rather than written style. The form must, however, have played a more important part than style since the second person plural *ye,* whether referring to one or more addressees, is not omissible. The omissibility of *thou* continued so long as *thou* was used, in some cases up to the late nineteenth and early twentieth centuries, especially if the addressee's name is mentioned.

The omission of the first person singular, as in *Thank you,* seems to have developed in the fifteenth century, if we can rely on our texts. It is, however, typically conversational, and the absence of earlier instances may simply be a reflection of the absence of conversational texts prior to the late ME period.

The structure of nominal expressions

NOUN SUBCLASSES

Gender. During the ME period the OE grammatical gender system gave way to the natural gender system used in NE. This means that the alternative natural gender system available for OE pronouns was generalized until it became the regular one. The change started in late OE but was not completed until late ENE. The preconditions for this change undoubtedly include the double pronominal gender system in OE, and the reduction in late OE and more extensively in ME of the case markers which simultaneously marked gender. There has been a great deal of rather speculative research on the various factors that brought about the change. It must suffice here to outline in the broadest terms some of the more convincing possibilities. Recently it has been suggested (Jones, 1967) that in certain dialects of the transitional period between OE and ME such as are represented by the OE *Lindisfarne Gospels* and *Durham Ritual,* the early ME *Peterborough Chronicle* (the entries for 1132–1154), *Southern Legendary* and *Layamon's Brut,* all of them texts that provide extensive source materials for the use of "unhistorical gender," certain specific inflections came to be associated with surface syntactic noun-verb relationships, regardless of the original gender of the noun to which they were attached. For example, *-ne* was the accusative inflection *par excellence* since it was unambiguously accusative; but it was also *par excellence* masculine and singular. In the dialects of the texts in question the accusativeness of *-ne* was taken to be its dominant feature and it was used extensively as the inflection marking accusative, hence usually objectivalized, nouns, whatever their original gender. The same nouns when in combination with a preposition were usually marked according to their original gender, presumably because in this instance the prepositions were the most distinct signals of the grammatical function of the NP. So we find in *Layamon's Brut* both *anne* (masculine accusative) *burh makede* 'a city built', and *in þere* (feminine dative) *burhe* 'in that city'; *burh* is only feminine in OE. In these dialects then, grammatical function overrides noun subclassification, so providing the conditions for loss or at least restructuring of the gender system.

The evidence is very convincing that syntactic considerations of this kind had a considerable part to play in the breakdown of the old gender system during the transitional period. They were, however, obscured by other factors. Within the case-marking system itself several changes were taking place. Among them was the merger of accusative and dative case markers as dative; so a *-ne* that was selected for its dominant accusativity in the transitional dialects itself gave way to the dominant dative inflection, and this in turn was lost except insofar as it was restructured as an oblique case in the pronominal system.

While case and gender were no longer being synthetically combined in one inflection in the same way as they had been, the natural gender system of the pronouns was being used more and more frequently when pronominal forms of NPs were selected. Important, too, was the influence of Latin and Scandinavian but especially of French. While the former, like English, had three genders, French had only two. French itself was not consistent; the Anglo-Norman dialect which first heavily influenced English did not always assign the same gender to nouns as did the Central French dialect from which words were later borrowed. Native words synonymous with foreign words sometimes did not have the same gender; for example, the native *mona* 'moon' was masculine while French *lune* and Latin *luna* were feminine. Mythology, symbolism, and allegory may also have played a part in sharpening the distinction between inanimate and animate (or personification of inanimates), so giving support to the already dominant natural gender system operating for pronouns. Nevertheless, as late as Shakespeare's time there are still traces of grammatical gender; in particular, borrowed words tend to retain their original gender, as, for example, *peace, rose,* and *victory,* which are regularly pronominalized by *she* in Shakespeare even in passages where personification is unlikely to be intended.

Number. In the previous chapter we saw that the agreement rules for number which normally operate between subject and verb were not always followed. This was particularly common in OE if the subject was a collective noun; shifts could occur in coordinate sentences from singular to plural verb markers without apparent change of meaning (see 3.43). This kind of situation where agreement fails across coordinated sentences persisted throughout ME and ENE; as in OE, the usual shift was from singular to plural, not vice versa. Agreement can also fail within one underlying sentence. Singular verbs quite frequently follow plural subjects throughout the history of English; it is, however, commoner in the sixteenth and seventeenth centuries than at any other time. At this period it is often used in rhyme, which suggests that the failure in agreement cannot be attributed to clerical error, as in:

4.54 Sh. Venus and Adonis 1127 She lifts the coffer-lids that close his eyes, / Where lo, *two lamps* burnt out in darkness *lies*.[10]

In many instances where number agreement seems to be violated,

[10] In the extreme North, *-es* was used as the regular marker of the plural as well as the singular verb from late OE on; there is no evidence that the *-(e)s* of 4.54–4.57 are of Northern origin, however.

specific grammatical conditions for the differences can be detected. For example, when the verb precedes the subject, it is frequently singular even where a plural might be expected; in such instances the constraining factor in assigning number to the verb is position rather than relationship to the subject:

4.55 Sh. Cymbeline V.v.233 How *comes* these staggers on me?
4.56 Sh. 2 Henry IV, II.iv.78 there *comes* no swaggerers here.
4.57 Nashe UT II.241.26 There *was* no more honorable wars in christendome then towards.

There is no evidence that at this time such constructions were considered colloquial or in any way substandard.

Occasionally we find a plural verb where we might expect the singular. Among instances of this kind are the following quotations cited by Visser (I:49):

4.58 Lydgate, Pilg. 10,890 Yt *are* but fantasmes that ye speke.
4.59 Malory, Morte Darthur (Caxton, ed. by Sommer) 134.16 it ben the damoyseles . . . that so name me.

In these "clefted" constructions we may postulate that there is the same kind of ordering of subjectivalizing and clefting as there is for structures like *There are three men over there;* if so, there is no lack of agreement in 4.58 and 4.59, only a different order of operations used in arriving at the surface structure from that normally used in clefted sentences, perhaps because the clefted sentences and the *there*-constructions were sometimes considered to have basically the same structural characteristics.[11]

DETERMINERS: DEFINITE AND INDEFINITE. During ME and ENE the use of the indefinite article *a* came to approximate more and more the modern usage, in which count nouns not previously mentioned and not modified by possessives, quantifiers, or the like, are marked by the indefinite article to indicate "first mention." There are nevertheless instances throughout the ME period of indefinite NPs without *a* where we would expect it:

4.60 PL III.255.30 (year?) Heydonis wyffe had chyld on Sent Petyr day.

By the sixteenth century absence of *a* was felt to be a distinct archaism; Spenser uses it deliberately in his attempts to recreate the older language.

[11] That the emphatic clefted *it*-construction was not fully differentiated at this period at least in the surface structure from the *there is* . . . construction is illustrated by the frequent use of *it* where we would expect *there* and vice versa. Consider Marlowe, *Edward II,* II.ii.102 *It* is no dealing with him now.

The definite article in its modern form *the* first appears in the transitional prose of the twelfth century, notably in the *Peterborough Chronicle:*

4.61 Chron. 263.24 (1137) Ðis gære for *þe* king Stephne ofer sæ to Normandi 'This year went the king Stephen over sea to Normandy'.

Here *the* is anaphoric, that is, it is used to refer back to the king, who has already been mentioned. *The* is also used in the *Peterborough Chronicle,* as in NE, to express the speaker's assumption that certain things are culturally known or accepted; for example, a man is known to have feet, therefore *the* is appropriate in:

4.62 Chron. 264.9 (1137) Me henged up bi *the* fet 7 smoked heom 'One hung up by the feet and smoked then'.

although the feet have not been mentioned before.

While the *Peterborough Chronicle* illustrates uses of *the* that are typical of NE, the modern use of *the* was not fully established in prose writings until Shakespeare's time. In the poetry of the sixteenth and seventeenth centuries many rather archaic structures still persist. These involve mainly the absence of *the* where we would expect it, for example in an NP that is the head of an *of* phrase (Sh. *Cymbeline* IV.ii.190 *Since death of my dear'st mother*) and in adverbial phrases of location (Sh. *Julius Caesar* I.ii.249 *He . . . foam'd at mouth*). In phrases not involving prepositions the absence of *the* is rare, even in poetry. Spenser uses it as one of his archaisms, as he does the absence of *a*. Shakespeare, in most but not all cases, apparently uses it to mock inept poetizing (as in Sh. *MND* V.i.221 *When lion rough in wildest rage doth roar,* a line from the mechanics' play).

As was pointed out in Chapter 3, *the* seems to have derived from the OE demonstrative *se, seo, þæt.* Although fundamentally a deictic or pointer, this demonstrative also has extensive anaphoric use, and it is precisely this kind of anaphoric function that the definite article *the* has. Once *the* developed as the anaphoric, it was usually fairly sharply contrasted with *that: the* was anaphoric, *that* almost exclusively deictic; at least this is what we may perhaps conclude from the infrequency of alternation between *the* and *that* in ME and ENE manuscripts.

Certain types of changes recur, and one of them is the development of the purely anaphoric use of demonstratives. In OE, *se, seo, þæt* developed purely anaphoric function; in ME the other demonstrative, *this,* did so in turn. The consequence is that we frequently find *the* and *this* interchanged in different manuscripts. There are, for example, the variant forms of Ch. *Nun's Priest* B.4601: Now am I come unto *the* wodes side (see Manly and Rickert, 1940, VII:611); and sometimes there are apparently synonymous uses within the same text (for example, there seems in most instances to be no difference between Chaucer's *in this world* and *in the world,* except that he prefers the former).

PRONOUNS. During NE the modern pronominal system became established. Most significant from the syntactic point of view was the loss of the grammatical gender system (p. 132) and the development of several changes in the expression of number.

The dual forms *wit* and *git* died out during the early part of ME. *Wit* does not seem to have survived much past 1200. *Git* hung on a little longer but disappeared by 1300.

Although the plural of the first person pronoun had been used in OE for the "authorial we" (*we* used for *I* by an author), based probably on a Latin model, it did not come to be used for the "plural of majesty" until ME. So while Alfred writes in the first person singular, as in 3.79 and 3.80, Henry III in his royal proclamation of 1258 speaks of himself as *we.* This use of "majestic" *we* for *I* seems to have originated in Byzantine Greek at the imperial court and to have spread all over Europe via late courtly Latin of the fourth century A.D. It is a product of feudal thinking when the king conceived of himself as the embodiment of the whole community.

Also new in the ME period, and probably also of Byzantine Greek origin, was the use of *ye* 'you' (plural) for the singular second person. One of the first instances in English occurs in the thirteenth century, but the use is not well established until the fourteenth century. Presumably this *ye* for *thou* is an extension from the majestic *we;* if the king speaks of himself in the plural, his subjects will address him in the plural too. The courtly origin of the usage is reflected in the fact that in ME honorific *ye* is used almost exclusively by upper class people. Chaucer has Melibee address his wife Prudence as *thou* (as wives were usually addressed) except when overcome by respect for her wisdom; Melibee, however, is addressed as husbands (including John Paston) usually were, with the honorific *ye* form. In Shakespeare's works *thou* is used in intimate conversation, by parents to their children and by masters to servants; *you* is used for the singular in formal speech among equals and by servants to masters. A change from *you* to *thou* in addressing a superior often signals a patronizing attitude, inappropriate intimacy, derogation, disdain, or even contempt. A well-known example of the latter is provided by Hamlet's cry addressed to Claudius whom he otherwise usually addresses as *you:*

4.63 Sh. Hamlet V.ii.336 Here, *thou* incestuous, murderous, damned Dane, / Drink off this potion.

Between lovers, however, a switch from *you* to *thou* signals change from reserve to more intimate feelings. A good example can be found in Shakespeare's *Much Ado* IV.i.252–331, the scene in which Benedick expresses his love for Beatrice. He starts with a reserved *you* but then changes to *thou;* then he shifts from one form to the other (*you* when he swears his love in mock ceremony, *thou* when he earnestly protests his love). Beatrice, however, maintains her distance throughout the scene with *you.*

Most of the remaining broad pronominal changes concern the form of the pronoun when marked for different cases. The personal pronoun system underwent the greatest surface changes; the most important were the development of the oblique forms (p. 122) and the replacement of OE *heo* by ME *she,* of OE *hie* by ME *they,* and of OE *ge* by ENE *you.* The introduction of *they* is particularly interesting as it represents the borrowing of a pronoun form from another language (Scandinavian); pronouns are rarely borrowed since they represent very basic parts of the grammatical system. *They, their,* and *them* all occur in early ME Northern texts; *they* spread to the South quite early, *their* not until the late fourteenth century and *them* not until the fifteenth. The motivation for the rapidity with which *they* was adopted in the South was presumably the ambiguity in many dialects between the singular *he* 'he' and plural *he, hie* 'they'; the plural genitive and oblique forms *here* and *hem* were in most dialects not ambiguous with the genitive and oblique singular feminine *hire* and the oblique singular masculine and neuter *him,* and therefore there was presumably less motivation to borrow the Scandinavian genitive and oblique plural forms.

As in OE, reflexives were usually not marked in any special way; see 4.51 and:

4.64 Sh. 1 Henry IV, I.ii.2 Thou art so fat-witted with . . . unbuttoning *thee* after supper.

Reflexive *-self* forms did, however, come to be used more and more during the ME and ENE periods. As in OE, *-self* does not occur with verbs of motion that have Agents and Patients in identity (those which have in NE a single NP with a double function) as in *Get thee out of my kitchen.*

Even when *-self* does occur in ME and ENE it rarely seems to function as the empty element it is now. As in OE it is usually emphatic and has many of the characteristics of the noun *self;* often it seems equivalent to expressions like *my jolly body, my proper person,* which are frequently found in ME but become less common during ENE.

Tense

As in OE and NE, the immediate past and nonpast were generally expressed by an inflection on the verb.[12] During ME, however, there developed two auxiliaries, *do* and *gin,* which, in one of their uses at least, were nothing but meaningless or "dummy" elements to which

[12] The forms of the tense inflections underwent considerable changes. Details can be found in any history of English under "morphology" or "accidence."

tense could be attached. In certain constructions *have + PP* also developed as the signal of past. While we still use *have + PP* in this way, as in *He seems to have left yesterday,* in NE the use of dummy *do* has been greatly restricted; *gin* was lost as a segmentalized carrier of tense as early as the sixteenth century.

The development in ME of the auxiliary *do* is one of the most interesting developments in the history of auxiliaries in English. Like the other auxiliaries we have looked at, *do* has various functions. Among them is the use of *do* as an optional carrier of tense in any construction, whether affirmative, negative, declarative, interrogative, or whatever; another is the use of *do* as an emphasizer of the truth of the proposition; yet another is the use of *do* as a causative. What the origin of the auxiliaries in their different functions is, is a matter of dispute; sometimes disputed, too, is the identification of the particular function of *do* in any particular sentence. Nevertheless, the existence of *do* in the various functions is fully agreed on. Here we will discuss chiefly the use of *do* as a tense-carrier, and then look briefly at its possible relationship to the other uses.

Do as a meaningless element, the only structural function of which is that of a tense-carrier, developed in early ME, especially in the Southern dialects. That it was meaningless is suggested not only by the absence of any clear correlation with particular types of discourse, such as emphatic discourse, but also by the interchangeability in different manuscripts of the same text of *do + Tense + Verb, gin + Tense + Verb* and simply *Verb + Tense.*

During earlier ME, this meaningless *do* was used extensively in poetry, but is not to be found frequently in prose until the end of the period. Chaucer, for example, uses this *do* a lot in his poetry but hardly at all in his prose. In the *Paston Letters* several instances can be found; nevertheless, nearly all putative examples could be causative or in a few cases strong affirmations.

By ENE, however, *do* was used extensively in all types of writing; some authors use it more than others, but all use it. Most grammarians of the time fail to mention it, perhaps because it was redundant, or because it was so common that it was felt not to merit discussion. What occasional mentions there are of it fully support the contention that there was a meaningless *do.* For example, in Palsgrave (1530) we find the comment: "*I do* is a verbe moche comenly used in our tonge to be put byfore other verbes: as it is all one to say 'I do speke . . .' and 'I speake. . . .' "[13] Jacques Bellot, a French contemporary of Shakespeare, notes that, in addition to the simple present the English "doe adde commonly the verb Faire, before the other verbes, for the replenishing and sounding of their tongues with more grace."[14] It is exactly this

[13] John Palsgrave, *L'éclaircissement de la langue française* (1530). Paris: Génin, 1852, p. 523.

[14] Jacques Bellot, "Le Maistre d'Escole Anglois," ed. T. Spira, *Neudrucke frühenglischer Grammatiken* 7, Halle, 1912, p. 29.

sort of stylistic variation that seems to be at work in 4.23 and 4.24 and in the following passage from Shakespeare's *As You Like It:*

4.65 Sh. AYLI III.ii.301 *Ros.* I'll tell you who Time *ambles* withal, who Time *trots* withal, who Time *gallops* withal and who he *stands still* withal.
Orl. I prithee, who *doth* he trot withal?
Ros. Marry, he *trots* hard with a young maid between the contract of her marriage and the day it is solemnized . . .
Orl. Who *ambles* Time withal?
Ros. With a priest that lacks Latin . . .
Orl. Who *doth* he gallop withal?
Ros. With a thief to the gallows . . .

By the late sixteenth century the use of *do* seems to be declining in affirmative declarative sentences, such as *I did run.* It is on the increase, however, in negative sentences, like *I did not run,* and especially in questions, like *Did he run? Do* is, however, optional in all these constructions. The recessiveness in the late sixteenth century of *do* in sentences like *I did run* is well illustrated in Salmon's study of Shakespeare's colloquial English (1965); she shows that Shakespeare used *do* in declarative affirmative sentences mainly in verse (where archaic language tends to be used), in "poetic" prose, in fixed formal phrases like *I do arrest you,* in supposedly archaic prose such as Falstaff's language, and in soliloquies. It is rarely used in the everyday speech of the bourgeoisie. Nevertheless, it was not until the NE period that this use of *do* was lost altogether.

Do in formal phrases like *I do arrest you* seems clearly related to another, meaningful *do* that asserts the truth of the proposition (the probable origin of our affirmative *do* in *I did go);* in NE, however, it is the stress, not the *do* that signals the affirmation. This *do* is paraphrasable as *truly* or *indeed.* As we shall see (p. 148), the subjunctive system partially broke down during ME and it appears that the function of the indicative as assertion of truth was in part taken over by *do + Tense + Verb,* while the expression of uncertainty or noncommitment was left to the simple *Verb + Tense. Do* is found especially in sentences involving various kinds of perception, such as *consider, discern, hear,* apparently to indicate that the speaker vouches for the correctness of his perception.

4.66 Del. Th. of Reading 300.17 consider, I pray thee good wife, that such as are in their youth wasters, *doe* prooue in their age starke beggars.

4.67 Nashe UT II.281.28 they dresse theyr iesters and fooles only in fresh colours, and saie variable garments *doe* argue vnstaiednes and vnconstancie of affections.

As might be expected, affirming *do* is most often found in passages vouching for the truth of something that the hearer might doubt, such as a dream or a miracle. It is probably such a use of *do* that we find in the following passages from *Hamlet:*

4.68 Sh. Hamlet I.i.114 A little ere the mightiest Julius fell, / The graves stood tenantless and the sheeted dead / *Did* squeak and gibber in the Roman streets.

4.69 Sh. Hamlet I.v.61 Upon my secure hour thy uncle stole, / With juice of cursed hebenon in a vial, / And in the porches of my ears *did* pour / The leperous distilment.

It is likely that the affirming *do* is derived from the causative *do,* as in *I did him go* 'I caused him to go', and that the dummy *do* in turn is derived from the affirming *do.* In OE there was, as at all stages of English, a verb *do*–'perform'; *to do the right thing* can be interpreted as 'to cause the right thing to be done', and so the development of a causative *do* is not remarkable. Causative *do-* first occurred in later OE but was not widely used until ME, as in:

4.70 PL II.93.34 (1448) he *dede* Davy sadillyn an oder hors 'he caused Davy to-saddle an other horse'.

Like many other verbs in OE and ME, causative *do* allowed the object of the causing to be deleted if it was indefinite: *I did someone saddle a horse* → *I did saddle a horse.* In such sentences the sense of causation is open to reinterpretation under the pressure of such complement structures as *I wanted to do it,* where the subject of the complement is identical with the subject of the main clause; by analogy, *I did pay them* is open to reinterpretation as *I did something: I paid them;* enough of the original sense of *do* remains, however, for sentences of this kind to mean *I did indeed pay them,* that is, the causative sense is lost but the implication remains that what I am saying happened did indeed happen. Consider, for example:

4.71 PL II.94.7 (1448) and she *ded* aske me after my master Berney, and I told here howe he was hurt.

Here the discourse almost certainly precludes the causative interpretation of *do* since a third person would then be involved who was caused to ask me after my master. The new auxiliary *do* meaning 'truly' came, like other auxiliaries of the period, to be closely attached to the main verb; hence *I did them pay* with preverbal object is usually interpreted by late ME times as 'I caused them to be paid', while *I did pay them* is interpreted as 'I say I truly paid them'. This *do* was itself open to reinterpretation, especially where it was redundant with adverbs like *truly* (for instance, *I did truly pay them*), as simply the dummy carrier of tense.

While many scholars (notably Engblom and Ellegård) agree in essence with the theory that dummy *do* originates in the causative, others (notably Visser III: 1488–1497) argue that the causative was itself rare before the thirteenth century, and that it developed primarily in the East, while dummy and affirmative *do* developed primarily in the Southwest. The latter therefore prefer to derive dummy and affirming *do* from the substitute-verb form *do* that right through English has been available as a replacement for a verb already mentioned (as in 3.21), or as an anticipator (and emphasizer) of action verbs, as in:

> 4.72 Or. 290.21 þa oferhogode he þæt he him aðer *dyde,* oþþe wiernde, oþþe tigþade 'then despised he that he to-them either should-do, either refused or conceded = then he despised doing either one or the other, refusing or conceding'.

The debate still continues and may never be resolved. I do not think the possibility should be excluded that the patterns of both the causative and the substitute-verb form of *do* may have reinforced the development of affirming and dummy *do*.

In any event, a dummy tense-carrier seems to have been a syntactic element highly favored in the ME period, since there developed beside *do* another dummy, *gin* (usually in the past tense form *gan*). Unlike *do* it is used almost exclusively as the carrier of past tense; it is also almost entirely restricted to poetry. This auxiliary originated in the OE verb *(on)ginn-* 'begin' and at least in some contexts has the aspectual quality of inception or starting, but more often it has no meaning at all; it may alternate with either *Verb* + *Tense* or *do* + *Tense* + *Verb* in different versions of the same manuscript. An example of the interchange of *did* and *gan* cited by the *Middle English Dictionary* (s.v. *ginnen* 3b) is:

> 4.73 Cursor Mundi 2009 (MS Göt.) A neu liuelad *gan* he bigin (MS Trin. *dud*) 'He began a new life' (auxiliary *gin* beside the main verb *bigin*).[15]

Gin developed first in the Northeast in the thirteenth century; in the fourteenth century it spread to the South. Unlike *do,* it was short-lived, although it was used very extensively in poetry in its heyday. By the late sixteenth century it is markedly archaic. Shakespeare, for example, uses it only in songs.

The third type of tense segmentalization to be discussed here is the use of *have* + *PP* as a marker of past tense. Consider NE *He appears to have left yesterday*. There is no such sentence as **He has left yesterday* because the perfective does not locate completion at a definite moment in time. What then is the *have* + *PP* of the previous sen-

[15] *Cursor Mundi* is a Northern text, dated ca. 1300–1325; MS Göt. is fourteenth century, MS Trin. is fifteenth century.

tence? It is simply the surface realization of past which would be lost by the rules of normal complementation with *to,* unless a segmentalized form was introduced in the surface structure. Similarly, *He must have left yesterday* involves not **It must be he has left yesterday,* but *It must be he left yesterday,* with *have + PP* as the realization of past. Constructions of this type came into being in ME, mainly in "contrary-to-fact" contexts such as in:

4.74 PL II.86.22 (1448) so that he myth *an* had mony to . . . 'so that he might have had money to . . .'.

With the development of structures like 4.74 we find the development of sequences of auxiliaries that in the surface structure allow modals (*may, can, shall, must,* and *will*) to be followed by *have + PP.* Such a sequence appears not to have occurred in OE; in ME, however, we find *have + PP* occurring after modals as the segmentalized expression of past (as in 4.74) and then as the segmentalized expression of perfect. Once sequences of auxiliaries had been established, the length of the possible sequences was increased at various stages of the language under certain structural limitations until in NE we allow such maximally generalized sequences as *The tense situation may have been being exacerbated by the police.* The development of these sequences is discussed under the relevant sections and summarized in Appendix B.

A very different kind of change in the structure of the tense system was the development in ME of the use of the "historic present." This is a stylistic device used chiefly in storytelling. It is especially frequent in the reporting of dreams or visions, but may occur in any narrative which treats past events as if they occurred at the time of the utterance. Unlike events actually occurring simultaneously with the time of the utterance, these narrated events are not treated as if they are in progress —that is, there is no progressive aspect and therefore no *be + PrP* auxiliary. For example, when giving an account of an event which is actually happening simultaneously with the utterance we might say *He is stabbing him again and again.* If, however, we are narrating a past event in the historic present we might say *He stabs him again and again.*

Since the historic present is not found until ME, and even then hardly at all until the middle period, some scholars have assumed it is a borrowing from French. As all Germanic languages use the historic present, however, the construction is likely to be native. Nevertheless, French literary models doubtless encouraged the use of this stylistic device in English writing. Perhaps Scandinavian models did too since the historic present occurs very frequently in Old Norse sagas. At first the historic present was largely confined to poetry. For example, Chaucer uses the historic present extensively in poetry, but hardly at all in his prose *Boece* and *Melibee.* The device became common in prose only in the later part of the ENE period.

Aspect

Distributive Habitual

With the loss during ME and in most dialects of a contrast between *beo-* and *wes-* (see p. 116), the realization of distributive habitual aspect came during the ME period to resemble NE standard educated literary usage fairly closely. It will not be discussed further here.

Progressive

During ME, *be + PrP* came to be used somewhat more frequently than in OE for progressive aspect. It remains relatively rare, however, until the NE period. According to Franz (1939:498), for example, Shakespeare uses *be + PrP* only very sparingly; the number of instances increases with the later plays, but even in the last play, *Henry VIII,* there are only a dozen or so examples. Action considered to be in progress at the time of the utterance is normally expressed, as in earlier English, by *Verb + Nonpast Tense* or *do + Nonpast Tense + Verb.*

During the ME period the progressive ceased to be expressed by a *be* verb + *ende,* and was replaced by a *be* verb + *ing*. The form *-ing* began to be used as the progressive marker at the end of the twelfth century in the South. By Chaucer's time it was the only form available in all but the cultural areas peripheral to Southern and Midland England.

There is considerable disagreement concerning the origin of the progressive *-ing*. It may have been derived in part from the "gerund" construction. This construction in earlier English involves a nominalized form of the verb expressing manner, as in *He came running* which expresses the way in which he came, and answers the question *How did he come?* In earlier forms of English this construction occurs with the preposition *on,* as in:

4.75 Nashe UT II.253.23 in a perspectiue glasse hee set before his eyes king Henrie the eight with all his Lordes *on hunting* in his forrest at Windsore.

The *on* was often reduced to [ə], giving such forms as *A-hunting we will go*. While it seems likely that this construction reinforced the progressive *-ing* construction, many scholars feel it is doubtful whether it actually gave rise to it since the gerund construction is used frequently only rather later than the progressive with *-ing*. The problem with claiming that the *-ing* progressive developed independently of this construction is that we are then forced to claim that *-ing* replaced *-ende* without a model; this is rather unlikely in view of the fact that speakers tend to use existing surface structures rather than to invent totally new ones, especially when no need for a new structure is apparent (*-ende* was not ambiguous, it was not phonologically weakened out of existence, and so on). Despite all the work that has been done on the replacement of

-ende by *-ing,* this still remains one of the mysteries of the history of English.

When the Agent is absent in an ENE sentence with progressive *be + PrP* and an action verb like *make, do, commit, bring, prepare,* a passive interpretation is often given to the sentence, as in:

4.76 Del. Gentle Craft 168.27 while meate *was bringing in* (= 'was being brought in').

According to Mossé (1938) this construction did not become common until the seventeenth century, although it can be found sporadically even four centuries before. Up to the eighteenth century the nonparticipial, nominal *-ing* constructions like *the church was in building* and *the church was a-building* were favored; of these, the former developed in earlier ME; the latter is current from ca. 1500–1700. Since the Agent is never expressed in participial constructions of the type illustrated by the passage from Deloney, they cannot strictly speaking be considered passives. The passive *was being built by X* with overt progressive auxiliary and optional overt Agent did not develop until the end of the eighteenth century and will be discussed in the next chapter (p. 178).

Perfect

As in OE, perfect in ME and ENE is realized as *have + PP* with nonmutative verbs; with mutative verbs the auxiliary is usually *be + PP,* though *have + PP* is used more and more frequently during the period. Of the mutative verbs that favored *be + PP* perfect, *come, become, arrive, enter, run,* and *grow* are some of the most resistant to *have + PP.* As late as Shakespeare's time *He is come* is far more frequent than *He has come* and continues in regular use until the late nineteenth century.[16] Some examples of mutative verbs with *be + PP* and nonmutatives with *have + PP* are:

4.77 Ch. Mel. B.2615 And in the same manere oure Lord Crist *hath woold and suffred* that thy three enemys *been entred* into thyn house . . . and *han ywounded* thy doghter.

4.78 PL II.137.21 (1450) as fer as I can undirstande, Danyelle *is come* in to this cuntre, for none other cause but for to have suche as the Kyng *hath gifen* hym in Rysyng.

4.79 Sh. 2 Henry IV, II.i.96 And didst thou not, when she *was gone* downstairs, desire me to be no more so familiarity with such poor people?

4.80 Del. Th. of Reading 279.28 What *is become* of my rare Iewels?

[16] For a summary of various scholars' views on the subject and some statistics for various authors, see Fridén (1948), especially pp. 64–65.

As we saw in the last chapter, *have + PP* was dominant over *be + PP* even in OE. It came to be generalized to more and more verbs. Fridén (1948:41–57) has shown that this generalization was not random for any verb in any construction, however. The kinds of conditions that obtain for *have + PP* to be favored where *be + PP* would be expected include, among others: (i) when the sentence is contrary-to-fact,[17] as in:

4.81 Sh. All's Well V.iii.110 Unless she gave it to yourself in bed, / Where you *have* never *come*.

(ii) in sentences with certain adverbs, for instance, adverbs of manner or place:

4.82 Ch. Mel. B.3000 For ye *han entred* into myn hous by violence.

and (iii) in the presence of the optional overt Patient in double Agent-Patient functions (if the Patient is not expressed, *be + PP* is preferred). Franz (1939:513–515) cites several pairs in Shakespeare illustrating (iii), such as *Romeo* II.i.3: He . . . *hath stol'n him* home to bed (Patient expressed); but *Macbeth* II.iv.25: Malcolm and Donalbain . . . / *Are stol'n* away and *fled* (Patient not expressed). In other words, the generalization of *have + PP* occurred via an intermediary stage of restricted conditioning. Only in later NE is *have + PP* used unconditionally for perfect in all environments.

The dominance of *have + PP* over *be + PP* may well have been reinforced by the fact that the perfect *be + PP* was in some contexts ambiguous with the passive *be + PP* and the resultative stative *be + PP* of, for example, *The door was closed all day yesterday*. Such ambiguity was rare in OE since the surface forms of most transitive and intransitive verbs were distinct (see pp. 75, 120), and since resultative statives were adjectival and therefore usually inflected (p. 93). With the rise of identical sounding transitives and intransitives, and with the loss of adjectival inflection, a considerable amount of ambiguity necessarily arose. Since nonmutative verbs outnumbered mutative ones and *have + PP* was not heavily loaded with different functions, the generalization of *have + PP* is a very natural change.

In early ME the perfective auxiliary *have + PP* (but not *be + PP*) came to be used in conjunction with the *be + PP* passive auxiliary, as in:

4.83 Ch. Mel. B.2683 the wronges that *han been doon* to yow.

In later ME *have + PP* also came to be used with the *be + PrP* progres-

[17] Nevertheless, if the action has not taken place but is expected, *be* is preferred, as in Sh. *1 Henry IV*, IV.iii.19 certain horse . . . *are not yet come up*.

sive auxiliary; this construction is almost entirely limited to poetry until the ENE period:

4.84 Ch. Knight A.929 We *han ben waitynge* al this fourtenyght.

The result of these changes is that *have* + *PP,* whether it functioned as the marker of perfect or of past (p. 141), was permitted in the surface sequence of auxiliaries after modals and before progressives or passive auxiliaries, just as in NE. The extension of *have* + *PP* to these environments shows that, as the perfective and the marker of past tense, this auxiliary had completely lost its original association with the *have* of possession.

The ME period saw the development of a further segmentalization of the perfective, as in *I have done gone*. The origins of this *do* + *PP* are as obscure as that of the other *do* auxiliaries. Possibly it is a restructuring of the causative *do*. If one has caused something, it has clearly already happened and is completed. Many instances of the *have* + *PP* followed by *do* + *PP* do indeed seem to retain a trace of a causative implication, as in:

4.85 PL II.20.19 (1425) Also he seyde . . . he *hadde do sherchyd* att Clunye 'Also he said . . . he had done searched at Cluny' (he had finished searching? he had caused someone to search?).

In the South, this construction did not survive past the fifteenth century. In Northern English it remained common, however. The *OED* (s.v. *do* B.31) cites from the sixteenth century:

4.86 Scot. Poems 16thC. II.189 (1578) And many other false abusion / The Paip (='Pope') *hes done invent.*[18]

Negation

In OE, as we have seen, *ne* was the most common realization of negation. This form continued to be used extensively in ME but was lost by ENE except when incorporated into another word (such as *never*). As in OE, it occurred preverbally:

4.87 Ch. Mel. B.2383 for they *ne* kan no conseil hyde.

A rival form was, however, developing: *not/nat,* a descendant of the OE emphatic *nawiht/nauht/noht* 'not-at-all' (analyzable as *ne-a-wiht* 'not-ever-anything'). In OE *noht* seems always to have maintained its full emphatic meaning:

[18] Here, as in some other instances, *do* does not require *PP* on the following verb. There is apparently no difference in meaning between *has done invent* and *has done invented.*

4.88 Or. 94.30 Ne geþyncð þe swelc gewin *noht* lustbære 'Not seems to-you such victory not-in-any-way attractive = Such victory does not appear attractive to you in any way'.

Since *noht* was emphatic it very often co-occurred in OE with other negatives, as in 4.88. By ME *noht* seems to have lost its emphatic quality in many instances. Chaucer regularly uses the double negative *ne . . . nat* . . . apparently without necessarily expressing emphasis. Typically, *not* occurs after the first auxiliary if there is one, otherwise after the main verb:

4.89 Ch. Mel. B.2315 he that is irous and wrooth, he *ne* may *nat* wel deme 'he that is angry and wrathful, he may not judge well (= he can not judge well)'.

Not also occurs independently of *ne* as in constructions like the continuation of 4.89:

4.90 Ch. Mel. B.2316 and he that may *nat* wel deme, may *nat* wel conseille (= 'advise').

Seventy years or so later in the *Paston Letters, not* without *ne* is preferred and is clearly not emphatic when it follows the verb or *Verb + Object Pronoun* (*I know him not* is regular; see p. 161). When used in other positions, however, it is emphatic, as in 4.1 and:

4.91 Sh. 2 Henry IV, IV.i.98 it *not* belongs to you.

As *not* came to be used regularly for the nonemphatic marker, a new form, *nothing,* in meaning much the same as *nawiht,* developed to replace the emphatic negative as in:

4.92 Del. Gentle Craft 254.11 but there his Mistris and he were so familiar, that it *nothing* pleased his Master.

The conditions for the loss of *ne* as an independent word expressing negation are probably several. *Ne* seems to have been typically unstressed, hence the elision in OE of its vowel with certain verbs like *habb-, wes-* and with quantifiers like *ænig*. Since *ne* was unstressed, it tended not to be heard and a phonologically more distinguishable marker was needed. *Not* could readily serve this need since by later ME its origin in *ne-a-wiht* was probably no longer sensed, owing to the phonological changes that the word had undergone partly under the effect of reduced stress; in any case it was close in meaning to *ne* even when it was still felt to be an emphatic. *Not* in turn came to be reduced to *n't* in unstressed position, but still had enough phonological structure (a consonant cluster) to be distinguishable. As we have seen, a new emphatic came to replace emphatic *not* as the latter became recessive.

As the examples have amply shown, multiple negation continued in use through ME and ENE. It was, however, becoming considerably less common already in late ME; by Shakespeare's time it was used mainly in coordinate phrases and sentences, as in:

4.93 Sh. 2 Henry IV, II.iv.100 I will bar *no* honest man my house, *nor no* cheater.

It does, however, occur emphatically in some other contexts, for example:

4.94 Sh. 2 Henry IV, IV.iii.88 There's *never none* of these demure boys come to any proof.

C. THE FORMATION OF COMPLEX SENTENCES

Coordination

In OE if a negative sentence was coordinated to a preceding negative, the coordinating conjunction was *ne* (see 3.74). This continued in use during ME but toward the end of the period was replaced by *nor;* the recessiveness of the coordinate conjunction *ne* very largely coincides with the recessiveness of the propositional negator *ne.*

It had also been possible in OE to delete parts of coordinate sentences without moving them into the first underlying sentence, as in 3.75 and 3.76. This is a distinctly OE structure; it was becoming recessive in the late OE period and disappeared almost entirely by early ME. It is no longer found in the writings of Chaucer or his contemporaries.

The result of these changes is therefore that coordination is expressed in ME and ENE very much as it is in NE. A reader of ME and ENE will, however, probably be struck by the frequency with which the word *and* is used to express underlying relationships that do not involve *and* coordination. Most conspicuous is the use of *and (if),* sometimes spelled *an,* which expresses condition, not coordination, as in 4.28, and in Sh. *1 Henry IV* I.ii.92: I must give over this life, and (*coordination*) I will give it over: by the Lord, and (*condition*) I do not I am a villain. This use of *and* is of early ME origin; it did not become common until ENE and then only in the sixteenth century. During NE it became recessive in all but some dialects, such as Scottish.

Complements

Indicative, Subjunctive, and Auxiliaries

During OE the inflectional distinctions between indicative and subjunctive came, like other inflectional distinctions, to be obscured by the tendency of unstressed vowels to be pronounced [ə]. With the loss of the contrast, the segmentalized auxiliary phrases with *scul-* and *will-*

that had already been used sporadically as alternates for the subjunctive came to be used more and more and to be generalized to more and more contexts; other auxiliary phrases also developed, as will be discussed below. By ENE the original inflectional subjunctives had been largely taken over by phrases with auxiliaries like *should, would, might, may*—especially *should.* There is also some evidence that the original subjunctive function was sometimes taken over by *Verb + Tense,* while the formula *do + Tense + Verb* was used with the function of the original indicative—to assert the truth of the proposition (see p. 139)—but this particular set of contrasts never became fully established, nor was it ever fully integrated with the factive versus nonfactive distinction.

Despite the recessiveness of subjunctive inflections, they are nevertheless found throughout the ME and ENE periods. They are observable only in the singular nonpast (subjunctive was marked in earlier ME by *-e,* later by absence of inflection, as opposed to indicative, which was marked *-eth,* later *-es*) and in forms of the verb *to be* (nonpast *be* for all persons, past *were* for first, second and third persons singular). Considering the old *beo-* verb still appears in some authors as late as ENE, however (see 4.11), it is in some circumstances hard to determine whether even a *be* verb is in the subjunctive if it is in the present tense. The examples below all have indisputable subjunctive forms, unless indicated otherwise, and are compared where appropriate with segmentalized auxiliary forms.

The subjunctive of wishing survived primarily in complements of the verb *wish,* and then especially when expressing a wish contrary to fact at the time of the wish, as in *I wish he were here:*

4.95 PL IV.141.7 (1465) I wold ryght fayn . . . that it *were* otherwyse bytwene you then it ys 'I would-wish right well . . . that it were different between you than it is'.

Wishes about the future are normally segmentalized by *should* and *would,* as in *I wish you would go.* In sentences with a suppressed wish-verb, subjunctive came to be retained largely in fossilized exclamations like *God bless you, Long live the king* (the latter with both subjunctive and Type 2 word order), and in prayers. The Lord's Prayer starts with a succession of wishes in the subjunctive, including *Thy kingdom come.* Other examples are:

4.96 PL III.290.17 (1461) *Please* yow to wete that . . . 'May-it-please you to know that . . .'.

4.97 Sh. 1 Henry IV, III.iii.47 God *reward* me for it!

In all, the exclamatory, almost hortatory, force of the subjunctive is quite marked—if you pray *Thy kingdom come,* you may in fact be exhorting God to bring it about that his kingdom come. This kind of exclamatory wish was segmentalized in early ME by *mote + Main Verb,* and later by *may* + *Main Verb*. Although the use of *may* in this construction is attested from the fourteenth century on, it did not become popular until the sixteenth century, when it replaced *mote*.

The original subjunctive of exhortation was maintained after verbs like *ask, bid, beseech,* but was also segmentalized by *should*. *Should* seems to have originated in such OE sentences as the following, where it expresses obligation, and is embedded in a main clause with the past tense of reported speech:

4.98 Chron. 138.4 (1008) Her bebead se cyng þæt man *sceolde* ofer eall Angel cynn scipu feastlice wyrcean 'In-this-year commanded that king that one should throughout all England ships constantly build'.

In ME, this *sceolde* was generalized to complements embedded to main clauses with nonpast; Visser (III:1656) cites as an early example:

4.99 ca. 1290. S. Eng. Leg. 420.7 Many gon naked and bidde þæt sum man heom *scholde biweue* 'Many go naked and ask that some person them should clothe'.

where little of the sense of obligation remains.

If the verb of exhortation is suppressed, either the subjunctive and Type 2 word order is used or, from the fourteenth century on, the segmentalized construction *let . . . Main Verb* (the first person plural auxiliary *uton* was lost in the thirteenth century). When exhortation was expressed by a subjunctive and Type 2 word order, if the surface subject of the exhortation was plural, then no inflection was available that contrasted with the indicative; word order alone then assumed the function originally signaled by subjunctive, as in *Sit we down*. Demonstrating the interchangeability of segmentalized and nonsegmentalized exhortations in Shakespeare's time, Franz (1939:536) cites:

4.100 Sh. Titus IV.ii.132 Then *sit we down,* and *let us all consult*.

Stage directions like *Enter a bear* appear to originate in exhortations, though it is doubtful whether they were always interpreted as subjunctives rather than conventionalized phrases.[19]

Right through ME and ENE, traces remain of the old subjunctive in complements of verbs of saying, reporting, thinking, hoping, wondering, and especially in negative contexts. Occasionally the subjunctive inflection is used, more often the segmentalized auxiliary phrase, especially with *should,* though sometimes also with *would*. The use of *should* mean-

[19] In an interesting paragraph on stage directions, Visser (II:807–808) discusses the interchangeability of the type *Enter Jacques, his sword drawne* with directions using *shall, must,* and *let,* and with non-subjunctive descriptive forms like *Manes enters later*.

ing 'was-said-to' (see 3.83) continues well into ENE, but is recessive by the seventeenth century and virtually lost by the eighteenth. Some examples are:

4.101 PL III.303.15 (1461) It is talkyd here how that ye and Howard *schuld* a' strevyn togueder 'It is said here how that you and Howard were-supposed-to have fought together'.

4.102 Sh. AYLI III.ii.167 But didst thou hear without wondering how thy name *should* be hang'd and carved upon these trees?

Whether negative verbs like *doubt* had subjunctive complements or not, they continued throughout the ME and ENE period to allow negative-incorporation into the complement. Many of the particular verbs that occurred in OE like *tweo-* 'doubt', *wand-* 'refrain from' dropped out of the language in ME and were replaced by borrowings from French and Latin, for instance, *doubt,* borrowed from French. The verbs borrowed from French themselves permitted negative-incorporation in the complement (for example: the modern French *Je doute qu'il ne fasse rien* 'I doubt that he'll [not] do anything') and so probably reinforced the construction, and kept it alive even when other forms of multiple negation were recessive. In ME we find:

4.103 Ch. Mel. B.2774 nature *deffendeth* (French) and *forbedeth* (English) by right that *no* man make hymself riche 'nature prohibits and forbids by right that not-any man make himself rich'.

with negative-incorporation, as opposed to the suppletive, but not negative-incorporated:

4.104 PL II.22.4 (1425) God *defende* (= 'forbid') that *any* of my saide kyn shuld be of swyche governaunce (= 'guidance') as he is of!

And in Shakespeare we occasionally find, besides the modern construction, also such forms as:

4.105 Sh. Errors IV.ii.7 First he *denied* you had in him *no* right (confused about identities, Luciana has claimed that Antipholus of Syracuse is her sister Adriana's husband; he has denied this, therefore has denied that Adriana [the *you* addressed in the quotation] has any right over him).

Although negative-incorporation into complements outlasted multiple negation, it too was recessive by the end of the ENE period and is hardly attested at all from 1700 in the standard dialects.

Subject and Object Complements

As the discussion of subjectivalization in general has shown, some form of subjectivalization or pseudo-subjectivalization was required in all but idiomatic phrases like *methinks* by the mid-sixteenth century. Subject-raising from the complement to the main clause, as in *It seems that he is a phoney* → *He seems to be a phoney,* came to be used extensively whereas in OE it is scarcely evidenced at all. Where subject-raising was not or could not be selected, pseudo-subjectivalization occurs; or, if the verb permitted it, the subjectivalization of a complement in the form of an infinitive complement, for example, *To vote is a privilege,* or of a gerund, for example, *Voting is a basic right* (both subjectivalized infinitive complements and gerunds were typical in OE). The subjectivalization of a *that* complement as in *That she writes so badly is a pity* seems still not to have been available at this period.

Object complements continued to have basically the same characteristics as in OE, although the use of anticipatory *that* or *it,* as in 3.91, fell into disrepute in literary style during ENE.

Relative Clauses

Full Clauses

The diversity of relative clause patterns in ME and especially ENE suggests there was considerable freedom in the use of relative clauses and extensive generalization of previously more limited forms. This generalization was later reversed and during NE constraints were re-imposed to allow much less flexibility than was available in ME and ENE.

The form *þe* occurs frequently in the ME part of the *Peterborough Chronicle* and other very early ME texts as a relative pronoun, but drops out almost completely by the end of the thirteenth century and is superseded by *that*. The OE *se, seo, þæt* relative is also superseded by *that*.

The generalization of *that* to contexts other than the relative pronominalization of nominative or accusative neuter singular nouns appears sporadically as early as Alfredian works, especially when the antecedent is a personal pronoun or proper name:

4.106 Or. 44.1 *Centauri* (plural) *þæt* sindon healf hors, healf men 'Centaurs that are half horse half man'.

It was regular with indefinite pronoun antecedents like *hwa* 'whoever'. In other contexts it is rare until early ME. For a very early example consider:

4.107 Chron. 264.24 (1137) I ne can . . . tellen *alle þe wunder ne alle þe pines* (plural) *ðæt* hi diden wreccemen on þis land

'I not know-how . . . to-tell all the wonders nor all the sufferings that they did to-wretched-men in this land'.

Here *ðæt* substitutes for *þe wunder* and *þe pines*. In later works *that* occurs in all contexts, whether restrictive or appositive relatives, whether the antecedent is a pronominal or nominal, a proper noun or not, and whether the function of the relative is adverbial or not:

4.108 Del. Th. of Reading 275.21 how can you like him *that* all women mislikes?
4.109 Sh. AYLI III.ii.172 since Pythagoras' time, *that* I was an Irish rat, which I can hardly remember.

At first it might appear that *that* is directly derived from the *se, seo, þæt* relative since it is identical in form to the nominative and accusative neuter singular. But there are functional differences. For example, ME *that* does not allow preposed prepositions whereas OE *se, seo, þæt* permitted them. This and various other differences suggest that the ME relative *that* perhaps originates in some other structure altogether, or, more probably, results from the conflation of the demonstrative *þæt* and some other structure. A likely candidate for this other structure is the subordinator *þæt* which was used in OE to indicate that complements were subordinate to the main proposition (as in *I know that he is coming*), and in causative subordinating phrases like *for þæm þæt* 'for that that = because'.[20] In ME this subordinator was generalized to all subordinate structures and came to be used with any other subordinator, for example, *if that, whether that, who that,* and so on.

During ME a series of "*wh*-relatives," *which, what,* and *who,* came into being. These probably derive from OE indefinites, like *hwilc* 'any', *hwæt* 'whatever', *hwa* 'whoever'. Although we distinctly prefer the *-ever* forms for indefinites in NE, we still find the earlier form in such proverbial expressions as *Who pays the piper calls the the tune*. For an ME example, see:

4.110 PL II.23-3 (1425) ye lyke to sende me redes lettres of alle the seyd matier . . . and *who* ye wil I be governed in this mater 'you please to send me advice letters concerning all the said matter . . . and whoever you wish I should-be governed (by) in this matter'.

In both cases *who* is, strictly speaking, *whoever,* but can also easily be thought of as *he that*—that is, as a reduced form of *Personal Pronoun + Relative*. The origin of the *wh-* relatives is presumably to be found in part in this kind of reinterpretation of the indefinites as *Personal Pro-*

[20] For discussion of this and many other problems connected with the history of relative pronouns in English see Klima (1965).

noun + *Relative*. The model of the interrogative *hwa* 'who?' *hwæt* 'what?' *hwilc* 'what kind of?' probably also played a part, though a smaller one. Consider, for example, the discourse *Who did it? He that did it was X* where *he that* on the surface seems to substitute for *who*.[21] The force of the interrogatives is not likely to have been as great as that of the definites because it was indirect. Some experiments with relatives of clearly interrogative origin are to be found, but they never became fully established, suggesting that the interrogative correlation was never fully accepted:

4.111 Ch. HF 375 And al the maner *how* she deyde . . . / Rede Virgile 'And for-all the manner how (in which) she died . . . read Vergil'.

There is little doubt that a further, and very important, influence was the Latin *qui, quae, quod,* and the French *que*. For one, the *which* and *what* relatives came to be used just at the time when the French and Latin influence was beginning to be strongly felt (ca. 1200); for another, it is hard to account for the fact that *who* did not come to be used extensively until the late fifteenth century whereas *which* and *what* were used from early ME on, unless we posit that the Latin models *qui* and *quod* supported the use of *which* and *what* owing to their phonological similarity, but not the development of *who* since it had little phonological similarity to any Latin form. That a separate relative other than *that* would have gained wide currency in ME regardless of Latin and French influence is, however, likely since *that* was too generalized to signal relative clause structure as opposed to any other kind of subordination.

Which was the first *wh-* form to be used more than sporadically as a relative although it did not become really popular until the fifteenth century. It is used for restrictive and appositive relatives and with both animate and inanimate antecedents. At first it occurs almost exclusively with a preposed preposition; this suggests that the *wh*-relative owes its origin in part to some desire to achieve a fuller surface subordination than *that* allowed. Chaucer and the Pastons still use *which* most commonly, but not exclusively, with prepositions. The following passages illustrate typical ME usage:

4.112 Ch. Mel. B.2234 as muche availleth to speken bifore folk *to which* his speche anoyeth, as it is to synge biforn hym *that* wepeth.

4.113 PL II.22.28 (1425) the engrossyng of *wyche* the messager of this bill myght nought abide 'the completing of which the messenger of this letter could not await'.

The rare usage without preposition is illustrated by:

[21] In fact, however, *X* is the real substitute for *Who* (not *He that*).

4.114 PL II.24.1 (1425) Mayster William Swan, *whiche* longe hathe be his procurator (= 'agent').

During the fifteenth and sixteenth centuries *which* came to be used more and more with inanimate antecedents, but several instances of *which* with human antecedents are still to be found in Shakespeare and other sixteenth-century writers:

4.115 Del. Th. of Reading 276.38 Now Tom Doue had all the Fidlers at a beck of his finger, *which* follow him vp and downe the Citie, as diligent as little Chickens after a hen.

Alternating with *Preposition* + *which* there developed in later ME the form *where* + *Preposition*. Expressions of this type are particularly common in the sixteenth century. Franz (1939:312) cites, among others, *whereof, whereby, whereon, whereupon, whereat, whereto, whereuntil, whereout, whereagainst, wherethrough* in Shakespeare's works.

The relative *what* is particularly favored after *all* and *nothing*. This usage dates back to OE. Chaucer uses it occasionally with other antecedents like *that,* and various authors like Pecock experimented with *what* after antecedent *it: after it what is write,*[22] presumably on the model of Latin *id quod,* but *what* never gained much currency except in popular writings such as the *Paston Letters.* Occasionally *that what,* and *nothing what* are found in literary ENE, but *what* is not used with a noun antecedent as in the modern nonstandard type: *the man what came.*

Who is the only relative that can be inflected. The nonnominative forms *whose* and *whom* came to be used as relatives in early ME. They are used mainly with animate antecedents until the later sixteenth century when we also find them with inanimate antecedents (usually suggesting personification):

4.116 Sh. Errors II.ii.178 Usurping ivy, brier, or idle moss / *Who* all for want of pruning, with intrusion, / Infect thy sap.

Like *which,* they are favored over *that* when the relativized noun is in construction with a preposition.

The unmarked (nominative) form *who* occurs only sporadically until the fifteenth century. It is not to be found in Chaucer. Even in the fifteenth century it appears not to have been used in informal style. In the earlier part of the *Paston Letters,* for example, *who* is used almost exclusively with the antecedent *God.* In the later correspondence it occasionally occurs in other contexts, but is rare:

4.117 PL VI.344.33 (1488) An inbacetour (= 'ambassador') fro

[22] Reginald Pecock, *The Repressor of Over Much Blaming of the Clergy,* ed. C. Babington. London: Longmans, Green, 1860, p. 2.

the kynge of Schottes *who* is now put in grete trobyll (='trouble, jeopardy').

The establishment of *who* as a regular relative in the mid-sixteenth century meant that three relatives were available: *that, who, which,* and to some extent a fourth: *what. Who* was usually used with animates, though certainly not exclusively. Franz (1939:229) notices that in Shakespeare the following inanimates occur especially often with *who* relative: *knees, ivy, brier, moss, casket, stones, wind;* not all instances suggest personification. The pressure of extensive use with animate antecedents not only reinforced the use of *who* with animates or personified inanimates, but also led to the recession of *which* with animate antecedents. The restriction of *who* to animate and of *which* to inanimate antecedents reduced the redundancy at the price of introducing a complexity in the grammar. On the other hand, *what* gave way to both *who* and *which,* resulting in the loss of *what* as a relative in standard English and hence in simplification.

All three relatives occur in ME with the subordinate *that*. In fact, *whom that, whose that* are commoner than *whom, whose* in the early part of the period when the *wh*-forms first come into use, presumably because the *wh*-forms were not felt to be full-fledged subordinators:

4.118 PL V.231.25 (1475?) he hathe seyd that he woold lyfte them *whom that* hym plese ('whom it may please him to raise').

Who that, on the other hand, is almost nonexistent, presumably because *who* was not used as a relative until the sixteenth century and this was the period in which the use of *that* after subordinators other than *so, such,* and the like became recessive. *Wh- that* relative forms no longer occur in Shakespearean English although only two centuries earlier they had still been very common, especially *which that,* as in:

4.119 Ch. Mel. B.2157 bigat upon his wyf, that called was Prudence, a doghter *which that* called was Sophie.

Definiteness is essential to relativization, since the relativized noun, being in identity with a noun in the higher sentence, is "aforementioned." It is hardly surprising then that the relative pronouns are sometimes preceded by *the*. Consider:

4.120 PL II.100.30 (1449) abok . . . *the queche* my seyd brother be hestid my moder 'a-book . . . the-which my said brother behested (asked of) my mother'.

4.121 Sh. 1 Henry IV, II.i.68 there are other Troyans that thou dream'st not of, *the which* for sport sake are content to do the profession some grace.

What may be surprising is that only *which* seems to allow this construction to be used regularly. Abbott (1870:185) and Franz (1939:301), for example, note only one instance of *the whom* in Shakespeare: *Winter's Tale* IV.iv.529: your mistress; from *the whom,* I see, / There's no disjunction to be made. This has suggested to some scholars that *the which* is modeled on French *lequel.* As in many other instances it is likely that the French reinforced the construction rather than brought it into being since its most common use is in appositive relatives when the antecedent is a whole sentence—a condition in which anaphoric marking is particularly necessary to show the connection between the parts of the sentence, as in:

4.122 PL II.171.23 (1450) we purpose to sende hym in to certaine places for to execute oure commaundement, for *the whiche* he ne may be attendant (= 'be on duty') to be in oure countees.

The following passage shows quite clearly the anaphoric character of both *the* and *wh-:*

4.123 Ch. Mel. B.2434 ye han broght with yow to youre conseil ire (= 'anger'), coveitise, and hastifnesse, *the whiche* thre thinges been contrariouse to every conseil honest and profitable.

It also suggests that relative subordinators are not necessarily always pronouns substituting for a noun; they may also be referential subordinators attached to, rather than substituting for, a noun and indicating identity with the head noun.

The use of *which* + *Noun* (that is, the referential rather than the pronominal relative) came to be almost a mannerism in the fifteenth century. While its use decreased in the sixteenth century, a considerable number of instances are still to be found in Shakespeare:

4.124 Sh. 1 Henry IV, V.iv.119 The better part of valour is discretion, *in the which better part* I have saved my life.

In OE we found *þe . . . Pronoun* constructions. In the ME period all relative clauses permit this kind of construction. It is most often found in poetry but is by no means limited to it:

4.125 PL II.103.27 (1449) ever deseryng to her of yowr wurschupfull ustate, *the whyche* All myghte God mayntayne *hyt* 'ever desiring to hear of your worshipful condition, which (may) all mighty God maintain'.

4.126 PL V.321.33 with other dyveres (= 'different people') *that* I know not *ther* names.

The construction is particularly frequently used when several clauses or coordinates intervene, and it is almost exclusively in this kind of context that *Relative . . . Pronoun* continues into ENE. At this period it is found chiefly in poetry:

4.127 Sh. M of V, IV.i.133 thy currish spirit / Govern'd a wolf, *who,* hang'd for human slaughter, / Even from the gallows did *his* fell soul fleet.[23]

In ENE another relative subordinator developed. This is the highly restricted equivalent of *Relative . . . Negative . . .* and occurs only if the relative clause is negative and is itself embedded to a negative or interrogative sentence. It is developed from *but* = *except* and from such phrases as *I do not know but that she went;* the relative function of *but* is clear in the following sentence where *but* is referential as well as negative:

4.128 Nashe UT II.264.27 no leafe he wrote on *but* was lyke a burning glasse to set on fire all his readers.

Reduced Relatives

In early OE texts adjectives occurred in either prenominal or postnominal position after relative clause reduction. In later OE, however, prenominal position came to predominate for uncoordinated adjectives and also for participles, provided they were preceded by a *be* auxiliary in the full clause. In ME postnominal adjectives came to be used more commonly again, largely under the influence of French. Most instances of postnominal adjectives in Chaucer, for example, are of adjectives borrowed from French, suggesting that not only the lexical items themselves but also their characteristic syntactic structures were borrowed; see 4.123 and:

4.129 Ch. Mel. B.2188 the los of oure othere goodes temporels.[24]
4.130 PL II.23.2 (1425) in alle haste resonable.

In Shakespeare's writings, too, postnominal adjectives are borrowings from either French or Latin, not native words:

4.131 Sh. MW of W IV.v.17 Speak from thy lungs military.

Nevertheless, so strong was the predominance of prenominal adjective and participle position that by the sixteenth century we begin to

---

[23] This punctuation follows the Folio and the first Arden edition. The second Arden edition (ed. J. R. Brown, 1959) treats *Even . . .* as an apposition and hence blocks interpretation of *who . . . his* as a relative; since relatives of the *who . . . his* type are still frequently to be found in ENE, there seems to be no valid reason for emending the Folio.

[24] The adjective *temporels* is itself plural; clearly the French construction was very much in Chaucer's mind here; *goodes* is, however, a native word so the whole phrase is not a borrowing.

find past participles of intransitives in prenominal position; these had previously always been avoided: The *OED* quotes 1562 *new comen up matter,* 1598 *a gone man,* 1548 *sour turned wine,* and even as late as 1827 *the transpired matters.* These prenominal participles obviously are derived from relative clauses with perfect realized by *be* + *PP*. That most constructions of this type were lost again is presumably to be accounted for along with the loss of *be* + *PP* as the realization of perfect (see p. 144).

During ME and ENE reduced relative clauses were frequently split if they were coordinate in structure (such as, *good men and true*) or if the underlying clause included the structure *be* + *Adjective* + *Complement.* The latter construction could be split so that the adjective or participle preceded the grammatical head, while the rest of the relative clause followed:

4.132 PL II.189.21 (1450) here ys a marveyllous disposed contree, and manye *evylle wylled* peple *to Sir Thomas Tuddenham* 'here is a remarkably (badly) disposed country and many evilly willed people to Sir T.T. = here is a country remarkably badly disposed and many people of bad will to Sir T.T.'.

4.133 Nashe, Strange News . . . I.262.25 his *decayed* eyes *with iniquitie.*

4.134 Nashe, Pref. to Green's Menaphon III.318.2 their *ouerfraught* studies *with trifling compendiaries.*

The split construction illustrates the tendency we saw in the last chapter to organize constructions according to modifier-head rather than according to sentence-groups.

While deletion resulting in prenominal adjectives was common from earliest times, deletion of the relative marker was unusual in other constructions until late ME; even so it did not gain full currency until the late sixteenth century. By late ME apparently any relative, whatever its function, is deletable; if it is followed by either the main verb *be* or the auxiliary *be,* that *be* is also optionally deletable. For a few examples of constructions not commonly found in NE, at least in written style, consider:

(i) with subject relative deleted:

4.135 Sh. M for M II.ii.34 I have a brother *is condemn'd to die.*

4.136 Sh. AYLI II.iv.70 Here's a young maid with travel much oppress'd / *And faints for succour.*

4.137 Nashe, Pierce Penilesse I.182.6 tis not their newe bonnets *will keepe them from the old boan-ach.*

(ii) with adverbial relative deleted:

4.138 PL II.172.5 (1450) unto tyme *he shal mowe be present.*

4.139 Nashe UT II.252.17 Erasmus . . . requested to see Tully in that same grace and maiestie *he pleaded his oration pro Roscio Amerino.*

While relative deletion clearly has its origin in OE, the construction may have been strengthened by contact with Scandinavian languages in the later OE period. The influence of Scandinavian on the lexicon of English does not really show until early ME; it is at this period too that relative deletion begins to be generalized. Considering it is typical of the Scandinavian languages of the early period, it is likely that the contact situation favored the generalization of an already existing rule. Whatever its origin, the development of relative reduction provides us with a very good example of the tendency toward generalization of a pattern, and hence simplification.

D. WORD ORDER

During ME the general characteristics of NE word order became established—that is, Type 1: *Subject (Auxiliary) Verb (Object)* was generalized to coordinate and subordinate clauses; Type 2: *(X) Verb + Subject (Object),* or *(X) Auxiliary + Subject + Verb (Object),* came to be used mainly for interrogatives; and Type 3: *Subject (Object) Verb (Auxiliary)* was virtually lost. In the transitional period between OE and ME we can only speak of tendencies. In the *Peterborough Chronicle* of the twelfth century, for example, the number of instances of Type 1 in subordinate clauses increases, but all the older patterns are still available. As much as three hundred years later we find Chaucer still using Type 3 order, as in 4.119, but only rarely. By ENE times Type 3 was found only very infrequently.

The association of Type 2 with interrogatives came to be so strong during ME that this order was generalized to nonsubordinate questions with *whether,* as in 4.26 and 4.27. In noninterrogative structures Type 2 continued to be used fairly extensively with certain negative adverbs like *scarcely* and with adverbs of time and place:

4.140 Sh. 2 Henry IV, II.iv.364 *Now comes in* the sweetest morsel of the night.

Pronoun objects continued one way or another to be treated differently from nouns as far as word order is concerned. Nonsubjectivalized pronominal Experiencers in impersonal constructions regularly occurred preverbally so long as impersonal constructions continued in use, as in 4.50, 4.51, and 4.118. Object pronouns not functioning as Experiencer sometimes still precede the verb as they did in OE; see 4.99 and:

4.141 Ch. Mel. B.2160 Thre of his olde foes *han it espyed.*

This construction is still used in ENE poetry but in prose it is extremely rare except for emphasis:

4.142 Sh. 1 Henry IV, II.iv.424 there is virtue in that Falstaff; *him* keep with, *the rest* banish (note the nominal as well as the pronominal object in preverbal position here).

The loss of preverbal position for pronoun objects is directly correlatable with the loss of Type 3 word order.

Certain rules still operate to prevent pronouns from occurring in final position in some structures. For example, an object pronoun regularly precedes *not* whereas a noun follows, as in *I know him not,* but *I know not your cousin.* This particular rule was lost with the development of *do*-support for negatives, but similar ones still persist, as in sentences with certain verb-particle constructions like *I looked up my friend: I looked my friend up, *I looked up her: I looked her up;* more subtly such rules account for the way in which most speakers find *I gave the book to the teacher* as good as or better than *I gave the teacher a book,* but *I gave the book to her* less comfortable than *I gave her the book.*

As in NE, special emphasis may override the general principles of unemphatic word order. In the written language we usually prefer clefting as a device for emphasizing; in earlier English emphasis was more readily expressed by simple word order shifts without clefting:

4.143 Sh. Twelfth Night I.v.60 *Clo.* Take her away. *Oli.* Sir, I bade them *take away you.*

5 THE DEVELOPMENT OF MODERN ENGLISH SINCE 1700

The beginnings of the Modern English period are often associated with the publication in 1668 of John Dryden's essay, *Of Dramatic Poesy,*[1] and Abraham Cowley's *Several Discourses by Way of Essays; in Verse and Prose.* More important than any one set of documents, though, in terms of the far-reaching consequences, are two extralinguistic developments – the spread of English and the growth of concern with good and bad usage.[2]

The growth of the British Empire inevitably resulted in the spread of English and the development of several major varieties: American, British, Canadian, Australian, Indian English, South African, and so on, each with its own dialects, whether geographical or socioeconomic. A few of the syntactic differences between British and American will be mentioned in the course of this chapter; most of the differences are tendencies rather than absolutes, and what syntactic distinctions there are have been somewhat clouded by numerous inter-dialectal borrowings, especially from American into British, and especially since the 1920s.[3]

Interest in English usage was not new in the eighteenth century. Sixteenth- and seventeenth-century grammarians had been concerned with spelling and pronunciation. Best known, perhaps, is Richard Mulcaster, who wrote his *First Part of the Elementarie* in 1582. Others of considerable importance, at least to our knowledge of ENE pronunciation, include, in the late sixteenth century William Bullokar and

[1] Dryden's prose has many characteristics of NE; his poetry, however, is relatively archaic and is more like ENE than NE.

[2] Discussions of this topic are numerous. Baugh (1957), Chapters 9 and 10, Leonard (1962) and McKnight (1928) provide excellent introductions with copious illustrations.

[3] For some general discussion see especially Brook (1963), Foster (1968), Kirchner (1957), and Schlauch (1959).

John Hart, and in the seventeenth Charles Butler, Christopher Cooper, Alexander Gill, and John Wallis. They had also been extensively concerned with vocabulary. Some, like Mulcaster, Sir John Cheke, and Roger Ascham, promoted "plain English"—that is, English "vnmixt and vnmangeled with borrowing of (from) other tunges."[4] Others, like Sir Thomas Elyot, promoted the augmentation of English especially with Latin words. At the end of the sixteenth century the argument between the two groups was virulent. In a sense both sides won the day: the augmenters, since a large number of borrowed words remained, like *confidence, education, maturity,* all lambasted by the purists as "obscure" and nicknamed "inkhorn terms"; and the purists, since many Latin and Greek borrowings dropped out again, like *fatigate* ('make tired'), *adjuvate* ('aid'), *collaude* ('recommend'). Nevertheless, it is not until the late seventeenth century and early eighteenth century that we find interest in prescribing grammatical as well as lexical structure and in suggestions like those of Defoe (*An Essay upon Projects,* 1697) and Swift (*A Proposal for Correcting, Improving and Ascertaining the English Tongue,* 1712) that an academy should be established to promote refinement, politeness, propriety, taste, and accuracy in the use of language. As a result of this new interest in legislating usage, a new genre of grammar, the "prescriptive grammar," came into being. Relatively few such grammars were written in the first half of the eighteenth century (Leonard [1962] claims only fifty or so grammars were written between 1700 and 1750, not all of them prescriptive), but by the end of the century this new genre had become extremely popular (Leonard claims more than two hundred were written between 1750 and 1800).

What led to the rise of this new interest in legislating usage and to the enormous popularity of prescriptive grammars? These are questions that ultimately can be answered only with reference to all aspects of the culture of the time. At the risk of gross oversimplification, it seems fair to say that three major issues were at stake: social, literary, and philosophical. Different grammarians appear to have been more or less influenced by each of these factors and to have been more or less willing to acknowledge each of them; all attempted to rationalize and to synthesize the differing views, and all in some sense failed to develop a fully rational system.

Perhaps the main social factor in the development of prescriptive grammars was the rise of the middle class. In urban communities the gentry felt threatened and sought ways to keep themselves apart from the middle class. They looked for overt behavioral tokens by which to single themselves out from others, tokens which would create barriers between themselves and the middle class. Language was an obvious vehicle for such an aim. So was good, "moral" behavior. But the notion of morality is always fuzzy and intuitive; when it becomes necessary

[4] Sir John Cheke; letter to Sir Thomas Hoby, prefaced to Hoby's translation of *The Courtier,* 1561; quoted by McKnight (1956:118).

to prove one's superiority, such tangible signals as language, diet, dress, and hair length become surrogates for morals and even identifiable with them. A particularly vocal defendant in public of the equation of language with morals was Swift.[5] In the *Proposal for Correcting . . . the English Tongue,* for example, he deplored the "Licentiousness which entered with the *Restoration;* and from infecting our Religion and Morals, fell to corrupt our Language."[6]

Most of the discussion on language and morals revolved around the use of words. Condemnation of a person's use of a particular word as "vulgar" could lead to condemnation of his language as a whole, and hence of the person himself. But sometimes sentence structure too came under scrutiny. If we can apply modern terms such as "competence grammar" and "felicity conditions" to eighteenth-century views of language, we can perhaps see in embryo the notion that if a man's linguistic performance matched exactly his linguistic competence he would satisfy all felicity conditions (see p. 49); he would never break promises; he would never command a person to do something without authority to do so; he would never lie. In other words, he would be a moral paragon (linguistically; in nonlinguistic action he might not be – he might murder his neighbor, but if he said nothing about it, he would not be violating his linguistic morality – but it is precisely the nonlinguistic morality that usually got left out of the equation). It was a problem to ensure ideal behavior when relatively little was known about linguistic systems, and even less about psychological ones. So it was easier to talk about words, metaphoric expressions, and the like, than about syntax.

While most of the prescriptivists dwelt on language and morality rather than on the immediate social issues, there can be no doubt that those social issues were in many cases the real cause for such concerns. For one, the country gentry, like Squire Weston in Fielding's *Tom Jones,* notoriously spoke just like the farmers. But Squire Weston had absolute authority so he had no need to develop elaborate codes correlating good birth with good language and good morals; good birth was enough. His urban counterparts, however, felt their authority eroding; it was they who needed codes. It was they who allowed such sentiments as the following to thrive:

> The best Expressions grow low and degenerate, when profan'd by the populace, and applied to mean things. The use they make of them, infecting them with a mean and abject Idea, causes that we cannot use them without sullying and defiling those things, which are signified by them. . . .[7] it is no hard matter to discern between the depraved Language of common People, and the noble refin'd expressions of the Gentry, whose condition and merits have advanced them above the other.[8]

---

[5] For a discussion of the differences between Swift's public stance and his practice, see Strang (1967).

[6] Swift IV.10.5.

[7] *Messieurs du Port Royal; The Art of Speaking; rendered in English.* London, 1676, p. 50. Cited by Leonard (1929:170).

[8] *Ibid.,* p. 41.

It is surely significant that it was for the edification of the urban gentleman that most of the grammars were written, to warn them against contamination with the vulgar. Hardly any were written at first for middle-class people to help them approximate the prestige model;[9] such an audience came to be addressed only in the late eighteenth and the nineteenth centuries when the gentry had all but lost the hold they had been desperately trying to maintain. Then the upper middle class adopted without much question the prescriptions that had been laid down for the gentry and used them as devices to separate themselves from the lower middle class, although the social, literary, and philosophical assumptions that had helped bring prescriptive grammars into being had almost vanished. So prescriptivism in the nineteenth century became primarily a tradition rather than the active response to an immediate situation that it had been. With the rise of nationalism and local individualism in the last couple of decades there has been a marked reaction to the use of language as a marker of social caste. Nevertheless, there are few societies that have come under Western influence since the eighteenth century where an "educated standard language" is not still identified with a specific prestige class.

There seems to be some sort of correlation between relative uninterest in linguistic prescriptivism and cultural pride, whether under the guise of regionalism, tribalism, nationalism, or the like. Although the conditions for mid-twentieth-century nationalism are totally different from those of the sixteenth century or even the ninth, these are the three periods when the notion of a fixed standard has been least important in the history of English and experimentation with the language has been most favored. In OE times Latin was the standard; along with his concern for establishing a nation of Englishmen came Alfred's desire to establish a vigorous (but scarcely standardized) style for literary expression that might become as good a vehicle for all subjects as Latin, but English was never felt to be as important a language as Latin. In the Middle Ages in England, French and Latin were the standard languages; apologies for writing serious works in English abound in later ME. With the Renaissance came a new surge of pride in English as a medium for all kinds of expression, including history, philosophy, and science, although apologies for using English still persist right through the sixteenth century. Fixing a standard was not of concern because it seemed more important to make the language vigorous, mature, and flexible. Experiments with English were, for the most part, heralded as signs of the strength of an emerging medium. By the end of the seventeenth century, however, few writers still questioned the acceptability of English as a medium for all subjects, nor did they question its vigor. They could therefore turn attention to refinement of a language they

[9] This does not mean that the middle class was ignored. On the contrary, as early as the beginning of the eighteenth century, Addison and Steele wrote the journal called *The Spectator* specifically to bring the language, morals, and culture of the gentry to the middle class. Addison and Steele were, however, not grammarians.

already assumed appropriate. Indeed, they could look back with some nostalgia at the past, and speak of linguistic traditions. In his *Proposal for Correcting . . . the English Tongue,* Swift praised the Elizabethan and Jacobean periods for fostering the greatest "improvement"; since then, he felt, English had declined. Others like Thomas Sheridan, Lord Monboddo, and later Noah Webster, less troubled than Swift by the licentiousness of the late seventeenth century, thought they saw in Restoration and Queen Anne English the "classical" or Augustan elegance they sought in language. Where Mulcaster and others in the sixteenth century had looked forward to the perfection of language, in the eighteenth century most looked back to the seemingly better past. Many, like Swift and Defoe, hoped to reverse the "decay" they thought they saw as social traditions changed. Others, like Dr. Johnson, saw that language changes inevitably and that it was therefore impossible to fix a language; but he too hoped to delay its decay, convinced as he was that change would bring corruption: "tongues, like governments, have a natural tendency to degeneration."[10]

Related to the development of a need for maintaining or creating social distance through language and with the development of a sense of linguistic tradition, was the rise of the literary war on wit. The innovative metaphor and surprising juxtapositions so typical of the sixteenth and especially the early seventeenth centuries were felt to be "false wit"; experiments with puns and metaphorical conceits were anathema to critics like Dr. Johnson. Instead, "true wit" was conceived as order, truth, decorum, or, as Pope put it, "Nature to advantage dressed"[11] (in some sense he seems to have thought of true wit as satisfying all the felicity and truth conditions). Tremendously important was the maintenance of decorum through faithful adherence to what were felt to be given, natural classifications – semantic categorizations that segmented the world and gave it orderliness. "Conceits" by definition violated such orderliness and therefore were a threat to the given way of things (just as on another level the rise of the middle class was a threat to the given, ordered social structure).

Inextricably bound up with the poets' and critics' ideas about true wit was the philosophers' notion of a single universal reason, matching a single universal truth and expressible in terms of "Universal Grammar." From earliest times there had been a nostalgic longing for the divine language that Adam and Eve and their descendants had spoken before the "confusion of tongues" that was supposed to have resulted from the pride embodied by the Tower of Babel. Such a divine language was variously thought to be Hebrew, Latin, or Greek, but little credence had been given to such theories. In the late seventeenth and early eighteenth centuries many rationalist philosophers believed that a uni-

[10] Johnson, Preface to the *Dictionary,* n.p.

[11] Alexander Pope, *Essay on Criticism,* 1.297 (1711).

versal language could not be reconstructed or recovered; instead it was possible, they thought, to create one.[12] Such a grammar was not supposed to supersede already extant languages, but would facilitate communication between people who spoke different languages; it would promote scientific research and clarify theological issues. Perhaps the most famous of such deliberately invented systems is that of Bishop Wilkins, described in his *Essay towards a Real Character, and a Philosophical Language* (1668).[13] Wilkins' Universal Grammar, like most others, was largely a formalized semantic system, a logical classification that was meant to be a model of the "*Internal* Notion or *Apprehension* of things" common to all men. Since in a Universal Grammar sound should ideally match sense, and related terms should have related expressions, Wilkins devised an elaborate system of sound combinations matching classificatory combinations.

Influenced by all these different developments, social, literary, and philosophical, the prescriptive grammarians attempted to devise a system for assisting the gentry in their attempt to maintain themselves as a class apart. Morality came for many to be a surrogate for social pressure. Metaphor was not the grammarians' immediate concern and so was usually left to the rhetoricians, but the relationship of the war on wit to prescriptivism can clearly be seen in the attempts to maintain pure, simple English and to avoid all "forced" expressions. Nearly all grammarians appealed to Universal Grammar in establishing their "rules." But since there was little clarity about what the syntactic rules of this grammar might be (the syntactic structure was barely formalized at all, unlike the semantic one), many grammarians appealed to Authority (tradition, whether Latin, Greek, or literary) and to usage (of the gentry). Perhaps the most famous of the prescriptive grammars were Bishop Lowth's *Short Introduction to English Grammar* (1762, 1775); Lindley Murray's *English Grammar* (1795), in part an imitation of Lowth's grammar; and Noah Webster's *A Grammatical Institute of the English Language* (2 parts, 1783–1784). Webster, and before him Joseph Priestley (in *The Rudiments of English Grammar,* 1761) were determined to support their prescriptivism openly from current usage; Lowth and Murray, however, preferred to refer to a largely mystical notion of Universal Grammar and to Authority – while in actual fact often basing their ideas on usage (with a considerable dose of personal preference in addition).

It is hardly surprising, given the variety of impetuses that led to prescriptivism and the vagueness of notions of Universal Grammar, that there was quite substantial disagreement on particulars. One thing that everybody did agree on, however, was that Universal Grammar did not tolerate redundancies or alternate structures with identical function. As

---

[12] For a detailed account of some theories of Universal Grammar, see Salmon (1966).

[13] For a résumé and discussion in terms of the seventeenth-century philosophical background of Wilkins' treatise, see Emery (1948).

we shall see, such redundancies as multiple negation were anathema to those who worked with the principles of Universal Grammar; so too were alternations such as the presence or absence of a meaningless tense-supporting *do* or the random interchange of *shall* and *will.* Yet redundancies in case, such as occur in *whom* versus *who,* were retained presumably because they approximated more readily than totally uninflected pronouns to the Latin and Greek models with their great variety of inflections.

There can be little doubt that the prescriptive notions developed in the eighteenth century, many of which are still to be found in present-day schoolbooks (despite radical changes in social conditions and ideas about literary form and style and about philosophy), have significantly affected educated written English. There is little evidence, however, that the spoken language has been anywhere near as greatly influenced. Much of the discussion in the following pages will in fact be devoted to showing how colloquial language has developed independently of prescriptivism.

Quotations in this chapter will be more limited than in the others, since the main issue is the development of forms that have already been discussed and illustrated in Chapter 2. For the same reason, what illustrative material is provided is taken from a wider selection of authors than in the other chapters.

Only those syntactic structures will be considered in which significant change has taken place since ca. 1700; hence there is no discussion of the performative of saying, or of case and its relationship to underlying functions, and so on.

A. THE PERFORMATIVE

Right through the NE period there has been marked concern with the use of the modal auxiliaries in all their functions. Only the broadest outlines of the issue are touched on here.[14]

Predicting versus Promising

During the seventeenth century and especially the eighteenth, several attempts were made to regularize what, as we have seen, was already a marked tendency. In his grammar, *Grammatica Linguae Anglicanae* (1653),[15] John Wallis had already stated that "simple futurity" (prediction of states and events not simultaneous with the time of utterance) should be expressed by *shall* in the first person, *will* in the second and third. But it was not until a century later that details were established.[16] Basing his comments mainly on usage, Lowth, for example, says:

[14] Extensive discussion and numerous examples are to be found in Visser (III:1581–1858), Jespersen (*Modern English Grammar* IV), and Poutsma (1904–1928, Part 2, Section II).

[15] A grammar written in Latin, but one of the least influenced by Latin models; it is primarily descriptive, very rarely prescriptive.

[16] For useful citations of prescriptive dicta see especially Visser (III:1581–1585).

> *Will,* in the first Person singular and plural, promises or threatens; in the second and third Persons, only foretells: *shall,* on the contrary, in the first Person, simply foretells; in the second and third Persons, promises, commands, or threatens. But this must be understood of Explicative Sentences; for when the Sentence is Interrogative, just the reverse for the most part takes place.[17]

It was not until the nineteenth century that such comments were taken as absolute rules.

Shall was from earliest English associated with obligation imposed by someone or something other than the subject of the sentence, whether by circumstances, fate, god, law, society, the speaker, or the like. *Will* was associated with one's own volition, hence with voluntary acts, or in a weaker sense, acts free from external compulsion. When one is foretelling something about oneself, one is usually predicting what circumstances will bring upon one; for example, if I predict my being twenty next Wednesday, I am predicting something in which my volition can play no part since I can have no control over it, hence the form *shall* in *I shall be twenty on Wednesday.* On the other hand, if I as speaker promise to do something, I am usually promising of my own volition, hence the form *will* in *I will go = I promise to go.* The distinction is clearly made in:

> 5.1 Cowper I.164.4 (1779) *I will* (promise) endeavour to say something now, and *shall* (prediction) hope for something in return.

When the subject of the sentence is something other than the speaker, the situation is different. If I, as speaker, take it upon myself that someone else will do something, then I am imposing my will on him, imposing an external obligation, hence *You shall go = I take it upon myself that you should go:*

> 5.2 Spect. 28, I.119.17 (1711) If you will (volition) be pleased to give me a good Word in your Paper, you *shall* (promise) be every Night a Spectator at my Show for nothing.

When predicting about someone else's future or habitual acts, one is not primarily concerned with the sense of external compulsion; it is true that if I predict his going he may not be free from obligation, but whether compulsion is present or not is irrelevant, and *will* is used, not *shall,* as in *He will go = I predict his going,* and also in:

> 5.3 Walpole I.35.21 (1744) I foresee there *will* be but little method in my letter.

[17] Robert Lowth, *A Short Introduction to English Grammar: with Critical Notes.* London, 1775 (rev. ed.), pp. 78–79.

The "proper" distinction between *shall* and *will* was taken in the eighteenth century as an infallible marker of good speech. Eighteenth-century editors of Shakespeare, like Pope, felt it was a blot on Shakespeare's language that he did not always observe the distinction and "corrected" his language. That opinions were so strong and that so many pages were spent on laying out the proper usage suggests that in actual practice the distinction was not rigidly adhered to. Where the distinction was not made, it was *shall* that usually predominated in the early part of the period. For example, Addison and Steele in the *Spectator* frequently use *I shall* instead of *I will* in a promissory way:

5.4 Spect. 10, I.44.15 (1711) Since I have raised to my self so great an Audience, I *shall* spare no Pains to make their Instruction agreeable.

One construction in which *shall* continued to be very common was the "generalized prediction," often involving habitual aspect, as in *You shall find that. . . .* In the *Spectator* we find both *shall* and *will:*

5.5 Spect. 53, I.225.34 (1711) 'Tis sure . . . that a sort of undistinguishing People *shall* banish from their Drawing–Rooms the best bred Men in the World.
5.6 Spect. 57, I.241.16 (1711) He is likewise a wonderful Critick in Cambrick and Muslins, and *will* talk an Hour together upon a Sweet–meat.

Concerned as they were with "future predictions," the grammarians had little or nothing to say about the habitual, distributive *shall/will* in predictions. They were, however, very common, and *shall* continued to be used interchangeably with *will* until the end of the nineteenth century when *will* took over almost completely.

It was always recognized that the prescriptive distinction between *shall* and *will* was primarily based on Southern British English. The Irish, Scottish, and Americans were known from the eighteenth century on not to differentiate between them in the same way. In American English *will* has for most people been generalized to both predicting and promising, whatever the subject; the one place where *shall* is still regularly found is in questions like *Shall I go?* (with the *shall* of compulsion, since in a question I am asking you to tell me whether there are external reasons for me to go). By contrast *Will I go?* is usually sarcastic, and is a negative response to an order, suggestion, threat, or the like.

Permitting

From the fourteenth century on, *may* has been the chief manifestation of permission; in the nineteenth century, however, another auxiliary, *can,* came to be used extensively. Despite objections to the ambiguity of *Can I go?* and hence the prescriptive advice to use *may* instead of *can* in questions, *can* is gaining ground and for some people is now the preferred form for permission.

May and *can* have interesting histories. In OE *mag-* was used to translate Latin *posse* 'have the (physical) power to'; *cunn-* was used to translate Latin *scire* 'know how to, have the (intellectual) power to'; as such they were contrasted in:

> 5.7 Chron. 264.24 (1137) I ne *can* ne i ne *mai* tellen alle þe wunder ne alle þe pines 'I not have-the-intellectual-capacity nor I not have-the-physical-capacity to-tell all the wonders nor all the tortures = I have neither the intellectual nor the physical capacity to tell all the wonders or all the tortures'.

and as late as the fourteenth century in:

> 5.8 Ch. Mel. B.2933 we preien yow and biseke yow as mekely as we *konne* (= 'know how') and *mowen* (= 'are able').

Early in ME, *mow* (OE *mag-*) and *koun* (OE *cunn-*), though still contrastable, merged in most contexts as alternate manifestations of 'be able to, have the capacity to, nothing prevents'. The alternation of *koun* with *mow* seems to derive from the use of *koun* with nonhuman subjects; in this context it lost some of its meaning of 'know' (since knowledge is assumed to be a quality of humans only) and was reinterpreted as 'be able to'; hence we get both *mow* and *koun* as 'be able to' in passages like the following:

> 5.9 PL II.73.27 (1445) porveythe therfor that thei *mow* be squarid there, and sentte hedre, for here *can* non soche be hadde in this conttre 'see-to-it therefore that they (the joists) may be squared there and sent hither, for here can none such be had in this part-of-the-country'.

The next step was that the sense of ability came to be extended to *koun* with human subjects, as in:

> 5.10 PL II.86.14 (1448) I am aferd that Jon of Sparham is so schyttyl wyttyd (= 'has wits like a shuttlecock'), that he wyl sett hys gode to morgage . . . but if (= 'unless') I *can* hold hym inne the better.

In the fourteenth century further changes took place. *Mow* was reinterpreted as expressing permission, but *koun* was not, presumably because some sense of the original distinction between physical and mental capacity remained: one can permit someone to do something, that is, not offer physical obstruction; but one cannot usually permit someone to know something intellectually. During the seventeenth century, *may* = *be able to* gave way almost completely to *can,* but continued to be used in the weakened sense of 'possibly' and as the permissive. Then in the nineteenth century *can* itself was reinterpreted (as *mow* had been in the fourteenth century) as the expression of permission. The shifts from the realization of "have the capacity" to the realization of the performative of permission, five hundred years apart as they are, represent the same kind of repeated change that has occurred in other languages too, for instance, German.

Commanding

No very significant changes have occurred in the manifestation of commanding. As far as imperatives are concerned, the main change is that forms like *You go* (with an overt addressee) which were common in OE and ME but dropped out almost entirely in the ENE period reappear at the beginning of the eighteenth century (Visser [I:17–18] claims he found no examples between 1475 and 1695). Visser finds the construction again first in Congreve:

5.11 Congreve, Love for Love I.1.7 (1695) you go to breakfast.

and speculates that at this period it was slang. It has persisted primarily in the spoken language and can be found in many fixed phrases such as *Never you mind, You take it from me,* usually with stress on the *you.*

The major change in question structures is in the word order. By the end of the nineteenth century such forms as *Came he?* are totally replaced by *Did he come?* in most dialects. The development of a predictable *do* in questions along with the generalization of the *Auxiliary + Subject + Verb . . .* word-order pattern is discussed on pages 176 and 185.

B. THE PROPOSITION

The Verb and Associated Arguments

The Verb

Perhaps one of the most marked characteristics of verbs in the NE period is the development of *Verb + Particle* phrases replacing single-word verbs. While this development is primarily of interest to lexicography, it is also important in syntax as it illustrates yet another type of segmentalization that has occurred in the history of English. Bureaucrats have long been accused of cultivating words like *finalize* which turn a phrase like *make final* into a one-word verb, but the main trend in everyday speech has in fact been the reverse.

Verb + Particle constructions date back to OE, but they were relatively rare before ENE. By the mid-eighteenth century Dr. Johnson noted that they were "more frequent in our language than perhaps in any other."[18] In British English after his time the construction seems to have been relatively unproductive. In America, however, it became increasingly productive during the NE period and is known as one of the major differences between British and American (though the distinction is becoming less and less clear with the continued borrowing of "Americanisms" into British English). Such *Verb + Particle* expressions as *build up* (in the meaning 'advertise, exalt'), *start up* (an engine), *fall for, brew up, lose out,* and especially the multi-particle constructions like *miss out on, meet up with* are either not listed in the British-English based OED or are, like *lose out,* marked as Americanisms. Several of the *Verb + Particle* constructions imply concentration on the end-point of the action (compare *drink:drink up; shut:shut up, shut down; burn: burn up, burn down*). The particle can in these instances be considered a kind of segmentalization of an underlying perfective meaning.

Other kinds of segmentalization involve the replacement of a verb by an auxiliary (or a semi-auxiliary) and an NP, as in *look at* → *have a look, call me* → *give me a call, launder* → *do the laundry.* It is quite an instructive (and amusing) exercise to experiment and see how many verbs are actually necessary in NE in order to communicate intelligibly. The number is remarkably small, and the verbs involved are nearly all like the following: *be, become, cause, do, get, give* (= *cause to have,* as in *I have a headache from reading* → *Reading gives me a headache*); in other words, verbs whose primary function is to express basic semantic-syntactic verbal structures.

Nominal Expressions

The functions of nominal expressions

PREPOSITIONS. The way in which nominal expressions in particular functions are manifested remains in essence the same from ENE through the present day. The chief change, as far as the structures we have been looking at are concerned, is the loss of *of* and *with* in nonsubjectivalized Agent expressions. In the early part of the eighteenth century, *with* is primarily associated with Instruments, but it also occurs with what we would consider Agentive expressions. Some authors allowed more variation than others, but many, like Dryden, used *by* with what we would think of as human Agents and *with* with nonhuman (but animate) Agents; so one may be bitten *by* a person but bitten *with* a snake. It may be, however, that, in keeping with contemporary definitions of the soul as human-specific, and of agency as a property of the soul, eighteenth-century writers who used *with* instead of *by* for nonhumans, did so because they did in fact not attribute agency to nonhuman animates—in other words, they may have considered nonhuman animates as capable of being only Instruments, not Agents. With the rise of romanticism in

[18] Johnson, Preface to the *Dictionary,* n.p.

the late eighteenth century, animals were once more endowed with a soul and were felt to be capable of agency; it is surely not coincidental that the *by* preposition came to be favored over *with* in passives in the early part of the nineteenth century. The changes involved here show well how cultural, including philosophical, changes may affect the particular syntactic realization of a pattern; the pattern itself remains unchanged, however.

Of particular interest is the sudden popularity at the end of the seventeenth century of a construction, sometimes called the "emphatic genitive," as in *one hell of a mess, a genius of a fellow*. The emphatic genitive originally developed in very late ME, probably as a borrowing from French. Mustanoja (1960:82) cites such examples as:

5.12 Malory, Morte Darthur (Caxton, ed. by Sommer) 117 he was a ryght good knyght *of a yonge man.*

It had never gained popularity and until the end of the seventeenth century was very rare. At that time, however, it became common and has remained productive ever since. Apparently the sudden increase in the use of the construction in the later seventeenth century was due to reborrowing from French.

SUBJECTIVALIZATION AND OBJECTIVALIZATION. Subjectivalization patterns were largely established in ENE and will not concern us here.

As we saw in the last chapter (p. 120), the proliferation of objectivalization was typical from ME on. Whether he was following his own personal dislikes or a trend of the times is not clear, but Murray objected in his *Grammar* to this proliferation, and in particular to such forms as *to agree the sacred with the profane;* he presumably would have objected also to Boswell's expression in:

5.13 Bos. 85.23 (1763) You *joked her* at his not dreading the English as gallants.

In British English there was a marked trend away from objectivalization in such constructions from the nineteenth century on. In American, however, objectivalization, especially of directional and locational functions, continued. In his study of British and American syntax, Kirchner (1957:37–38) cites the following as Americanisms: *slip the notice, wonder the same thing, stay the course, fly the Atlantic, walk the streets,* and points out that constructions of this kind came to be largely idiomatic or technical in British English before the influence of American English reintroduced them in their literal meanings in the 1920s; for example, *to walk the streets* means (or meant) in British English only to be a prostitute, whereas in American English it meant both to be a prostitute and literally to walk around the streets.

The trend has not all been away from objectivalization, however.

In neither British nor American are the following typical eighteenth-century locutions current any more: *I accept of your offer, I miss of it,* and *I consider of the matter.* The changes are ultimately specifiable only in terms of particular lexical items and the particular functions associated with them, not of large categories, so we can only note a tendency, not a distinct change.

The structure of nominal expressions

NUMBER. Where number agreement of verbs with collective nouns is concerned, there has been some divergence between British and American. In British English collectives like *government, team, group,* and so on tend to have plural agreement, in American singular. The kind of switch from plural to singular as in *the group were X and was Y* that we found in earlier English (pp. 85 and 133) is no longer common.

PRONOUNS. In NE the form *you* totally replaced *thou* except in religious and archaic contexts, whatever the social status of the addressee. In what Leonard claims to be one of the first prescriptive statements, George Fox (*A Battle-Door for Teachers and Professors to Learn Singular and Plural,* 1660) had attacked the use of *you* for a singular addressee in the mid-seventeenth century, but such protests had no effect.

A distinction between informal and formal second person singular was, nevertheless, maintained elsewhere in the system after the *thou–you* contrast was no longer available. If the pronoun contrast was lost, the distinction between singular and plural verb forms was not – with the loss of *thou* the second person singular *-st* verb inflection was lost too, but the third person singular *-s* form was used as a replacement of *-st*. Speaking of himself in his diaries with the familiar *you,* Boswell says:

5.14 Bos. 199.10 At night you *was* clear and resolved to go on manly.

and, in more elegant vein, Horace Walpole writes to his friend George Montagu:

5.15 Walpole I.192.19 (1768) I wish you *was* still more a Tartar, and shifted your quarters perpetually.

Many grammarians attacked such usage on the grounds that *you* is a plural form and therefore should have a plural verb; Lowth, for example, condemned *you was* as "an enormous Solecism"; but others like Noah Webster defended it. It became unfashionable in the nineteenth century and is now considered nonstandard.

The desire to make some distinction at least between second singular and second plural, if not between second singular informal and second singular formal, has led to the development of new distinctions, such as *you-all* (U.S. Southern and Midland), *you-uns* (U.S. Midland), and *youse* (Scottish, Anglo-Irish and U.S. Midland), but none has gained full acceptance in standard dialects.[19]

Tense

Of main interest is the development of *do,* the meaningless tense-carrier that was so frequently used in later ME and ENE. By 1700 the modern English system was very largely established, with *do* as a tense-carrier in negatives, questions, and emphatic affirmations, but not in simple assertions; nevertheless, the older system, where *do* was optional, continued in use especially in negative constructions, through the nineteenth century among some authors and in some dialects (for example, Southwestern dialects of British English). Perhaps the commonest construction in which the conservative use of a negative without *do* occurs is *X know(s) not:*

> 5.16 Walpole I.129.15 (1761) Houghton, *I know not* what to call it, a monument of grandeur or ruin!

Absence of *do* with *know* had been typical from earliest times and continued well into the late nineteenth century and even the twentieth.

In the mid-eighteenth century, Dr. Johnson condemns *do* in assertions, apparently largely on the grounds that it is redundant: "*Do* is sometimes used superfluously, as, *I* do love, *I* did *love;* simply for *I love,* or *I loved;* but this is considered as a vitious mode of speech."[20] He then follows up his criticism with the observation that *do* is frequently used in negatives, but its chief use is in interrogatives. Dr. Johnson's comments suggest that the ENE system was perhaps more prevalent in the spoken language than we might be made to think by the more elegant style of contemporary writings, or even some of the earlier grammars, like those of Alexander Gill (*Logonomia Anglica,* 1662) and John Wallis (*Grammatica Linguae Anglicanae,* 1653), which claim that *do* is intensive only.[21]

In the history of *do* we see a set of changes that brought into being a new auxiliary and then restricted it again. If we concentrate simply on the presence or absence of *do* we can observe in the development of

---

[19] Kurath (1949) uses the term Midland for the area of the Delaware Valley spreading West to the Upper Ohio Valley, Western North and South Carolina; this area has very distinctive linguistic characteristics that sharply differentiate it from both North and South.

[20] Johnson, "A Grammar of the English Tongue," prefaced to the *Dictionary,* n.p.; section entitled "Of the Verb."

[21] Gill and Wallis were probably either mistaken or being prescriptive without acknowledging it, since many instances of *do* occur which can hardly be intensifiers.

auxiliary *do* an elaboration at the phrasal level (a new segmentalization), and later an elaboration in the specification of the contexts in which *do* could occur. If we think of the function of *do* in the grammar as a whole, however, we can see that when *do* was restricted to certain obligatory specifiable contexts, such word orders as *Subject + Verb + not, Verb + Subject + X* no longer operated side by side with *Subject + Auxiliary + not + Verb, Auxiliary + Subject + Verb + X.* In respect of word order, therefore, the grammar was considerably simplified by the restriction of *do.* For more details on word order, see page 185.

The only exception to the obligatory presence of *do* is in sentences with *be* and *have,* but even with these, dialects vary considerably. *I do be happy* is a form that has never been accepted in Southern British or standard American dialects; nevertheless, it does occur in Anglo-Irish and in various nonstandard dialects, as in *I do be afeard* and before auxiliary *be:*

> 5.17 Synge, Playboy I Is it often the polis do be coming into this place?

It was well into the nineteenth century before the main verb *have* came to be acceptable with *do.* Most Americans use *do* in the appropriate structures where any *have* verb is concerned, but in British English *do* is not usually used if *have* is the *have* of inalienable possession; for example, British *Hasn't she (got) blue eyes? She has blue eyes, hasn't she?* versus American *Doesn't she have blue eyes? She has blue eyes, doesn't she?* Aspect also makes a difference for the presence or absence of *do* with *have* in British, though not American speech; in British English *When have you to leave?* is a question about obligation on one particular occasion, but *When do you have to leave?* is a question about a recurrent habit. The way in which generalizations of a syntactic element (in this case *do*-support) operate on underlying rather than surface structures (alienable versus inalienable possession, habitual versus nonhabitual) is very well illustrated once again by these examples. The resulting differences in surface forms present the kind of condition that encourages change; perhaps it is not just borrowing from American English that has resulted in many people's using *do* with *have* whether inalienable or not, whether momentary or not, but the pressure of other verbs, since *do* is regularly used with all of them (except, of course, *be*).

Aspect

Distributive Habitual

For some developments in the realization of distributive habitual associated with other elements in the sentence, see the section on predicting.

Progressive

By about 1700 *be* + *PrP* was restricted in Southern British roughly as it is now to the expression of ongoing activity at a moment of time. In some dialects *be* + *PrP* was extended to other contexts; for example, it is used in Irish both as the progressive and as the marker of simple nonpast tense, as in *It's the books, I'm thinking,* perhaps under the influence of Celtic.[22] The use of *be* + *PrP* with normally stative, non-action verbs to express the meaning *behaving as if X were Y* (as in *Do you think I am being a fink?*) is apparently largely a late nineteenth-century development.

One of the main developments involving progressive is the emergence of an overt passive progressive construction of the type *It was being discussed by the panel.* In the last chapter (p. 144) we saw how phrases of the type *It was building* are often interpreted as passives although the absence of an overt Agentive phrase brings into question their status as true passives. Constructions of this type were typical of eighteenth-century English:

> 5.18 Swift, Gulliver XI.96.25 I guessed *there was some Mischief contriving.*

but did not always meet the approval of the pundits. Dr. Johnson, for one, considered it a "vitious expression";[23] presumably he preferred active constructions like *I guessed someone was contriving some mischief.* By the end of the century the passive progressive suddenly appears in letters, as in:

> 5.19 Southey I.249.24 (1795) like a fellow whose uttermost upper grinder *is being torn out* by the roots by a mutton-fisted barber.

The opprobrium was great at first; the construction was considered "unharmonious" at best, "clumsy," "a philological coxcombry," even "a monstrosity," "illogical, confusing, inaccurate, unidiomatic."[24] Nevertheless, it was used extensively in informal letter style in the early part of the nineteenth century (Macaulay, for example, uses it in his letters but not in his literary works where he prefers the *It was doing* construction), and by the end of the nineteenth century it was fairly well established even in literary works, although some opposition continued until the end of the century. The development of progressive passives represents the generalization of the whole auxiliary system to passives, and as such is an excellent example of simplification by generalization (see p. 14).

---

[22] Both Irish and Welsh have phrasal constructions corresponding to our *be* + *ing* form that are used to express habitual, progressive and simple nonpast with statives.

[23] Johnson, *op. cit.*, "Of the Verb."

[24] R. G. White, *Words and Their Uses,* 1871, pp. 334–363; quoted by Mossé (1938:157).

Perfect

The use of the *be* + *PP* perfect became more and more recessive until it was lost entirely in standard English during the twentieth century. As late as the mid-eighteenth century Dr. Johnson, however, considers it the proper perfect for "neuter verbs," that is, intransitive verbs, and cites *I am risen, I was walked out.*[25]

There are some difference between British and American English in the use of *have* + *PP* that reflect the kinds of constructions we found in earlier English. It is often pointed out that the perfect frequently has no overt expression as an auxiliary in American English if an adverb like *just* is present: *I just got here, Your friend just came,* whereas in British English forms like *I have just got here* are preferred. As we saw, absence of *have* + *PP* where we would expect it was typical in OE and usual in ME and ENE; it is still quite usual in the eighteenth century:

5.20 Walpole I.131.12 (1761) their very language *is polished* since I lived among them (= 'has become polished').

In respect of the absence of *have* + *PP,* then, American English is more conservative than British English (by contrast, it is more innovative in the use of *do*).

Negation

Little need be said here except that multiple negation was rarely used in standard English by 1700. As in ENE, the one construction in which it was found at all frequently was in coordinations:

5.21 Walpole I.71.27 (1752) I have not lost one enamel, *nor* bronze; *nor* have not been shot through the head again.

Basing their opinions no doubt in part on standard usage, but ostensibly on the notion that Universal Grammar followed the rules of logic, the grammarians legislated that multiple negatives "absolutely prove what you mean to deny"[26] and were not to be tolerated in polite speech. They have continued in use in most nonstandard dialects, however.

C. THE FORMATION OF COMPLEX SENTENCES

Complements

Relics of the Subjunctive

Looking back at earlier NE we find examples like the following of what appear to be regular descendants of the old inflectional subjunctive. By this time the inflection has no overt form except in the verb *be,*

[25] Johnson, *op. cit.,* "Of the Verb."

[26] John Clarke, *Rational Spelling Book,* 1796, p. 83; quoted by Leonard (1929:93).

but clearly contrasts with the indicative in the nonpast (subjunctive *He ride* versus indicative *He rides):*

5.22 Spect. 143, II.65.6 (1711) if a Servant is order'd to present him with a Porringer of Cawdle or Posset-Drink, by way of Admonition that he *go* Home to Bed.

It is interesting to see how varied opinions on the subjunctive were in the eighteenth and nineteenth centuries. Many grammarians, like Lowth and Priestley, speak of a subjunctive of doubt, hesitation, condition, possibility, and so on, subsuming both the auxiliaries and the inflection under subjunctive, that is, giving a primarily semantic definition of the subjunctive. Many grammarians felt that what I am calling the inflectional subjunctive was in fact not inflectional, but a verbal phrase with a modal auxiliary deleted. Among those who adhered to this view were Priestley and William Cobbett. In his *Grammar of the English Language in a Series of Letters* (1818), Cobbett carried the theory so far as to rule that forms like *Were he rich* should not be used at all since there is no reason for *were;* for example, it cannot be derived by deletion of a modal (Letter 19).

Others regarded some of the forms that were not readily accounted for by deletion of a modal as purely conventional. For example, in the first edition of his *Grammatical Institute of the English Language,* Webster cites subjunctive forms for the verb *be,* but in the second he does not; instead he simply states that *be* is the form used after *if* and other conjunctions, as in *if he be there.* It may not be wholly idle to speculate that he associated this *be* with the reflex of OE *beo-* that occurred in some dialects since he calls it indicative but "vulgar."

All agreed that the subjunctive (that is, the inflection) was rare. Dr. Johnson went so far as to say it was almost "wholly neglected" at his time, but was used "among the purer writers of former times after *if, though, ere, before, till,* or *until, whether, except, unless, whatsoever, whomsoever,* and words of wishing."[27] There is no question that the subjunctive was recessive, though it was not "wholly neglected."

Subjunctives in complements without overt main clauses were the most recessive. Wishes have not survived except in phrases like *Long live the President!* and a multitude of expletives like *Damn you!* Exhortations have survived only in a few fixed phrases like *Please you to go, Fare you well* (with Type 2 word order). With main verbs other than *wish* they very largely died out except in highly formal prose and legal language. Jespersen (*Modern English Grammar* IV:161) quotes as an excellent example of the distinction between subjunctive and indicative surviving in formal language the following congressional resolution reported in a newspaper of 1896:

5.23 That the President *be* and *is* hereby requested to invite negotiations with any Government.

[27] Johnson, *op. cit.,* "Of the Verb."

Be expresses an intent, *is* the fact that a request is made.

Recently there has been a trend in American English to favor the subjunctive once more as opposed to the indicative or the segmentalized *should,* especially in complements of verbs like *suggest, insist, recommend,* as in:

5.24 I suggest that Ronnie forge (subjunctive) checks (a kind of exhortation).

as contrasted with:

5.25 I suggest that Ronnie forges (indicative) checks (he actually does it).

The subjunctive as in 5.24 was retained after 1600 mainly in the spoken language of the Pilgrim Fathers and their descendants (although it is rarely attested in written documents after ME), so the form is not an innovation, only an example of the reversal of the trend away from subjunctives. What *is* an innovation is the word order in negative subjunctive complements:

5.26 I suggest that Ronnie not forge that check.

since *not* always follows the verb in earlier English. Its position can be explained by arguing either that a modal auxiliary has been deleted or that the *not* is emphatic. Since modal auxiliaries are not deleted before *not* in other constructions the first argument simply leaves us with another question. The second is not entirely satisfactory either, but at least suggests affinities with structures elsewhere in the system which emphasize an element by putting it at the beginning of the clause, as in *Not laugh but cry is what I feel like doing.*

The auxiliary *should* remained during the eighteenth century the chief replacement of the subjunctive inflection. It was not until the nineteenth century that *would* came to be used extensively for second and third person subjects. Nevertheless, the last hundred years or so have seen a significant reduction in the use of *should* and *would* where OE had the subjunctive; in complements of nonpast main clauses, *shall* or *will* is used, or just nonpast instead of *should* or *would.* Consider, for example, how strange the past auxiliary sounds to us in:

5.27 Wycherley I.79.4, Love in a Wood I.i. But I am afraid this double plot of yours *Should* fail.

Subject Complements

It is apparently during the NE period that factive complements of the type *(the fact) that . . .* began to occur in subject position, as in *The fact that he used the gun is obvious.* When they first occur is not discussed in the standard grammars. Jespersen (*Modern English Grammar* III: 24–27) regards *The fact that . . .* constructions, with the whole underlying factive structure in overt form, as a later development than subjectivalized factives introduced by *that* alone, as in *That he used the gun is obvious.* Jespersen calls the presence of *the fact* a device to prop up the clause, and gives the following quotation from Macaulay apparently as one of the first instances known to him:

5.28 Macaulay, History I.31 But the fact that it was thought necessary to disguise these exactions under the names of benevolences and loans sufficiently proves that the authority of the great constitutional rule was recognized.

In any event, such subjectivalized factives are fairly late developments in the history of English and are found mainly in formal and scientific writing. The *it*-construction continues to be favored for factives. Subject-position is still not available for nonfactives of the *that* . . . type:

5.29 *That he witnessed the accident is likely.

Relative Clauses

In the eighteenth century there was considerable debate about the appropriate form of the relative pronoun and also about when relative pronouns could be deleted. Most modern standard dialects, at least those exemplified in informal writing, are characterized by a system close to that agreed on by the eighteenth-century grammarians, perhaps partly under the influence of those grammarians, but doubtlessly also in part because the grammarians based their prescriptivism on dialects closely connected with modern standard English. Nonstandard dialects and often the conversational style of standard dialects resemble the ENE system more closely than the grammarians' system, however.

Full Clauses

In the *Spectator,* no. 78 (1711), Steele published what purported to be a letter from a correspondent, but which was probably his own. It is entitled "The humble Petition of *Who* and *Which,*" and is an attack on the use of *that* as a relative. Steele argues that *that* was a "Jack-sprat" (upstart) that had ousted *who* and *which.* He was of course wrong in claiming that the *wh-* forms were older. It is true, however, that *that* had once more become extremely common as the relative in the seventeenth century. Franz (1939:304–305), for example, shows that many of the *wh-* forms in the Shakespeare Quarto editions were replaced by *that* in the Folio. What is interesting is that this "petition" expresses a whole set of notions that still persist in many grammar books: that *that* should not be used too much (the restriction of *that* to restrictive relatives is not one of Steele's suggestions, however; that change seems to have occurred spontaneously); that *who* should be restricted to human antecedents, *which* to nonhuman. Steele objects vehemently to the "misuse" of *which* in the Lord's Prayer: *Our father which art in heaven.* Not all agreed with him about the Lord's Prayer, preferring to respect tradition rather than grammar in ritual prayers, but they agreed fully with the distinction between *who* and *which* in contemporary language; they went on to argue that *whose* is the genitive only of *who* and not of *which,* a notion that is not fully reflected in modern English and never has been. In his edition of Shakespeare's plays Pope "corrected" *who* with nonhuman antecedents to *which,* sometimes even where personification was involved. He also "corrected" *what* to *which;* here he was responding to a social distinction that was already fairly well developed in the eighteenth century—*nothing what* was by then largely "uneducated" usage. The distinction Pope made between *who* and *which* was probably not such a sociolinguistic response, but derived from his philosophical attitude to Agents and the concept of voluntary versus nonvoluntary action, responsibility versus absence of responsibility, an attitude we have already seen in the section on the use of prepositions.

If opinions were strong about *who* versus *which*, they were stronger still about *who* versus *whom.* Pope, for example, seems to have observed the formula:

A. Nongenitive relative and interrogative: *who,* if subject or predicate nominal; *whom* elsewhere.

He emended *who* to *whom* wherever it occurred in Shakespeare in nonsubject and nonpredicate nominal function, whether it was the relative *who* or the interrogative *who.* Here the appeal was clearly to the model of Latin and other inflected languages where nominative was associated with the subject and predicate nominal functions.

The general drift of the language was, however, in just the opposite direction. In ENE the system generally was:

B. i. Nongenitive relative: *who,* if subject or predicate nominal; *whom* elsewhere.
   ii. Nongenitive interrogative: *whom,* if object of preposition; *who* elsewhere.

though very few authors showed complete consistency in their use of *who* and *whom.* One of the few who did was Wycherley, writing in the latter part of the seventeenth century, just at the transition between ENE and NE. During the eighteenth century more and more "conversational" writings show a tendency for the relatives to have the same pattern as the interrogatives:

C. Nongenitive relative and interrogative: *whom,* if object of preposition; *who* elsewhere.

In other words, we find the generalization of a system based on position rather than function, as we saw also in the distribution of the personal pronouns *I* versus *me,* and so on (p. 125). In many people's spoken, but not written language, a further generalization has taken place that has resulted in the optional extension of *who* to all contexts; it is only in nonstandard dialects that this generalization has led to the total loss of *whom* as in *To who did he give it?* The simplification resulting from this generalization can readily be seen in the formula:

D. Nongenitive relative and interrogative: *who.*[28]

Another prescriptive notion that did not take hold was that prepositions should be moved with the relativized noun as in *The man for whom I voted.* Lowth and other eighteenth-century grammarians favored the co-occurrence of relative and preposition, but most of them saw that the language favored splitting the two, as in *The man whom I voted for.* It is not until the nineteenth century that prescriptivists insisted that the split was wrong; there is little evidence this this dictum had any substantive effect on the spoken language.

In previous chapters we saw that it was relatively common to use the uninflected relative together with a personal pronoun to substitute for the relativized NP. By the beginning of NE such constructions became obsolete in standard English; they did, however, continue in use in nonstandard dialects. Franz (1939:298) cites various nineteenth-century authors using it to capture the "uneducated" English of their time, including:

5.30 Dickens, Martin Chuzzlewit XL.316 As a good friend of mine has frequent made remark to me, *which her* name, my love, is Harris.

Reduced Clauses

Once again, a sharp distinction must be drawn between the written and the spoken language in the NE period. For most speakers the ENE system that permits deletion of any relative still persists, though many educated speakers who are more conscious of the way they write than the way they speak may actually think that their use of this construction is considerably more limited than it is.

In the written language, and in spoken language influenced by written language, however, a whole set of restrictions now operate, resulting in a much more complex set of relative reduction rules than existed earlier. For example, the relative may be deleted only if it functions as the object of the verb or preposition, or if it functions as the subject of *be + Adjective* or *be + Adverb;* if a subject relative is deleted, *be* must

[28] The history of interrogative and relative *who* is discussed in great detail in Klima (1965).

be too. The development of such elaborate constraints may in part result from attempts to avoid the ambiguities that may result from the more generalized deletion rules, as in:

5.31 I saw the man voted (that he voted, *or* the man who voted).

and the perceptual complexities of such nonambiguous sentences as:

5.32 The fellow over there just voted is an FBI agent.

(Most listeners would interpret the first part as a complete sentence and would have to reprocess the utterance on hearing *is an FBI agent.*)

Connected with the development of constraints on the reduction of relatives is the recessiveness during NE of prenominal past participles. Largely derived as these were from perfects, when the *be* + *PP* perfect was no longer used, and when a subject relative could be reduced only if followed by a *be* verb, the conditions for prenominal past participles no longer obtained, except when they had underlying passive structures. So we do not find **the disappeared seals*, **the arrived letter* but we do find *The captured convict*. Such constructions as *the fallen leaves* nearly all involve stative resultatives rather than pure perfects and are derivable from relative clauses of the type *The leaves which are fallen;* they are therefore not counter-examples to the widespread loss in NE of prenominal perfect participles.

As we have seen, from OE times on there has been a tendency for adjectives to follow the noun if they have complements but to precede if they do not. It was only in NE that this restriction became obligatory. Such phrases as *the citizen responsible* versus *the responsible citizen*, the *stars visible* versus *the visible stars* are not exceptions, as in all instances of seemingly postnominal adjectives there is very clearly an underlying complex structure that has been suppressed; it includes such elements as "at that particular time" and complements like "(visible) specifically to us," "(guilty) specifically of that deed".

D. WORD ORDER

Numerous minor changes in word order have occurred during the last two or three centuries. Perhaps the most significant in terms of the structures we have been looking at is the generalization of the word order in yes–no questions and in negatives. From the OE period on there were two word orders for yes–no questions, one for sentences with auxiliaries, one for sentences without; similarly, with the development in ME of *not* as the main negative, there came to be two orders from the ME period on for negative sentences, one for those with auxiliaries, one for those without:

A. Yes–no Question i. Auxiliary Subject Verb . . .
ii. Verb Subject . . .

B. Negative   i. Subject Auxiliary not Verb . . .
    ii. Subject Verb not . . .

When *do* developed as the causative auxiliary, the dummy tense-carrier, and as the manifestation of *truly*, it patterned with the auxiliaries. Meaningless, dummy *do* may well have come to be used as extensively as it was in part because it provided a means for generalizing the auxiliary pattern.

The coexistent systems of questions with just main verbs, and questions with dummy *do* and main verb were, for most speakers, simplified as early as 1700 with the loss of A. ii. The coexistent systems in negative sentences were for most speakers simplified by about 1900 with the loss of B. ii. (For a gross sketch of the changes, see Appendix B.) Once more we find an example of the way in which similar changes may affect different parts of the syntactic system at different times as part of an overall drift toward generalization.

Another change that we have seen is in relative clause constructions. Where earlier an *Adjective + Complement* could follow the noun as in *a man friendly to me* and could even occasionally be preposed to the noun as in *a friendly to me man*, in NE *Adjective + Complement* is almost exclusively postnominal and the simple adjective is prenominal. Again we have a reduction in available choices, and hence a simplification, though when we also take into account the fact that adjectives without complements typically occur prenominally we can see that maximum simplification has not occurred; a simpler system yet would be one where all adjective expressions are preposed to the noun – a system close to this is actually to be found in German – or one where all adjectives are postposed.

One rather frequently mentioned difference between British and American word order may be of interest here in demonstrating how a certain type of simplification may occur in one dialect but not in another. In sentences of the type *I* (Agent) *gave the letter* (Patient) *to Jane* (Goal), the Patient is objectivalized, that is, follows the verb without a preposition; a further rule will allow the "indirect objectivalization" of Goal so that it occurs without preposition between the verb and the object:

5.33 Give the letter to Jane (objectivalization only).
5.34 Give Jane the letter (objectivalization + indirect objectivalization).

In many dialects of American English, if one or both of Patient and Goal are pronouns, the same patterns occur:

5.35 Give it to Jane.
5.36 Give it to her.
5.37 Give her the letter.
5.38 Give her it (usually pronounced as an ellided *Giverit*).

In earlier English, however, the order had been somewhat different. In particular, indirect object pronouns usually followed the object pronouns as in:

5.39 Nashe UT II.254.8 He shewed *her* (object) vs (indirect object) without anie more adoe, sicke weeping on her bed.

It is this particular order that is still characteristic of British English. So while we find in British English all the sentence types 5.33–5.37, instead of 5.38, we find:

5.40 Give it her.

The American pattern illustrates the generalization of the nominal to the pronominal order and as such is a considerable simplification over the British system.

E. POSTSCRIPT ON "BLACK ENGLISH"

As I was writing this book, I became increasingly interested in the similarities I had observed between earlier English and Black English of the so-called "street-speech" variety, that is, colloquial Black English, spoken largely in the ghettos in situations where standard English forms are either ignored or openly militated against. Extensive descriptive work is being done on present-day Black English, particularly with attention to the socioeconomic factors that correlate with dialect variation, but little has been done on the historical backgrounds. What historical investigation there has been recently has largely involved arguments about whether Black English is so like other varieties of English as to have the same underlying structure, at least in modern times (see Rosenbaum, 1964), or whether it is so dissimilar that it does not have the same underlying structure as other dialects of NE, but rather one much closer to its "creole" and "pidgin" origins (see especially Dillard, 1968, and Stewart, 1968).[29] Proponents of the first view tend to relate Black English directly to British-based dialects of English spoken mainly in the Southern United States in the seventeenth and eighteenth centuries; proponents of the latter view concentrate on the African origins of Black English and pay very little attention to the British backgrounds. At the present time it seems premature to opt for one position or the other (see Loflin, 1969)—we simply know too little as yet about the structure of Black English or, indeed, in many cases about the structure of those dialects of English with which Black English has had most contact. It is clear that there are still elements in the lan-

[29] As far as earlier studies are concerned, it was for a long time assumed that Black English was derived directly from seventeenth- and eighteenth-century English; differences were felt to be "errors," "confusions," and so on. Little serious attempt was made to prove direct influence of earlier English, however, and no attention was paid to the creole aspects of Black English. For some discussion see Herskovitz (1958), Chapter 8.

guage that have African, and particularly creole, origin. What is not so clear is the extent to which Black dialects have been decreolized, in other words, whether only superficial approximation to English has taken place with little restructuring as Stewart (1968) argues, or whether considerable restructuring has occurred resulting in relatively close approximation to English not only on the surface but also in the underlying structure, as Dillard (1968) suggests may actually be the case. Other questions that are still largely unanswered are: With which dialects of English has there been most contact? And when did that contact occur?

Before going on to discuss particular syntactic structures in Black English in terms of their similarities both to earlier English and to creoles, it may be useful to characterize creoles briefly. Creoles have relatively little inflectional structure, are highly segmentalized, have few alternate variants for underlying structures, and tend to show little syntactic redundancy. Contrary to popular opinion, their underlying structure is as complex as that of other languages; the only way in which they are inferior is in the social status afforded to them and to the speakers of creoles. Typically creoles are spoken where there are several groups of people with different ethnic backgrounds (for instance, African and Indonesian), all of them of socially inferior position; the creole is used among these groups and in communication with the socially dominant group, who usually derive from yet other ethnic backgrounds (for instance, European).

The origins of individual creoles are somewhat in dispute. Some scholars argue that they originated directly in a pidgin – a simplified language typically learned to fit the needs of bare survival in a trading situation. Pidgin English, for example, would have been learned by African slaves needing to communicate the bare necessities to their white masters or overseers (who themselves usually used the pidgin in response). The children of pidgin speakers may learn the pidgin as their own native language. In learning the pidgin they will restructure it, as children will restructure any language they learn; in this case, however, the restructuring is extensive and involves extensive elaboration, not the usual simplification (see p. 11). Other scholars argue that as at least the European-related creoles tend to have remarkably similar characteristics – for example, tense marking is minimal in all, but aspectual marking is quite extensive – it may be that each creole did not develop independently from different pidgins, but rather that all creoles go back to one original creole (and possibly one pidgin). Since a few Portuguese forms appear scattered through most creoles, it has been argued that this original creole was the Portuguese-related *lingua franca* called Sabir that flourished from the Middle Ages up to the beginning of the present century. Present-day English-, French-, Dutch-, Spanish-, and other-related creoles have basically the same structure as Sabir, it is argued, but in each case the vocabulary and to some extent the surface syntactic structures have been modified to approximate the prestige language.[30] The arguments both for and against the theory that Sabir is the original "Proto-creole" are well presented in DeCamp (1968) and will not detain us here since they do not affect the discussion to follow in any crucial way.

Whatever their origins, there are many creoles extant in the world. They are found, for example, in the Philippines, the West Indies, in Africa, India, and also in the United States: Gullah is a creole that is still spoken by Negroes mainly in Georgia and the low country of South Carolina, both areas where blacks greatly outnumbered whites for two centuries. The different kinds of possible interrelationships between creoles and other languages in one area can be illustrated by comparing two groups of countries in the Caribbean in which English is the prestige language. On the one hand we find throughout St. Lucia, Grenada, and Dominica both French- and English-related creoles and also a continuum from the English-related creole to standard English; on the other hand we find in Trinidad a continuum from an English-related creole to standard English, but only pockets or enclaves of French and Spanish creoles in isolated areas. If the political situation changes and no one prestige language continues to exist in a given area, the creole will become a noncreole language with the full range of socioeconomic gradings that are found among any other language. This kind of situation is occurring in the South American country of Surinam where Dutch has ceased to be the prestige language and Sranan (an English- and Dutch-related creole) is coming to be used as the national language. If, however, the political situation does not change radically, the creole may become decreolized and undergo restructuring such that it approximates the prestige language very closely and eventually may become subsumed within it. This sort of decreolization has definitely occurred in Black English; the question is how far the process has gone in Black English of the street-speech variety (it is virtually complete in nearly all other varieites).

The question regarding how far decreolization has occurred in the street-speech variety is still open for a number of reasons. In the absence of extensive reliable historical data there is, for one, the general problem of how far English-related creoles that have been in existence for several hundred years were in the first place influenced by the syntactic structures characteristic of earlier stages of English. Then there is the particular problem that when structures appear in present-day Black English that have similarities with those available both in creoles and in earlier forms of English, it is not always clear exactly what significance should be attached to these similarities. Some resemblances may stem from universal similarities between languages and may therefore be found in any pair of compared languages. Other resemblances may be purely coincidental. Others again may represent restructuring toward the English model. This restructuring may be complete, but it

[30] This process has been called "relexification."

will more often be partial, since the speakers are making hypotheses about external, skewed data; hence a structure in Black English that is typical of creole languages and also has many similarities with seventeenth- and eighteenth-century English but is not identical with the English form is not necessarily of creole origin.[31] A further complication is that Black English itself influenced dialects spoken by whites, so that presence of a form in both white and Black dialects does not necessarily always mean that the form is of English origin (see Dillard, 1967). Another problem, of course, is why decreolization did not take place in certain structures. Various factors must doubtless be considered, such as frequency—for example, Modern English retains several archaisms such as vowel alternation to signal plural in *foot–feet* apparently because of the pressure of the statistical frequency with which this noun is used. Among these factors is the possibility that supposedly persistent creole forms have been reinforced by English forms that already in the eighteenth century were nonstandard or subsequently became so, or even dropped out of use altogether in white dialects; in such cases the lack of decreolization is only apparent. Cases such as these are perhaps the hardest to prove, but they are also the most interesting—most of the examples in the following pages are of this kind.

Any serious study of the history of decreolization of Black English in America must take into account not only the problems discussed in the last paragraph, but also the linguistic conditions among white settlers in seventeenth- and eighteenth-century Virginia, Maryland, Georgia, North and South Carolina, and other states; it must take into consideration whatever little documented evidence there is of earlier Black English, of Gullah both past and present, of creoles and African languages, and so on. Above all, it must consider the social conditions of plantation life from the seventeenth century on and the subsequent effects of migrations to the North and of urban life. Such a complex investigation is not likely to be completed in the near future without cumulative evidence from many studies of individual problems. I offer here a very brief list of some much-studied structures found in the street-speech variety of contemporary Black English which seem to me to have more than random connection with some of the earlier forms of English that we have been looking at in the course of this book, in the hope that they might be suggestive enough to encourage further investigation into the problem of which English dialects influenced which structures during the decreolization process.

Most of the structures we will be looking at resemble Northern English and Scottish forms. This is hardly surprising when we consider that many white Southerners were Ulster-Scots who had migrated to the

---

[31] Consider, for example, the fact that the OE segmentalized perfect was probably reinforced by Latin, although the Latin *hab-* + *PP* perfect was still used primarily with verbs of mental experience; some scholars have even gone so far as to claim borrowing from Latin into OE, despite the distributional differences (see Chapter 3, n. 11).

United States in the 1720s, landing first in the Delaware Bay, but then spreading rapidly west to the Alleghenies and Ohio Valley, and south through Maryland and Virginia to the Carolinas. Originally farmers and tradesmen, the Ulster-Scots settled in the South as indentured servants and farmers. With the growth of the plantations some became overseers, others were pushed out of their farms by the plantation system and became the class now called the "poor whites." It is surely only natural that the Negro slaves would have spoken primarily with their overseers, rather than with the owners, most of whom originated in Southern England and spoke dialects closer to standard British dialects than to the Scotch-Irish "folk-speech" many of the overseers used.

Perhaps one of the best known characteristics of Black English is the use of the uninflected *be* as in:

5.41 It don't usually *be* that way.[32]
5.42 I never *be* in fights.
5.43 When the teacher *be* rappin' to me . . .

Uninflected *be* is sometimes said to be a clearly creole form since it has no equivalents in standard English.

The contexts in which this *be* is used are not fully understood—but this is hardly surprising if we consider that the use of these forms is not native to most of the investigators, and anyway the contexts for the use of such forms as *shall* and *will* are not fully clear even for those who do use them. In the main, invariant *be* is used to express habitual, especially distributive, actions or states; it typically occurs with *when (ever), sometimes, most of the time, usually, always, never,* very rarely with such nondurative, nonhabitual time adverbs as *right now* (though it can occur there too), and never in identity (**She be my mother*). The situation is remarkably similar to one that existed in many creoles, in which expression of aspect rather than tense is very important; but it is also similar to the situation in OE and ME, with relics in Northern ENE, when *beo-* and *wes-* were contrasted. Is this pure coincidence or can we postulate that the creole and English forms reinforced one another? The continuation of *I be* versus *I am* in Scottish ENE dialects (see 4.12) suggests that possibly *be* is not as untypical of English as most investigators assume. This also applies to the form *he/they bes* as in:

5.44 The guys that *bes* around the park with us.

This form is found in Scottish ENE usually for prediction, but some-

[32] My data from Black English is drawn very largely from Labov *et al.* (1968). The observations on creole come from scattered sources, particularly discussions with Miss Lilith Haynes, a speaker of the English-related creole of Guiana; at the time of writing she was engaged in research on creole languages at Stanford University; any misrepresentations are of course solely my responsibility.

times also for habitual aspect. In Black English it is primarily habitual (Labov, *et al.*, 1968:228–243). Restriction to the habitual use of *be/bes* might well be due to the fact that only the aspectual, not the performative, use had similar surface properties in both earlier English and in creole. The restriction to aspectual use certainly does not *de facto* preclude English influence.

The fact that it is largely preadolescents, not adults, who use *be* and *bes* might suggest that the form is innovative rather than conservative. But then neither creole nor English could have any immediate relevance since postulating either English or creole origin presupposes a historical continuum. As *be* is a stigmatized form, having no correspondence in standard English, the lack of it in adult speech may be the result of teen-age concern with emulating prestige forms, and not at all the result of innovative forces.

Constructions with modal auxiliaries also show possible reinforcement by earlier English. Quotation 4.7 illustrates how two modal auxiliaries could occur together in ME, as in *I shall may go.* While constructions of this kind dropped out in the standard language, they remained in some nonstandard dialects during ENE and are still used in white Southern nonstandard, as in:

5.45 I *may can* go out (= 'I may be able to go out').
5.46 You *might ought* to do that.
5.47 I *might could* be worse.

Labov *et al.* (1968:260–263) show that in Black English this double construction has been extended to situations not found in white Southern nonstandard (or in earlier) English, for instance:

5.48 You *must didn't* read it too good.

and consider 5.48 an example of an extension of the double modal in 5.47. Arguing that the constructions are basically parallel, they cite both together in:

5.49 You *might could* go to the church and pray a little, but you—that still *might don't* help you.

Labov *et al.* treat the double modal of 5.47 as having no tense marker (hence *may* and *might* are two different modals, not the same one marked by different tenses), and the *Modal* + *do* construction of 5.48 as an innovation where tense is marked and *do* supports it. Another possibility worth investigating is that constructions like *might could* represent the spread of past tense agreement to the second modal (rather like the spread of the past tense from the auxiliary to the main verb, as in late ME *I did write* → *I did wrote,* and like the spread of the past participle from the auxiliary to the main verb in late ME *I have done finish* → *I have done finished* [see p. 146]). It is also possible that *might don't* is historically not a generalization of *might can, might could,* or the like, but rather a restriction of an already extant English form. In ME modals could not only be followed by other modals; they could also be followed by *do.* Among the many instances of *Modal* + *do* that occur in ME, very few indisputably involve noncausative, tense-supporting *do.* One example is:

5.50 PL IV.149.37 (1465) more playnly than I *may do wryte* at thys tyme.

in which the *do* may or may not be causative.[33] In ENE a modal followed by indisputably noncausative *do* is found chiefly in Scotland; the OED cites as a Scotticism a modal followed by noncausative *do* as early as 1513 (s.v. *do,* 31):

5.51 Douglas, Æneis XIII, x.103 (1513) Onto his ceptre thou *sall do succeid.*

In Black English, according to Labov *et al., Modal* + *do* occurs only in negative sentences whereas in Scottish it occurs in affirmative sentences as well. Another problem is that this structure also appears in creoles. If the construction is of creole origin, then it is not the innovation Labov *et al.* suggest. But the question then arises why it was not decreolized. One reason might be extension of the double modal structure (thus accepting Labov *et al.*'s suggestion in principle but modifying it to fit the hypothesis of creole origin); another might be reinforcement by an earlier English form such as 5.51 and association of *do* with negative (and interrogative and emphatic) structures, but not with affirmative declarative ones.

If *do* could follow modals in ME and ENE, it could follow the perfect *have* + *PP* auxiliary even more readily (see 4.85 and 4.86). In ENE most examples of *have* + *PP* + *do* (+ *PP*) are to be found in Northern English and Scottish texts. Is it too much to speculate that the perfective construction exemplified by:

5.52 We *done got* this far (= 'We have got this far').

is at least influenced by the surface string *X has done V* + *PP*? It is true that many creoles have forms like:

5.53 Him *finish done* (= 'He has quite finished').

and, as a partial alternate, though with less emphasis on the completion:

5.54 Him *done finish* (= 'He has already finished').

---

[33] Margaret Paston is known to have used scribes frequently.

What is important is that Black English does not have 5.53, which is the more usual creole form. Even if 5.52 originated in forms like 5.54, we can explain the generalization of 5.52 (which is not found in standard English) as at least reinforced by the earlier English double perfect structure. That 5.52 has in fact been completely restructured to the English form is reasonably clear considering that the past participle form is used in Black English while it is absent in creoles (the creole form of 5.52 is *We done get this far*). In modern Black English, 5.52 may be accounted for by the same rule that accounts for the optional absence of *have* and *be* in those positions in which standard English may reduce them, for example, *I've done it,* but **What do you've to eat?* Black English *I done it,* but **What do you to eat?* In the light of such observations it seems unnecessary to insist that Black English *He done gone* and similar phrases are exclusively creole in origin, whereas, for example, the Northern British Glasgow dialect *He done gone* is not creole by any stretch of the imagination.

Negation is another area which may reflect earlier English as well as creoles. Multiple negation is common in both Black English and white dialects. Labov *et al.* (1968:273) cite the following sentences with just one underlying negation from Southern white nonstandard speech:

5.55 I *ain't* gonna sit in *no* chair and let *no* crazy lawyer tell me *no* lies about *no* law that *no* judge has in *no* law books that *no* smart politician wrote or *nothin'* like that, *nohow.*

Such constructions are typical of Black speech too. The difference is that where multiple negation is optional for nearly all white nonstandard dialects, for Black English of the street-speech variety in its pure unhypercorrected form, it seems to be obligatory, even to the point of requiring the spread of negative-incorporation into the complement, as in:

5.56 We *ain't* askin' you to go out and ask *no* pig to leave us alone.

Standard English has generalized forms without multiple negation; Black English has generalized those with; other dialects reflect the more elaborate system of earlier English when multiple negation was optional.

Several more similarities between Black English and certain ENE and early NE dialects could be mentioned, even if the comparisons were restricted solely to the kinds of structures discussed in this book. The cumulative effect of these similarities seems to me highly persuasive that earlier British dialects did influence Black English in more than superficial ways; but exactly how far-reaching these influences were cannot be fully determined at the moment in the absence of substantive information about earlier Black English, and especially about its creole origins. One thing these similarities clearly show is that forms which may be stigmatized at one period may be fully acceptable at another, and that stigmatization is purely a function of social conditions, not of the language itself.

APPENDIXES

A THE MODAL AUXILIARIES AND DO

In the course of this book the modal auxiliaries have been treated as the manifestations of underlying structures such as performatives. This approach, designed as it is to demonstrate the continuity of underlying structures as contrasted with surface changes, is rather unusual in anything but theoretical linguistics. A more usual approach is to start with the surface forms, for instance, *can,* and to inquire what functions *can* had at various times; this view anchors on the word for its view of continuity, and as such is a view concentrating on surface forms. It has the advantage of suggesting how, given certain data, younger generations may hypothesize about the structure of the language and sometimes restructure it. While some attempt has been made to incorporate surface considerations of this sort, a clear picture of the changes may not have emerged. This appendix is designed to provide in the grossest terms the major uses of *do* and of the modal auxiliaries discussed in this book, starting from the surface form. For far completer studies, see the major articles and books on the subject, such as those by Ehrman, Ellegård, Fridén, Jespersen, Poutsma, Visser, and others.

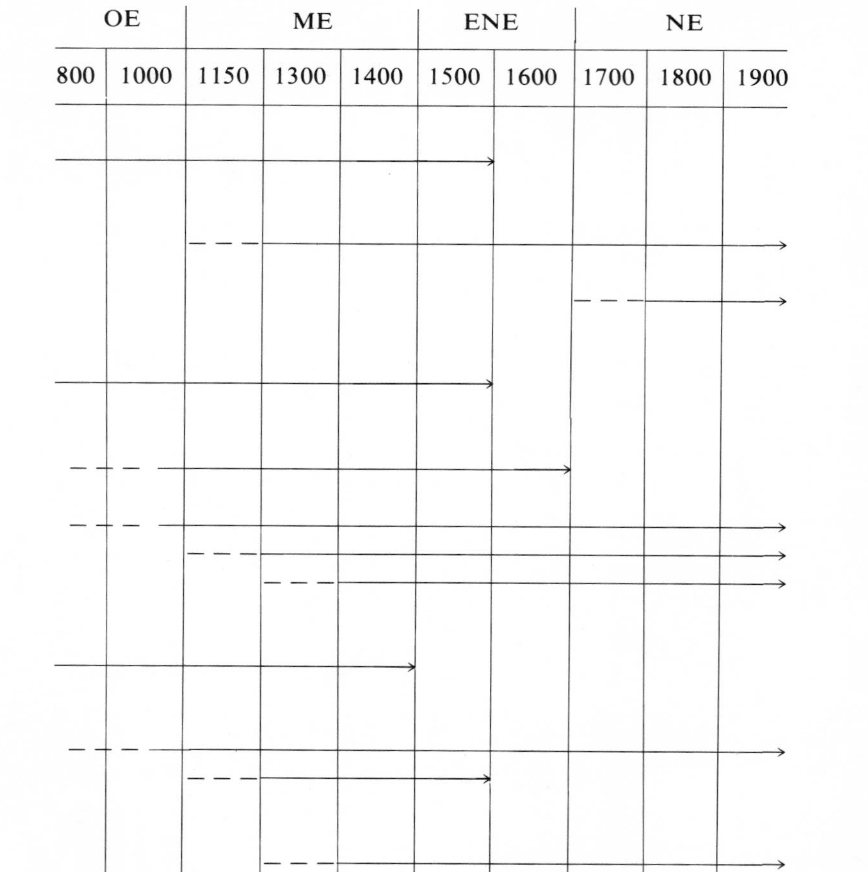

Sense	Example
CAN	
a. have intellectual power to	OE he cann riden (= He knows how to ride).
b. have capacity to	He can ride (= is able to).
c. permission	You can go now.
MAY	
a. have physical power to	OE he mæg ridan (= He has the strength to ride).
b. have capacity to	He may ride (= is able to).
c. eventuality ('maybe')	I may go.
d. permission	You may go now.
e. wish	May you succeed!
MUST	
a. permission	OE he mot gan (= I permit him to go).
b. obligation	He must go.
c. wish	ME Mote I long liuen (= May I live long!)!
d. inferred certainty	They must be married by now.

	OE		ME			ENE		NE			
	800	1000	1150	1300	1400	1500	1600	1700	1800	1900	
SHALL											
a. obligation, necessity (V → Aux)											Six years thou shalt (must) sow the land.
b. promise, resolve											He shall go.
c. prediction											I shall go.
WILL											
a. want, desire (V)											Will him to go. Do what you will.
							(very limited)				
b. volition (Aux)											We won't go (refuse to).
							(mainly in negative sentences)				
c. promise, resolve											I will go.
d. prediction											He will go.
DO											
a. make, put (V)											Do the deed.
b. substitute verb											I laughed and Bill did so too.
c. causative											I did him die.
d. "truly, indeed"											I believe they do like warfare.
e. optional tense-carrier											He did go (= He went).
f. obligatory, dummy auxiliary in questions											Did he go?
g. obligatory, dummy auxiliary in negatives											I didn't go.

B WORD ORDER

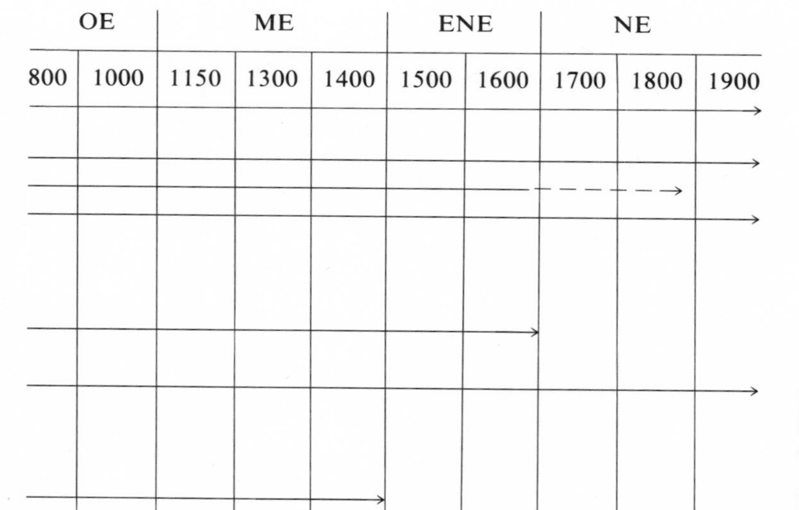

* *Not* is an ME form; in OE the chief negative was *ne* (usually associated with Type 2 order).
**X = certain adverbs of time and place, negative adverbs like OE *ne*, and *scarcely, hardly*.

C MAXIMAL SEQUENCES OF AUXILIARIES

The order is specified in terms of Type 1 order. In OE when two auxiliaries co-occurred, the construction was split and the progressive or passive usually followed the Main Verb (V).

Parentheses signal optional elements; curly brackets mean each line within the brackets is mutually exclusive with the other lines within the brackets. *Inf* is the infinitive marker required by Modals on the following verb in OE.

1. ACTIVE SENTENCES

[*be* + *PP* = the perfective auxiliary]

OE:

$$\left\{\begin{array}{l}\text{(Modal + Inf) (be + PrP)}\\ \text{(have + PP)}\\ \text{(be + PP)}\end{array}\right\} \text{V}$$

ME, ENE:

$$\left\{\begin{array}{l}\text{(Modal) (have + PP)} \left(\left\{\begin{array}{l}\text{be + PrP}\\ \text{do*}\end{array}\right\}\right)\\ \\ \text{(be + PP)}\end{array}\right\} \text{V}$$

NE: (Modal) (have + PP) (be + PrP) V

2. PASSIVE SENTENCES

["Passive" = *be* + *PP*]

OE: (Modal) Passive + V

ME, ENE: (Modal) (have + PP) Passive + V

NE: (Modal) (have + PP) (be + PrP) Passive + V

* If it followed *have* + *PP, do* was sometimes expressed as *do* + *PP*.

D NUMBER, CASE, AND GENDER INFLECTIONS IN OLD ENGLISH

DEMONSTRATIVE + NOUN

Nouns have different inflectional markers for number, case, and gender according to their form in earlier Germanic and ultimately in Indo-European. Typical noun declensions may be illustrated by the masculine noun *stan* 'stone', the feminine noun *talu* 'tale', and the neuter noun *scip* 'ship'. Each noun paradigm is cited with the demonstrative *se, seo, þæt* 'that'.

General Masculine Declension

	Singular	*Plural*
Nominative	se stan	þa stanas
Accusative	þone stan	þa stanas
Genitive	þæs stanes	þara stana
Dative	þæm stane	þæm stanum
Instrumental	þy stane	þæm stanum

General Feminine Declension

Nominative	seo talu	þa tala
Accusative	þa tale	þa tala
Genitive	þære tale	þara tala
Dative	þære tale	þæm talum
Instrumental	þære tale	þæm talum

General Neuter Declension

Nominative	þæt scip	þa scipu
Accusative	þæt scip	þa scipu
Genitive	þæs scipes	þara scipa
Dative	þæm scipe	þæm scipum
Instrumental	þy scipe	þæm scipum

THIRD PERSON PRONOUN

	Singular			*Plural*
	Masculine	*Feminine*	*Neuter*	*Common*
Nominative	he	heo	hit	hi
Accusative	hine	hi	hit	hi
Genitive	his	hire	his	hira
Dative	him	hire	him	him
Instrumental	him	hire	him	him

SELECTED BIBLIOGRAPHY

A. GENERAL BIBLIOGRAPHY

Abbott, Edwin A. *A Shakespearian Grammar* (1870). New York: Dover, 1966 (repr.).

Austin, J. L. *How to Do Things with Words.* Edited by J. O. Urmson. Cambridge, Mass.: Harvard University Press, 1962.

Bacquet, Paul. *La Structure de la Phrase Verbale à l'Époque Alfrédienne.* Paris: Les Belles Lettres, 1962.

Barber, Charles. *Linguistic Change in Present-day English.* Edinburgh: Oliver and Boyd, 1964.

Baugh, Albert C. *A History of the English Language.* New York: Appleton-Century-Crofts, 1957. 2d ed.

Bolinger, Dwight L. *Aspects of Language.* New York: Harcourt Brace Jovanovich, Inc., 1968.

Boyd, Julian, and J. P. Thorne. "The Semantics of Modal Verbs." *Journal of Linguistics,* 5:57–74 (1969).

Brook, G. L. *English Dialects.* London: Andre Deutsch, 1963.

Brunner, Karl. *Die Englische Sprache; ihre geschichtliche Entwicklung,* Vol. 2. *Syntax.* Tübingen: Niemeyer, 1962.

Burling, Robbins. *Man's Many Voices; Language in its Cultural Context.* New York: Holt, Rinehart and Winston, 1970.

Chomsky, Noam. *Aspects of the Theory of Syntax.* Cambridge, Mass.: M.I.T. Press, 1965.

———. *Language and Mind.* New York: Harcourt Brace Jovanovich, Inc., 1968.

Closs, Elizabeth [Traugott]. "Diachronic Syntax and Generative Grammar." *Language,* 41:402–415 (1965). Rev. version in D. Reibel and S. Schane, eds., *Modern Studies in English.* Englewood Cliffs, N.J.: Prentice-Hall, 1969.

DeCamp, David. "The Field of Creole Language Studies." *Latin American Research Review,* 3, 3:25–46 (1968).

Dillard, J. L. "Negro Children's Dialect in the Inner City." *Florida Foreign Language Reporter* 5, 3:7–10 (1967).

______. "Non-standard Negro Dialects – Convergence or Divergence?" *Florida Foreign Language Reporter,* 6, 2:9–12 (1968).

Ehrman, Madeline E. *The Meanings of the Modals in Present-day American English.* Janua Linguarum Series Practica, No. 45. The Hague: Mouton, 1966.

Ellegård, Alvar. *The Auxiliary* Do: *The Establishment and Regulation of its Use in English.* Stockholm: Almqvist and Wiksell, 1953.

Emery, Clark. "John Wilkins' Universal Language." *Isis,* 38:174–185 (1948).

Engblom, Victor. "On the Origin and Early Development of the Auxiliary *Do.*" *Lund Studies in English,* 6, 1938.

Fasold, Ralph W. "Tense and the Form *BE* in Black English." *Language,* 45: 763–776 (1969).

Ferguson, Charles A. "Diglossia." *Word,* 15:325–340 (1959).

Fillmore, Charles J. "The Case for Case." In E. Bach and R. T. Harms, eds., *Universals in Linguistic Theory.* New York: Holt, Rinehart and Winston, 1968.

______. "Types of Lexical Information." In *Working Papers in Linguistics* 2, Ohio State University, 1968; and in F. Kiefer, ed., *Studies in Syntax and Semantics.* Dordrecht: Reidel, 1970.

Fillmore, Charles J., and D. Terence Langendoen, eds. *Studies in Linguistic Semantics.* New York: Holt, Rinehart and Winston, 1971.

Foster, Brian. *The Changing English Language.* London: Macmillan, 1968.

Franz, Wilhelm. *Die Sprache Shakespeares in Vers und Prosa; Shakespeare Grammatik.* Halle/Saale: Max Niemeyer, 1939. 4th ed.

Fridén, Georg. *Studies on the Tenses of the English Verb from Chaucer to Shakespeare, with Special Reference to the Late Sixteenth Century.* Cambridge, Mass.: Harvard University Press, 1948.

Fries, Charles C. "On the Development of the Structural Use of Word-Order in Modern English." *Language,* 16:199–208 (1940).

Greenberg, Joseph H. *Language Universals, with Special Reference to Feature Hierarchies.* Janua Linguarum Series Minor 59. The Hague: Mouton, 1966.

Halliday, M. A. K. "Notes on Transitivity and Theme in English." *Journal of Linguistics,* 3:37–81, 3:199–244 (1967), and 4:179–215 (1968).

Herskovits, Melville J. *The Myth of the Negro Past.* Boston: Beacon Press, 1958. 2d ed.

Huchon, René. *Histoire de la langue anglaise.* 2 vols. Paris: A. Colin, 1923–1930.

Hungerford, Harold, Jay Robinson, and James Sledd, eds. *English Linguistics: An Introductory Reader.* Glenview, Ill.: Scott, Foresman and Co., 1970.

Jacobs, Roderick A., and Peter S. Rosenbaum, eds. *Readings in English Transformational Grammar.* Waltham, Mass.: Ginn, 1970.

Jespersen, Otto. *Growth and Structure of the English Language.* New York: Doubleday, 1955. 9th ed.

______. *The Philosophy of Grammar.* London: Allen and Unwin, 1924.

———. *A Modern English Grammar on Historical Principles* (1909–1949). 7 Parts. London: Allen and Unwin, 1961 (repr.).

Johnson, Samuel. *A Dictionary of the English Language: in Which the Words are Deduced from their Originals, and Illustrated in Their Different Significations by Examples from the Best Writers. To Which are Prefixed, a History of the Language and an English Grammar.* London: J. Jarvis, 1787 (6th repr.).

Jones, Charles. "The Grammatical Category of Gender in Early Middle English," *English Studies,* 48:289–305 (1967).

Katz, Jerrold J., and Paul M. Postal. *An Integrated Theory of Linguistic Descriptions.* Cambridge, Mass.: M.I.T. Press, 1964.

Kellner, Leon. *Historical Outlines of English Syntax.* London: Macmillan, 1892.

King, Robert D. *Historical Linguistics and Generative Grammar.* Englewood Cliffs, N.J.: Prentice-Hall, 1969.

Kiparsky, Paul. "Linguistic Universals and Linguistic Change." In E. Bach and R. T. Harms, eds., *Universals in Linguistic Theory.* New York: Holt, Rinehart and Winston, 1968.

———. "Tense and Mood in Indo-European Syntax." *Foundations of Language,* 4:30–57 (1968).

———, and Carol Kiparsky. "Fact." In M. Bierwisch and K. E. Heidolph, eds., *Recent Developments in Linguistics.* The Hague: Mouton, 1970.

Kirchner, Gustav. "Recent American Influence on Standard English: The Syntactical Sphere." *Zeitschrift für Anglistik und Amerikanistik,* 5:29–42 (1957).

Klima, Edward S. "Negation in English." In J. A. Fodor and J. J. Katz, eds., *The Structure of Language: Readings in the Philosophy of Language.* Englewood Cliffs, N.J.: Prentice-Hall, 1964.

———. "Studies in Diachronic Transformational Syntax." Unpublished Ph.D. dissertation, Harvard, 1965.

Kurath, Hans. *A Word Geography of the Eastern United States.* Ann Arbor: Michigan University Press, 1949.

Labov, William. "Contraction, Deletion, and Inherent Variability of the English Copula." *Language,* 45:715–762 (1969).

———. *The Social Stratification of English in New York City.* Washington: Center for Applied Linguistics, 1966.

———, Paul Cohen, Clarence Robins, and John Lewis. *A Study of the Non-Standard English of Negro and Puerto Rican Speakers in New York City.* 2 vols. Cooperative Research Project No. 3288. New York: Columbia University, 1968 (mimeographed).

Lakoff, George. "Linguistics and Natural Logic." *Studies in Generative Semantics I.* Phonetics Laboratory, University of Michigan, 1970.

———. *Irregularity in Syntax.* New York: Holt, Rinehart and Winston, 1970.

Lakoff, Robin. *English as a Language* (forthcoming).

Langacker, Ronald W. *Language and its Structure: Some Fundamental Linguistic Concepts.* New York: Harcourt Brace Jovanovich, Inc., 1968.

Langendoen, D. Terence. *Essentials of English Grammar.* New York: Holt, Rinehart and Winston, 1970.

———. *The Study of Syntax; The Generative-Transformational Approach to the Structure of American English.* New York: Holt, Rinehart and Winston, 1969.

______. "The Syntax of the English Expletive 'It.'" In F. P. Dinneen, ed., *Georgetown Monograph Series on Language and Linguistics,* 19:207–216 (1966).

Lass, Roger, ed. *Approaches to English Historical Linguistics: An Anthology.* New York: Holt, Rinehart and Winston, 1969.

Leonard, Sterling A. *The Doctrine of Correctness in English Usage, 1700–1800* (1929). New York: Russell and Russell, 1962 (repr.).

Loflin, Marvin D. "Negro Nonstandard and Standard English: Same or Different Deep Structure?" *Orbis,* 18:74–91 (1969).

Lyons, John. *Introduction to Theoretical Linguistics.* Cambridge: Cambridge University Press, 1968.

McIntosh, Angus. "The Relative Pronouns *þe* and *þat* in Early Middle English." *English and Germanic Studies,* 1:73–87 (1947–1948).

McKnight, George H. *The Evolution of the English Language; from Chaucer to the Twentieth Century* (1928). New York: Dover Press, 1968 (repr.).

McLaughlin, John C. *Aspects of the History of English.* New York: Holt, Rinehart and Winston, 1970.

Mitchell, Bruce. *A Guide to Old English.* Oxford: Basil Blackwell, 1965.

______. "Syntax and Word-Order in 'The Peterborough Chronicle' 1122–1154." *Neuphilologische Mitteilungen,* 65:113–144 (1964).

Mossé, Fernand. *Histoire de la forme périphrastique être + participe présent en Germanique.* Paris: Klincksieck, 1938.

______. *Manuel de l'anglais du moyen âge: des origines au XIVe siècle.* 2 vols. Paris, Aubier, 1945–1949. [English translation of Vol. I by J. A. Walker, *Handbook of Middle English.* Baltimore: Johns Hopkins Press, 1952.]

Mustanoja, Tauno F. *A Middle English Syntax.* Helsinki: Société Néophilologique, 1960.

Myers, L. M. *The Roots of Modern English.* Boston: Little, Brown, 1966.

Palmer, Frank R. *A Linguistic Study of the English Verb.* London: Longmans, 1965.

Postal, Paul M. "On the Surface Verb 'Remind.'" *Linguistic Inquiry,* 1:37–120 (1970).

Poutsma, H. *A Grammar of Late Modern English.* 2 parts. Groningen: Noordhoff, 1904–1928.

Price, H. T. "Foreign Influences on Middle English." *University of Michigan Contributions in Modern Philology* 10. Ann Arbor: University of Michigan Press, 1947.

Pyles, Thomas. *The Origins and Development of the English Language.* New York: Harcourt Brace Jovanovich, Inc., 1964.

Quirk, Randolph, and Charles L. Wrenn. *An Old English Grammar.* London: Methuen, 1957. 2d ed.

Reibel, David A., and Sanford A. Schane, eds. *Modern Studies in English; Readings in Transformational Grammar.* Englewood Cliffs, N.J.: Prentice-Hall, 1969.

Reskiewicz, Alfred. "Split Constructions in Old English." In *Studies in Language and Literature in Honor of Margaret Schlauch.* Warsaw: Polish Scientific Publishers, 1966.

Robertson, Stuart, and Frederick C. Cassidy. *The Development of Modern English.* Englewood Cliffs, N. J.: Prentice-Hall, 1954. Rev. ed.

Rosenbaum, Peter S. "Prerequisites for Linguistic Studies on the Effects of Dialect Differences on Learning to Read." *Project Literacy Reports,* No. 2. Ithaca, N.Y.: Cornell University, 1964.

Ross, John R. "On Declarative Sentences." In R. A. Jacobs and P. S. Rosenbaum, eds., *Readings in English Transformational Grammar.* Waltham, Mass.: Ginn, 1970.

Salmon, Vivian. "Language-Planning in Seventeenth-Century England; Its Context and Aims." In C. E. Bazell *et al.,* eds., *In Memory of J. R. Firth.* London: Longmans, 1966.

———. "Sentence Structures in Colloquial Shakespearian English." *Transactions of the Philological Society,* 1965, pp. 105–140.

Schlauch, Margaret. *The English Language in Modern Times (since 1400).* Warsaw: PWN–Polish Scientific Publishers, 1964. 2d ed.

Scott, Charles T., and Jon L. Erickson, eds. *Readings for the History of The English Language.* Boston: Allyn and Bacon, 1968.

Searle, John R. *Speech Acts: An Essay in the Philosophy of Language.* Cambridge: Cambridge University Press, 1969.

Sørensen, Knud. "Latin Influence on English Syntax; A Survey with a Bibliography." *Travaux du Cercle Linguistique de Copenhague,* 11:131–155 (1957).

Stewart, William A. "Continuity and Change in American Negro Dialects." *Florida Foreign Language Reporter,* 6, 1:3–18 (1968).

Stevick, Robert D. *English and its History: The Evolution of a Language.* Boston: Allyn and Bacon, 1968.

Stockwell, Robert P., Paul Schachter, and Barbara Hall Partee. *Integration of Transformational Theories on English Syntax.* 2 Vols. Los Angeles: University of California, October, 1968 (Mimeographed).

Strang, Barbara M. H. *A History of English.* London: Methuen, 1970.

———. "Swift and the English Language: A Study in Principles and Practice." In *To Honor Roman Jakobson; Essays on the Occasion of his Seventieth Birthday, Oct. 11th, 1966.* Vol. 3. Janua Linguarum Series Maior 33. The Hague: Mouton, 1967.

Traugott, Elizabeth Closs. "Toward a Theory of Syntactic Change." *Lingua,* 23:1–27 (1969).

Turner, Lorenzo D. *Africanisms in the Gullah Dialect.* Chicago: University of Chicago Press, 1949.

Visser, F. Th. *An Historical Syntax of the English Language.* 3 Vols. to date. Leiden: Brill, 1963–1969.

Weinreich, Uriel, William Labov, and Marvin I. Herzog. "Empirical Foundations for a Theory of Language Change." In W. P. Lehmann and Y. Malkiel, eds., *Directions for Historical Linguistics: A Symposium.* Austin: University of Texas Press, 1968.

Wolfram, Walter A. *A Sociolinguistic Description of Detroit Negro Speech.* Washington: Center for Applied Linguistics, 1969.

Wyld, Henry Cecil. *A History of Modern Colloquial English.* Oxford: Blackwell, 1936. 3d ed.

B. PRIMARY TEXTS

(Texts quoted by abbreviated titles)

Ælf. Coll. = *Ælfric's Colloquy,* ed. G. N. Garmonsway. New York: Appleton-Century-Crofts, 1966.

Ælf. Gr. = *Ælfric's Grammar.* In *Ælfrics Grammatik und Glossar,* ed. J. Zupitza (1880). Berlin: Max Niehans, 1966.

Ælf. Hom. = *The Homilies of Ælfric.* In *Homilies of the Anglo-Saxon Church,* ed. B. Thorpe. London: Ælfric Society, 1844–1846.

Bo. = *King Alfred's Old English Version of Boethius' "De Consolatione Philosophiae,"* ed. W. J. Sedgefield. Oxford: Clarendon Press, 1899.

Bos. = *Boswell in Holland 1763–1764,* ed. Frederick A. Pottle. New York: McGraw-Hill, 1952.

Ch. = *The Text of the Canterbury Tales,* 8 vols, ed. J. M. Manly and Edith Rickert. Chicago: Chicago University Press, 1940; and *The Works of Geoffrey Chaucer,* ed. F. N. Robinson. Boston: Houghton Mifflin, 1957. 2d ed.

Chron. = *Two of the Saxon Chronicles Parallel,* 2 Vols., ed. Charles Plummer and John Earle. London: Oxford University Press, 1892–1899.

Cowper = *The Correspondence of William Cowper; Arranged in Chronological Order, with Annotations,* 4 vols, ed. T. Wright. New York: AMS Press, 1968 (repr.; originally published 1904).

CP = *King Alfred's West-Saxon Version of Gregory's "Pastoral Care,"* ed. H. Sweet, EETS 45 and 50. London: Trübner, 1871.

Del. = *The Novels of Thomas Deloney,* ed. M. E. Lawlis. Bloomington: Indiana University Press, 1961.

Nashe = *The Works of Thomas Nashe,* 5 vols, ed. R. B. McKerrow. Oxford: Basil Blackwell, 1958.

Or. = *King Alfred's Orosius,* ed. H. Sweet, EETS 79. London: Trübner, 1883.

PL = *The Paston Letters: A.D. 1422–1509,* 6 vols, ed. James Gairdner. London: Chatto and Windus, 1904.

Sh. = *The Arden Edition of the Works of Shakespeare,* 38 vols. London: Methuen, 1903–1969. (Where there is more than one edition the more recent is used, unless otherwise specified in the footnotes.)

Southey = *The Life and Correspondence of the Late Robert Southey,* 6 vols, ed. C. C. Southey. London: Longmans, 1849. 2d. ed.

Spect. = *The Spectator,* 5 vols, ed. D. F. Bond. Oxford: Clarendon Press, 1965.

Swift = *The Prose Writings of Jonathan Swift,* 14 vols, ed. H. Davis. Oxford: Basil Blackwell, 1957–1964.

Synge = *The Plays and Poems of J. M. Synge,* ed. T. R. Henn. London: Methuen, 1963.

Walpole = *A Selection of the Letters of Horace Walpole,* 2 vols, ed. W. S. Lewis. New York: Harper, 1926.

Wycherley = *The Complete Works of William Wycherley,* 4 Vols. ed. M. Summers. London: Nonesuch, 1924.

INDEX

The index is restricted to subject-matter. The only lexical items listed are the main auxiliary verbs: *be, can, do, have, may, must, shall, will;* these are cited both in their Old English and in their modern forms. The page on which a major term is defined is indicated by italics.